Counseling
Troubled
Older Adults

Counseling Troubled Older Adults

A Handbook for Pastors and Religious Caregivers

Harold G. Koenig, M.D.
and
Andrew J. Weaver, Ph.D.

Abingdon Press
Nashville

COUNSELING TROUBLED OLDER ADULTS:
A HANDBOOK FOR PASTORS AND RELIGIOUS CAREGIVERS

Copyright © 1997 by Abingdon Press

This book is printed on recycled, acid-free paper.

Library of Congress Cataloging-in-Publication Data

Koenig, Harold George.
  Counseling troubled older adults : a handbook for pastors and religious caregivers / Harold G. Koenig, Andrew J. Weaver.
      p.   cm.
  Includes bibliographical references and index.
  ISBN 0-687-01731-9 (pbk. : alk. paper)
  1. Mentally ill aged—Pastoral counseling of—Handbooks, manuals, etc.   2. Geriatric psychiatry—Handbooks, manuals, etc.   3. Mentally ill aged—Religious life.   I. Weaver, Andrew J., 1947– .
  II. Title.
  BV4461.K64   1997
  259'.4—dc 20   96-36718
                                                                                                  CIP

Scripture quotations, unless otherwise indicated, are from the New Revised Standard Version Bible, copyright © 1989 by the Division of Christian Education of the National Council of the Churches of Christ in the United States of America.

Scripture quotations noted NIV are taken from the Holy Bible: New International Version. Copyright © 1973, 1978, 1984 by the International Bible Society. Used by permission of Zondervan Bible Publishers.

97 98 99 00 01 02 03 04 05 06 — 10 9 8 7 6 5 4 3 2 1

MANUFACTURED IN THE UNITED STATES OF AMERICA

To Charmin, Jordan, and Rebekah, with love
—H. K.

To Linda with love and gratitude
—A. W.

Contents

Preface

I t was Goethe who observed, "As people grow older, often they feel less inclined to enter upon any new work. To grow old, however, is in itself to enter upon a new business."

In an industrialized society with technological medicine guaranteeing greater longevity to life, this "new business" requires an extraordinary project for the elderly and for their caretakers. This mammoth business is made even more complex and challenging in a democracy where quality of life and respect for persons are integral parts of the philosophical foundation on which most of the culture's institutions are built.

One of the many institutions being called upon to help care for the nation's elderly is the religious establishment. That there are dynamic and intricate relationships between aging, religion, and health can no longer be denied or overlooked. Indeed, much contemporary research demonstrates overwhelmingly that religion and aging are for many American citizens interwoven realities, often of life-and-death proportion. Standing at the interface of religion and aging is a cadre of caregivers—physicians, specialists in geriatrics, nurses, psychologists, psychiatrists, social workers, professional counselors, clergy, and mental health specialists of many kinds.

The particular focus of this volume is on pastors and other religious caregivers and the roles they might play in this "new business" of a nation of older persons, many of whom find this developmental phase of life difficult to negotiate. Their difficulties, as the authors show, take sundry forms—depression, anxiety, substance dependency, psychoses, abuse, and so on. And, sooner or later, all must deal with what some existentialist philosophers and psychologists claim to be the base of most, if not all, of our human dilemmas—death and dying.

At times the sheer demographics of an aging population and the resulting problems and issues—physical, mental, spiritual—can generate an overload difficult for caregivers to carry. Contemporary health care dialogues illustrate this reality, often in dramatic ways. To say that *all* helping professions will be needed to meet the needs of the elderly seems axiomatic. Yet the reality exposed in much of contemporary research dealing with the cooperation between the mental health establishment and faith communities bespeaks otherwise. Indeed, there have been times when resistance to cooperative efforts have been massive, resulting in a variety of false assumptions and generalizations about both mental health and religion.

Fortunately, in the following pages the authors move far beyond the diagnosis and blame arenas found in much of the past literature. Recognizing the inextricable relationship between mental health and religious faith, the authors deal with just what such a link means in the work of practitioners, particularly in the everyday activities of religious caregivers. And they do so without oversimplifying the technical factors implicit in the lives of troubled older adults or treating religious professionals in a condescending fashion.

Acutely aware of research findings that focus on the mental health/religion dynamic, much technical material is translated into real lives and into practical implications. Such terms as bipolar disorder, post-traumatic stress disorder, and dementia with delusions become more than psychiatric jargon. In the mode of the "living human document," these conditions are depicted in the experiences and behavior of 72-year-old Thelma, or 64-year-old Jim, or 79-year-old Nellie.

The reader learns the nature of enlightened assessment, including diagnostic nuances; possible treatment implications, particularly within a faith community; referral possibilities and procedures, both within and beyond the religious congregation; and treatment possibilities, again within the faith community or in concord with specialists in mental health.

These descriptive and prognostic topics in themselves ought to prove immensely helpful to religious professionals eager to contribute to the counseling of troubled older adults. But the authors' added contributions of *specific* resources—local, national, self-help, and cross-cultural—make this truly an authentic and comprehensive *handbook*.

Orlo C. Strunk, Jr., Ph.D.
Professor Emeritus, Boston University
Managing Editor, *The Journal of Pastoral Care*
Pastoral Psychotherapist, the Coastal Samaritan Center, Inc.,
Myrtle Beach, South Carolina

How to Use This Book

Counseling Troubled Older Adults is designed to be a pastoral care text for those in training for pastoral ministry as well as a useful resource casebook for those engaged in pastoral work with older persons. The book addresses mental health problems commonly found among elderly people. Part 2 is presented in case vignette format in much the same style used to train mental health professionals. The case vignettes employ a multidisciplinary approach, integrating current clinical knowledge in psychology, psychiatry, medicine, pastoral care, family therapy, and social work with the latest advances in research on how individuals utilize religion to help them cope with emotional distress in later life. This book is written for persons of all faiths, with a sensitivity to the multicultural reality of North America. The authors are both committed Christians who work as specialists in mental health. Dr. Koenig is a geriatric psychiatrist and researcher in religion and mental health. Dr. Weaver is a clinical psychologist and ordained United Methodist minister who has served rural and urban parishes.

This book is designed so that the reader may quickly and easily locate information about different mental and emotional conditions for which older persons and their families seek help. It is a practical guide on how to assess problems and what to do about them. The table of contents provides the titles and subject content of cases that exemplify common mental health problems experienced by older adults. Alternately, the reader may look up a condition in the index, which will refer them to the page numbers in the book where the problem is discussed. National organizations that provide information and support for persons with mental or emotional problems are also listed for rapid identification. Perhaps the best way for busy pastors to use this book is to carefully examine the table of contents to see which kinds of problems we address in this book and then turn to specific sections when the need arises. Seminarians and pastoral students, on the other hand, should read each section carefully and consecutively to become familiar with the range of conditions.

Pastors will find information about the important role they play in geriatric mental health care and their need for special training on how to recognize and meet the needs of older adults and families in the first section of the introduction (part 1). Those wanting to review recent research examining the relationship between religion and emotional or mental health can turn to the section entitled "New Confirmation of Old

Beliefs"; this material may be helpful for pastoral caregivers as they interact with medical or mental health professionals; and it will be particularly useful to chaplains working in hospital settings, who need scientific validation of the importance of their work. A discussion of the relationship between aging and religious belief and practice concludes the introduction; this section underscores the importance of religion to older persons and the crucial impact that the pastor can have on their emotional health because of this.

The heart of this book is part 2, which provides twenty-nine cases of common mental and emotional problems frequently experienced by older persons and their families. Each case provides an example of an older adult with a specific mental or emotional syndrome who is seeking help from his or her pastor. Included in each case is information about how a pastor (or other religious caregiver) would assess the problem, how to gently and professionally conduct the assessment, what aspects about the case are most important, how to make the diagnosis, general information about the condition, and specific directions about what the pastor can do, what the congregation can do, when to refer for professional assistance, and information (often addresses and telephone numbers) about other local and national resources that provide help with the problem.

The last section is devoted to how to network with mental health providers and make referrals. If there are words or terms that are unfamiliar to the reader, he or she should turn to the glossary in part 3, in which technical terms are defined.

Throughout the book, the abbreviation *DSM IV* refers to the *Diagnostic and Statistical Manual of Mental Disorders*, fourth edition (Washington, D.C.: American Psychiatric Press, 1994).

PART ONE

Introduction

The Role of the Clergy in Geriatric Mental Health Care

Religion, Mental Health Services, and Seniors

Religion and spirituality are central to the lives of most older Americans. Eighty percent of persons aged 65 or older are members of a church or synagogue and over half (52 percent) worship at least once a week. Nine out of ten seniors indicate they "pray frequently" when faced with worries or personal problems. Among religiously involved seniors over half reported that 80 percent or more of their closest friends come from their church. A recent survey found that 67 percent of elderly men and 79 percent of elderly women living in rural Iowa reported attending church once a month or more despite limitations of mobility due to health.[1]

The mental health needs of older persons are increasingly becoming the central counseling concern of those in ministry. By the year 2000, 50 percent of the members of mainline Protestant churches and American Judaism will be 60 years of age or over.[2] Experts estimate that 10 to 30 percent of older adults have emotional problems that are readily reversible when recognized and treated promptly. It is of great concern that less than 20 percent of seniors with a mental health diagnosis receive professional mental health care. This often results in chronic mental health deterioration.[3]

Clergy are in a particularly useful position to counsel troubled seniors as well as assist them in finding the specialized care they require. A recent study by the National Institute of Mental Health found that a person aged 65 or older with a mental health problem is more likely to seek clergy help than to seek out a mental health specialist.[4] Pastors are often in long-term relationships with individuals and their families, enabling them

1. J. R. Cerhan and R. B. Wallace. "Predictors of Decline in Social Relationships in the Rural Elderly," *American Journal of Epidemiology* 137 (1993): 870-80.
2. C. E. Custer, "The Church's Ministry and the Coming of the Aged," *Circuit Rider* (September 1991), 4-6.
3. B. A. Husaini, S. T. Moore, and V. A. Cain, "Psychiatric Symptoms and Help-Seeking Behavior among the Elderly: An Analysis of Racial and Gender Differences," *Journal of Gerontological Social Work* 21, no. 3 (1994): 177-95.
4. Cited in A. A. Hohmann and D. B. Larson. "Psychiatric Factors Predicting Use of Clergy," in *Psychotherapy and Religious Values*, ed. E. L. Worthington Jr. (Grand Rapids, Mich.: Baker Book House, 1993), 71-84.

to observe changes in behavior that may indicate early distress. Clergy are frequently sought for counseling in a crisis such as a personal illness or injury, a change in the health of a family member, or the death of a spouse, family member, or close friend.

This frequent use of the clergy by seniors should not be a surprise, given the ready availability and accessibility of clergy. According to the United States Department of Labor, there are approximately 312,000 Jewish and Christian clergy serving congregations in the United States (4,000 rabbis, 53,000 Catholic priests, and 255,000 Protestant pastors). In a recent review of ten separate studies, clergy reported that they devote between 10 and 20 percent of their forty- to sixty-hour work week on pastoral counseling.[5] Annually, this allocation totals 148.2 million hours of mental health services. To match this time allocation, each of the almost 77,000 members of the American Psychological Association (practicing clinical psychologists) would need to be delivering services at the rate of 38.5 hours per week. This estimate does not take into account the work of the nearly 100,000 nuns in full-time religious vocation in the Roman Catholic Church. Undoubtedly, older persons in distress go to clergy and other religious caregivers in large numbers because they are representatives of communities that offer a sense of continuity with centuries of human history, a feeling of being a part of something greater than oneself, and an established pattern of responding to human needs.

Congregations Provide Services for Seniors

Research indicates that churches and synagogues are widely used to provide services for older persons. Among a group of 212 Jewish and Christian congregations in the northeastern United States, 84 percent of the congregations had visitation programs for the homebound elderly, 80 percent had visitation programs to nursing homes, 70 percent offered regular hospital visits for seniors, 44 percent provided transportation, 37 percent gave telephone reassurance calls and 16 percent provided home-delivered meals.[6] More than seven in ten congregations in the study believed that programs for older persons will be a priority in the next five to ten years. Active lay leadership and joint sponsorship with community agencies were the principal predictors of the presence of programs for seniors in the congregations.

The role of the clergy is particularly vital for seniors in rural or small community settings where mental health services are the most sparse and there is often little separation between church, community, and family. In

5. A. J. Weaver, "Has There Been a Failure to Prepare and Support Parish-Based Clergy in Their Role as Front-Line Community Mental Health Workers? A Review," *Journal of Pastoral Care* 49 (1995): 129-49.
6. N. W. Sheehan, R. Wilson, and L. M. Marella, "The Role of the Church in Providing Services for the Aging," *Journal of Applied Gerontology* 2 (1988): 231-41.

rural America, churches often function as the community counseling resource. According to a comprehensive study of Catholic, Lutheran, and Methodist pastors in North Dakota, about one in four of these pastors' churches had 40 percent or more of their parishioners aged 65 or over.[7] Almost 100 percent of the pastors surveyed made regular home visits to the elderly, 87 percent indicated they had weekly or monthly services at local nursing homes, 72 percent made transportation available to elders, 70 percent worked with hospices, and 44 percent were involved in meals-on-wheels programs. The older members in these churches were also very involved in voluntary activities. Eighty-three percent helped in worship services, 74 percent taught in the educational program, 81 percent served in the telephone ministry, 70 percent served in hospices, 51 percent assisted refugee resettlement, and 38 percent delivered meals. These high rates of involvement are consistent with other research showing that church and synagogue participation is by far the most common form of voluntary activity for older Americans.

Religious Commitment and Ethnic Minority Seniors

Turning to ethnic minority communities, studies indicate that the church is an integral component of both the African American and Hispanic American community support networks, particularly among seniors. A recently published study of older Hispanic Americans reveals a pattern of high religious commitment and participation. In this survey of 178 older Hispanics (mostly Mexican Americans) residing in San Antonio, Texas, 82 percent indicated they had attended church that week, and 88 percent indicated that they regularly used prayer to cope with stress or sadness. These older Hispanic Americans indicated a high level of helpfulness gained from their religious beliefs and involvement. Overall, 78 percent reported that their faith was a "very important" sustaining resource in their lives while only 4 percent indicated religion had not been helpful. Moreover, older Hispanic Americans reported they had become more involved in religious activities as they had grown older.[8] In a second study of 1,805 Hispanic Americans (mostly of Mexican, Cuban and Puerto Rican heritage) over the age of 55, researchers discovered that those surveyed were twice as likely to seek help from the church than from any other community service when addressing family problems, depression, worry, and fear.[9]

7. M. Samuel and G. F. Sanders, "The Role of Churches in the Supports and Contributions of Elderly Persons," *Activities, Adaptation and Aging* 16, no. 2 (1991): 67-79.
8. D. Maldonado, "Religiosity and Religious Participation Among Hispanic Elderly," *Journal of Religious Gerontology* 9 (1994): 41-61.
9. R. A. Starrett, D. Rogers, and J. T. Decker, "The Self-Reliance Behavior of the Hispanic Elderly in Comparison to Their Use of Formal Mental Health Helping Networks," *Clinical Gerontologist* 11 (1992): 157-69.

In a national sample of 581 older African Americans, about 95 percent considered themselves "very or fairly religious" and indicated they prayed almost daily.[10] About 80 percent of these older African Americans reported receiving emotional or financial support from fellow church members in times of need. In fact, when ill or requiring advice and encouragement, they were more likely to find help from their church than from family members.[11] In a second extensive study of 635 African American churches in the northern United States, a remarkable 38 percent of the congregations had a working relationship with the local mental health department; in contrast, only 9 percent had programs designed for older members.[12] Research indicates that Black and non-Black churches whose pastors have lower levels of information about the needs of the elderly also develop fewer programs for older members.

Clergy Knowledge About the Elderly

Given the important function the church serves in the personal support system for older Americans, and given the large numbers of older persons seeking clergy counsel, pastors require a high level of knowledge about issues affecting persons in this age group. Unfortunately, the vast majority of clergy (70 to 80 percent) have received no seminary course work in gerontology-related topics.[13] This situation continues despite a promising increase in the number of seminaries offering courses that focus on ministry to the aging. In a 1989 survey of 113 accredited seminaries in the United States, 59 percent offered courses dealing with the concerns of older persons.[14] This figure is three times greater than one found in a similar survey conducted fourteen years prior. One recent, puzzling study of 160 midwestern pastors found that those who were self-educated and participated in continuing education events about seniors had more knowledge of the needs of older persons than the 30 percent exposed to seminary course work. This research raises questions regarding the adequacy of seminary training being offered in this area.[15]

Increased exposure of clergy to gerontological knowledge, primarily in the form of self-study and continuing education classes, has had positive

10. R. J. Taylor and L. M. Chatters, "Nonorganizational Religious Participation among Elderly Black Adults," *Journal of Gerontology* 46, no. 2 (1991): S103-11.
11. R. J. Taylor and L. M. Chatters, "Patterns of Informal Support to Elderly Black Americans: Family, Friends, and Church Members," *Social Work* 31 (1986): 431-38.
12. S. B. Thomas, S. C. Quinn, A. Billingsley, and C. Caldwell, "The Characteristics of Northern Black Churches with Community Health Outreach Programs," *American Journal of Public Health* 84, no. 4 (1994): 575-79.
13. H. G. Pieper and T. Garrison, "Knowledge of Social Aspects of Aging among Pastors," *Journal of Religious Gerontology* 8, no. 4 (1992): 89-105.
14. E. D. C. Brewer, "A National Study of Gerontology in Theological Education," in *Gerontology in Theological Education*, eds. B. Payne and E. D. C. Brewer (Binghamton, N.Y.: Haworth Press, 1989), 15-29.
15. Pieper and Garrison, "Knowledge of Social Aspects of Aging Among Pastors," 89-105.

results among some clergy. Researchers surveyed 221 United Methodist, Southern Baptist, and Evangelical Lutheran pastors. Only 20 percent of these pastors had seminary course work or internship experience related to aging issues, whereas 80 percent had taken continuing education classes on aging issues. These pastors had positive attitudes toward and high levels of knowledge about seniors' needs.[16] Again on a promising note, these scores represent a marked improvement over those found in a similar group of clergy less than a decade earlier. It may be that both a greater awareness of aging issues and high rates of older persons involved in their churches focused these pastors' attention on the need to educate themselves. One-third of the pastors in this study spent 30 to 50 percent of their work time in ministry to seniors. The vast majority of these clergy felt very strongly that additional training in gerontology was necessary, and half expressed an interest in enhancing counseling skills with the elderly. The overwhelming majority of these pastors strongly advocated that all seminaries require a course that would expose students to the needs of older persons and would introduce pastoral approaches to working with the aging.

What Mental Health Training Do Pastors Need?

Most people who seek pastoral counsel report that they find clergy effective when offering emotional support and encouragement. In fact, when Americans are asked to compare psychologists and psychiatrists to clergy on interpersonal skills, they rate clergy as warmer, more caring, more stable, more professional, and similar in listening skills.[17] Given these findings, it would be reasonable to suggest that pastors have much to teach mental health professionals about relating effectively to those they serve. Aside from the fact that they serve a potentially very large constituency, the issue that clergy need to address is that they are limited as helpers to seniors and others because they generally lack the knowledge to identify the mental health problems they are asked to minister to. It is the primary aim of this book to address these deficits in training by presenting clear and thorough diagnostic information about the most common mental health issues found among seniors.

The single most important factor in increasing pastoral counseling effectiveness with seniors is training in diagnostic skills. The more accurately clergy can evaluate the needs of the elderly seeking help, the more appropriately they can respond. After eleven years of training an estimated 25 percent of the clergy in the Cleveland, Ohio, area, educators concluded:

16. J. K. Guiledge, "Gerontological Knowledge among Clergy: Implications for Seminary Training," *Educational Gerontology* 18 (1992): 637-44.
17. F. Schindler, M. R. Berren, M. T. Hannah, A. Beigel, and J. M. Santiago, "How the Public Perceives Psychiatrists, Psychologists, Nonpsychiatric Physicians, and Members of the Clergy," *Professional Psychology: Research and Practice* 18 (1987): 371-76.

Even some clergy with years of counseling experience did not utilize the concept of evaluating and defining a problem before making a referral. . . . They were unable to formulate major issues, discriminate between acute and long-term aspects of a situation, weigh the resources and weaknesses of either an individual or a family, or establish hypotheses regarding aspects of the problem which were not immediately evident. They often felt under pressure to act or provide some kind of advice before they had sufficient information upon which to base their recommendation or course of action. . . . The clergy were unfamiliar with public and private mental health resources with the exception of a few social agencies. They did not view themselves as part of the mental health resources within the community, and were uncomfortable in discussing issues of referral, both with mental health professionals and with congregants.[18]

These researchers found that training clergy in diagnostic skills enhances their ability to assist those who come to them in distress and increases clergy effectiveness when making referrals.[19]

It is promising that when clergy are offered continuing education experiences to enhance their knowledge about seniors, they express strong interest in the topic. A study of 132 experienced urban and suburban clergy in Rochester, New York, found almost three-fourths had an interest in an extended workshop on ministry to the aged. Afterward, half of the clergy requested that the workshop offer additional skills in counseling older adults and their families. There was also a high interest in information on services for elders offered by local agencies working with seniors. When extended training in ministry to seniors has been conducted among religious caregivers, marked increases in program development and planning for seniors in the congregations have taken place.

Summary and Conclusion

The number of older Americans is growing more rapidly in churches than in the general population. The rural and ethnic minority elderly have particularly high rates of church involvement. Despite limitations in training, clergy act as primary counselors for millions of older Americans. Unfortunately, clergy generally have poor mental health evaluative and referral skills, and most of those seeking clergy help are counseled in isolation from mental health professionals. Clergy who have higher levels of knowledge about older persons are more likely to have church programs designed for seniors in their congregation. Experienced clergy strongly advocate for required seminary courses in gerontology and indicate a high interest in continuing education, particularly in counseling older adults and their families. Much of this volume will focus on enhancing diagnostic and referral skills for clergy working with older persons.

18. M. Wasman, R. B. Corradi, N. A. Clemens, "In-Depth Continuing Education for Clergy in Mental Health: Ten Years of a Large Scale Program," *Pastoral Psychology* 27, no. 4 (1979): 255-56.
19. A. W. Klick, P. M. Ladrigan, and N. D. Fenity, "Clergy Request Linkage: Implications for Planning Ministry with Older Adults," *Educational Gerontology* 13 (1987): 437-42.

The United States population is aging rapidly. The graying of America is largely due to the aging of the 76 million member baby-boom cohort (born 1945–1965) and a decrease in birthrate compared with earlier generations. Of particular concern are the high rates of depression, anxiety, suicide, and substance abuse among baby boomers. If rates of mental disorder remain stable in this population group, by the year 2020 there will be epidemic numbers of older persons with mental illness, particularly depression, alcoholism, and drug abuse. Who will provide the mental health services needed by this group?

In the early 1980s, rates of mental disorder among older persons were at an all-time low; consequently, only 3 percent of the Medicare budget over the past decade has gone toward mental health services. This percentage has remained relatively constant from 1980 to 1992, when the total Medicare budget increased astronomically from $38 billion to $134 billion. The rapidly increasing Medicare budget has caused frantic efforts by those in Washington to stem any further growth in this program. Furthermore, other priorities, such as the need to reduce the federal deficit, have drawn attention away from the elderly and caused lawmakers to look for further cuts in the Medicare budget. This comes at a time of increasing numbers of older persons with both physical and psychological illnesses in need of services.

Even now, access of elderly persons to formal mental health services is becoming more and more restricted. Medicare currently pays only one-third of the fees that mental health professionals can collect from younger patients with private insurance. Because of these low reimbursement rates, psychologists and psychiatrists are now beginning to turn away older adults from their practices. Are Medicare rates likely to increase over the next thirty years to the point that they are competitive with private insurance or fees paid by managed care programs? This is quite unlikely. Mental health needs are not all that will place a drain on the Medicare budget. Rapidly escalating rates of disability, dementia, and other chronic physical illness are expected to consume even greater proportions of Medicare funds than will mental health concerns. Unfortunately, these physical disorders are precisely the ones that are associated with high rates of depression, anxiety, and substance abuse; consequently, rates of emotional disorders and demand for services from distressed elders are likely to increase even higher than projected.

Thus, we can expect government resources to be increasingly inadequate to meet the mental health needs of older adults in this society. Who, then, will provide these services? Are there resources within the community that might be tapped to help meet the need? As in the past the church has reached out to vulnerable groups in society, so again the church must respond to the brewing mental health crisis ahead. Whether society will recognize the church as an important resource, as a friend rather than a foe, is less certain.

Are religious beliefs and behaviors conducive to mental health? The forebears of modern psychology and psychiatry as well as a number of present-day leaders in these fields have argued otherwise. Indeed, they claim that religion is a neurotic influence and often fosters—rather than alleviates—mental illness.[1] Religious persons have been portrayed in the psychiatric literature as rigid, closed-minded, and intolerant of others—contrasting markedly with the emotionally healthy individual with a flexible, tolerant, and fluid belief system. Those in the religious community, on the other hand, offended by such negative attitudes toward them, have come to distrust mental health professionals. Rather than induce neuroticism, they claim, religious doctrines and lifestyles breed healthy individuals, enhance family solidarity, and provide a solid basis for stable and fulfilling relationships in the community.

New Research Evidence

Speculations concerning religion's neurotic influence have been based largely on personal opinion and experience with religious subjects who were mentally ill. Most of the earlier research that found positive associations between religiousness and mental distress involved primarily younger populations and college students. Over the past ten years, systematic surveys of "normal" or non–mentally ill adult populations have reported different results. This is especially true for studies of older adults. We will now review research that objectively and scientifically examines whether devout religiousness enhances or diminishes physical health and emotional well-being in later life. The point to be learned from this review is that clergy and pastors already have within their hands a powerful tool that can be used to combat depression, anxiety, and other emotional disorders.

Physical Health

It is one thing to claim that religion helps one stay healthy, but quite another to demonstrate that it actually does so. Nevertheless, over two hundred studies now demonstrate a link between religion and health.[2] Strength of childhood religious training and importance of religious beliefs

---

1. S. Freud, *The Future of an Illusion* (1927), in *The Standard Edition of the Complete Psychological Works of Sigmund Freud*, ed. J. Strachey (London: Hogarth, 1962), 43-44; A. Ellis, "Psychotherapy and Atheistic Values: A Response to A. E. Bergins's 'Psychotherapy and Religious Values,' " *Journal of Consulting and Clinical Psychology* 48 (1980): 642-45.
2. J. S. Levin and P. L. Schiller, "Is There a Religious Factor in Health?" *Journal of Religion and Health* 26 (1987): 9-36.

are particularly important for older adults' self-perceptions of good health.[3] The relationship between physical health and religiousness, however, is a complex one. As health deteriorates, many older persons turn toward religion as a source of comfort. Therefore, when investigators examine the relationship between religion and health at any one point in time (e.g., a cross-sectional study), they often either find no relationship or find that the sicker persons are more religious. This is because physically ill subjects use religion to help them to adapt to distress caused by illness. In a study of patients hospitalized with acute, severe health problems, we found that use of religion as a coping behavior was most common in individuals with the most severe illness.[4] Thus, changing religiousness in response to increased physical illness and disability may cancel out or conceal any direct beneficial effects that religion may have on health.

One way to circumvent this problem is to examine patients with a medical illness that has few physical symptoms that might cause distress and alter coping behavior; this would avoid the problem of persons turning to religion *in response to* poor health. High blood pressure is a condition that has relatively few overt physical symptoms and provides an excellent model in which to study the religion/health relationship. This relationship has important implications for public health because of the devastating long-term effects of high blood pressure on the heart, kidneys, and brain. We examined the relationship between blood pressure, importance of religion, and church attendance in a sample of 407 adult men surveyed in the 1960s.[5] We found that men who reported that religion was very important to them and who attended church frequently had the lowest blood pressures. Particularly striking was the difference in mean *diastolic* blood pressure in older men; those more religiously active had an average diastolic pressure 6 mm. of mercury lower than that of other men; this difference is a medically significant one. More recently, these results have been replicated in a sample of medically ill older adults, in which a link was found between higher blood pressure and lower religiosity.[6]

Reflecting these beneficial effects on health, a number of studies have now documented longer survival and lower mortality rates among the highly religious. D. M. Zuckerman and her colleagues at Yale, studying 400 chronically ill older adults living in Connecticut, found that mortality rates were significantly lower among those reporting that they received "strength from religion."[7] Other studies have demonstrated lower rates of

3. B. Hunsberger, "Religion, Age, Life Satisfaction, and Perceived Sources of Religiousness: A Study of Older Persons," *Journal of Gerontology* 40 (1985): 615-20.
4. H. G. Koenig, *Aging and God* (Binghamton, N.Y.: Haworth Press, 1994), 169.
5. D. B. Larson, H. G. Koenig, B. H. Kaplan, R. F. Greenberg, E. Logue, and H. A. Tyroler, "The Impact of Religion on Blood Pressure Status in Men," *Journal of Religion and Health* 28 (1989): 265-78.
6. H. G. Koenig, D. O. Moberg, and J. N. Kvale, "Religious Activities and Attitudes of Older Adults in a Geriatric Assessment Clinic," *Journal of the American Geriatrics Society* 36 (1988): 362-74.
7. D. M. Zuckerman, S. V. Kasl, and A. M. Ostfeld, "Psychosocial Predictors of Mortality Among the Elderly Poor: The Role of Religion, Well-Being, and Social Contacts," *American Journal of Epidemiology* 119 (1984): 410-23.

cancer among White Protestant clergy and members of specific religious groups (50 to 75 percent of those in the general population).[8] While these findings are often attributed to diet and lifestyle, it is not clear that this explanation is entirely sufficient; indirect effects from positive influences on mental health may be particularly important.

Mental Health

When random samples of persons over age 65 are asked, "How do you cope with the stress of physical illness and other unpleasant changes in your life?" approximately 20 to 30 percent will spontaneously offer a religious response.[9] When asked a direct question about whether religious belief helps them cope, almost 90 percent of older adults indicate that it does.[10] Once again, just because persons report that religion helps them cope does not necessarily mean that it actually does; such individuals may be deluded into thinking that it helps them when, in fact, it could have the opposite effect. Is there any objective evidence that religious beliefs or behaviors facilitate adjustment to stressful life changes? Both cross-sectional and longitudinal studies have now documented such effects.[11] These studies are important for pastors and clergy to know about because they provide objective evidence of beneficial effects of Judeo-Christian beliefs and activities on mental health.

For example, the relationship between well-being, church attendance, and intrinsic religiosity was examined in 830 midwestern community-dwelling (noninstitutionalized) older adults.[12] After controlling their study for the effects of health status, social support, and income, the researchers found that both frequent church attendance and intrinsic religiosity were associated with higher well-being. More recently, we published a report in the *American Journal of Psychiatry* on 850 acutely ill, hospitalized older adults with medical illness that provides objective evidence of a relationship between religious coping and mental health.[13] At the same time, we also examined the relationship in 161 younger hospitalized patients. From this study of over 1,000 patients, the conclusions

8. J. W. Gardner and J. L. Lyon, "Cancer in Utah Mormon Men by Lay Priesthood Level," *American Journal of Epidemiology* 116 (1982): 243-57; H. King and F. B. Lock, "American White Protestant Clergy As a Low-Risk Population for Mortality Research," *Journal of the National Cancer Institute* 65 (1980): 1115-24; J. F. Mayberry, "Epidemiological Studies of Gastrointestinal Cancer in Christian Sects," *Journal of Clinical Gastroenterology* 4 (1982): 115-21.
9. H. G. Koenig, L. K. George, I. C. Siegler, "The Use of Religion and Other Emotion-Regulating Coping Strategies Among Older Adults," *The Gerontologist* 28 (1988): 303-10.
10. Americana Healthcare Corporation, *Aging in America: Trials and Triumphs* (Westport, Conn.: Research and Forecasts Survey Sampling, 1980-81), 83.
11. H. G. Koenig, *Research on Religion and Aging* (Westport, Conn.: Greenwood Press, 1995), 33-83.
12. H. G. Koenig, J. N. Kvale, and C. Ferrel, "Religion and Well-Being in Later Life," *The Gerontologist* 28 (1988): 18-28.
13. H. G. Koenig, H. J. Cohen, D. G. Blazer, C. Pieper, K. G. Meador, F. Shelp, V. Goli, and R. DiPasquale, "Religious Coping and Depression in Elderly Hospitalized Medically Ill Men," *American Journal of Psychiatry* 149 (1992): 1693-1700.

were clear. Religious behaviors such as prayer, reading the Bible, or having a strong faith in God appeared to protect both younger and older medically ill patients against the emotional stresses of hospitalization and acute illness. This effect was particularly noticeable in older men who were physically disabled. The finding persisted even after we controlled for the effects of fifteen other health and social variables. More important from a medical standpoint, severe depression (major depressive disorder) was also less common among religious copers.

It is possible that as persons become depressed they simply lose interest in religion, just as they typically lose interest in other areas of life. This phenomenon could artificially create a relationship between low religiousness and depression, yet have nothing to say about religion's positive or negative effects on mental health. Perhaps the most exciting discovery was made in the second phase of our study, when we followed 200 patients for an average of six months after hospital discharge. We found that patients who were strong religious copers at the start of the study were much less likely than other patients to become depressed over time. In fact, religious coping was the only factor out of many other health and social variables that independently predicted lower depression scores six months later. This finding suggests that the inverse relationship between religious coping and mental health cannot be explained by a lowered interest in religion due to depression; rather, religious coping either prevented depression from developing or helped it resolve more quickly. If this were an isolated finding, it could be explained as a fluke. Similar results, however, have been reported by a number of other investigative teams working throughout the United States and Canada.[14]

Besides protection from depression, frequent involvement in a religious community's activities or in private activities such as prayer and Scripture reading has been associated with lower rates of alcoholism; furthermore, if addicted to alcohol, persons who are more religiously devout have greater success breaking this habit.[15] According to widely renowned Harvard psychiatrist George Vaillant, religion acts as a "substitute addiction" that compensates for the benefits previously obtained from drinking alcohol.[16] One of the reasons that older persons drink alcohol is to obtain relief from the emotional pain that losses of loved ones and increasing disability and dependence can cause. Studies have now shown that elders who attend church frequently, both because of their beliefs and because of the social support they receive there, are less likely to

14. Koenig, *Research on Religion and Aging*, 33-83.
15. Koenig, *Aging and God*, 381-90.
16. G. E. Vaillant and E. S. Milofsky, "Natural History of Male Alcoholism," *Archives of General Psychiatry* 39 (1982): 127-33.

experience problems with anxiety and worry.[17] Thus, religion may help to relieve or prevent the psychological problems that lead older persons to abuse alcohol.

Summary and Conclusions

The heart of America's 76 million baby boom population will reach age 65 in about 25 years. Despite being raised during a time of unprecedented economic prosperity and intellectual advancement, baby boomers have experienced higher rates of drug and alcohol abuse, depression, and suicide than any previous generation. Even now, when rates of mental illness are lower among older persons than in any other age group, federal and state agencies are having more and more difficulty meeting the mental health needs of this population. We are concerned about the situation in future years when government resources will be even scarcer and baby boomers will reach age 65 with declining health and declining economic prosperity.

If commitment to religious beliefs and activities based in the Judeo-Christian tradition produces greater well-being and lower levels of depression and anxiety in later life, then religious bodies are crucial resources that will increasingly be relied upon to help meet emotional needs. Whether churches and synagogues will be prepared to meet the overwhelming psychological needs of older adults in the twenty-first century (or even will desire to do so) remains an unanswered question. It certainly underscores the need for pastors and other religious caregivers to learn (1) how to competently recognize emotional and psychiatric disturbances in later life, (2) how to train members in their church to provide emotional support to these persons, (3) what local and national resources are available to assist the elderly, and (4) when to refer persons to professionals for treatment.

17. H. G. Koenig, L. K. George, D. G. Blazer, and J. Pritchett, "The Relationship Between Religion and Anxiety in a Sample of Community-Dwelling Older Adults," *Journal of Geriatric Psychiatry* 26, no. 1 (1993): 65-93; see also H. G. Koenig, *Is Religion Good for Your Health? Balm of Gilead or Deadly Doctrine* (Binghamton, N.Y.: Haworth Press, 1997).

Normal Aging,
Religion, and the Clergy

The process of normal aging begins at birth and ends at death. While we are all aging, most of us associate the aging process with the latter one-third of the life span. The latter one-third of life is often associated with gain: the acquisition of wisdom, knowledge, and self-control through experience; the reduction of pressure from responsibilities once shouldered; more time to participate in hobbies and relationships that bring enjoyment and fulfillment; grandchildren that can be loved and enjoyed (without the responsibility of parenthood); and the opportunity to pass on wisdom and experience to others.

Nevertheless, this time in life is not always associated with gain. It is during this period, age 60 and beyond, when changes in physical and mental health and social relationships are most noticeable. Change in this respect usually means loss: loss of physical strength, endurance, flexibility, memory, and for some, independence; loss of occupational prestige (with retirement), social position, and at times, position within the family; loss of finances and sometimes home; and loss of friends and family (through death or relocation). During times of loss older adults look back on their lives and evaluate whether it has all been worth it; this is called life review. From this life review either a sense of integrity or a sense of despair results. It is during periods when losses outweigh gains that elders begin questioning the purpose and meaning of their lives.

"What purpose and meaning does my life have now?" asks the widower whose spouse and lifelong companion has died, or the elderly woman with chronic pain from crippling arthritis. "What use am I to anybody now?" asks the disabled older adult who is dependent on others for the fulfillment of basic life needs. These questions of meaning, purpose, and usefulness must be answered positively if the older adult is to obtain integrity, fulfillment, and happiness. When the answer is negative, however, this forms the foundation for the development of depression, anxiety, loneliness, despair, hopelessness, and most of the other mental disorders that we will be discussing in this book. Pastoral caregivers are confronted over and over with these questions from older congregants and their families. You will need to answer these questions, and it would be most helpful if the answer you gave were reasonable, believable, and effective. How do you respond, then? Can you answer these questions?

We believe that you can. The answer lies in Jesus' response to the inquirer who asked him what was the greatest commandment: " 'You shall love the Lord your God with all your heart, and with all your soul, and with all your mind.' . . . [and] 'You shall love your neighbor as yourself ' " (Matthew 22:37, 39). Relating this commandment to the older adult's questions about life meaning and purpose involves three steps: (1) helping the older person develop a strong faith and a deeper personal relationship with God, (2) helping the individual identify the gift or talent (no matter how small or seemingly inconsequential) that God has given them at this particular time in their life that can be utilized to serve God, (3) helping that person use that gift on a daily basis to serve God and others. Compared with doctors, nurses, social workers, or psychologists, why are pastors the most likely, if not the only, professionals to communicate effectively this message that provides a basis for meaning, purpose, and usefulness to many in later life? Because most older adults are religious, have more exposure to their pastor than to any other professional, and are unlikely to hear this message from other professionals. Are older adults really more religious than younger adults, and if so, why? Do people become more religious with age?

Religious Beliefs

The vast majority of persons of all ages in most countries around the world believe in some type of higher power or universal spirit.[1] In the United States, the proportion claiming a belief in God or a universal spirit has fluctuated between 94 percent and 99 percent for the past thirty-seven years.[2] More than 70 percent of Americans believe in some form of life after death (with 11 percent undecided). Recently, George Barna surveyed the religious beliefs of 1,005 randomly sampled adults in the United States. One of the questions he asked was, " 'There is a God who watches over you and answers your prayers.' Do you agree strongly, agree somewhat, disagree somewhat, or disagree strongly with that statement?" Responses differed by age, with agreement noted by 84 percent of those aged 18-25, 91 percent of those aged 26-54, 89 percent of those aged 55-64, and 96 percent of those aged 65 or over. Barna also asked, "Please tell me whether or not the word 'religious' accurately describes you." In response to this question, 49 percent of those aged 18-25 answered yes, compared with 88 percent of participants aged 65 or older.[3] During the 1983-1984 National Institute of Mental Health (NIMH) Epidemiologic Catchment Area Survey, approximately 1,300 persons aged 60 or over were asked whether religion was "very important," "somewhat

1. Princeton Religion Research Center, *Religion in America* (Princeton, N.J.: The Gallup Poll, 1976), 13.
2. Princeton Religion Research Center, *Religion in America: 50 Years (1935-1985)* (Princeton, N.J.: The Gallup Poll, 1985), 22, 42.
3. G. Barna, *What Americans Believe* (Ventura, Calif.: Regal Books, 1991), 176-78, 207-9.

important," or "not important" to them; 88 percent responded that religion was "very important."[4] There is little doubt, then, that religious beliefs are more common in old age than at any other time in life.

Religious Behaviors

Religious behaviors such as prayer and Scripture reading are also prevalent among older Americans. Ninety-five percent of persons aged 65 or older pray at least once daily;[5] and many spend time reading religious Scriptures, particularly those persons with physical disabilities or chronic health problems that preclude regular church attendance. The Barna Report found that 38 percent of Americans aged 18 to 44 read the Bible weekly or more often, compared with 61 percent of those over age 65.[6] Older adults also frequently watch or listen to religious programming on TV or radio. The NIMH Epidemiologic Catchment Area survey reported that almost one-third of older adults watch or listen to religious TV or radio at least several times per week, compared with only about one-tenth of persons under age 45.[7] Likewise, Barna found that the majority of older Americans (58 percent) watched religious TV once or more in the previous year;[8] this percentage has not changed noticeably over the past five years despite the bad press involving televangelists.

Church Attendance

Church attendance and participation in small prayer or Scripture study groups are by far the most common forms of voluntary social activity among older adults in America. In fact, membership in religious organizations exceeds that in all other voluntary social groups combined.[9] Half of all persons aged 65 or older attend church at least weekly.[10] They do so despite often having to overcome serious health and mobility problems. For some older persons, the emotional support provided by church members is even more important than that provided by family members. We examined the sources of social support relied on by 106 consecutive elderly patients attending a geriatric family medicine clinic in Springfield, Illinois. More than half of these patients reported that nearly all their closest

4. H. G. Koenig, L. K. George, D. G. Blazer, and J. Pritchett, "The Relationship Between Religion and Anxiety in a Sample of Community-Dwelling Older Adults," *Journal of Geriatric Psychiatry* 26, no. 1 (1993): 65-93.
5. Princeton Religion Research Center, *Religion in America* (Princeton, N.J.: The Gallup Poll, 1982).
6. Barna, *What Americans Believe*, 288.
7. H. G. Koenig, S. Ford, L. K. George, D. G. Blazer, "Age Differences in the Relationship Between Religion and Anxiety Disorder in Community-Dwelling Adults," *Journal of Anxiety Disorders* 7 (1993): 321-42.
8. Barna, *What Americans Believe*, 127-29.
9. S. J. Cutler, "Membership in Different Types of Voluntary Associations and Psychological Well-Being," *Gerontologist* 16 (1976): 335-39.
10. Princeton Religion Research Center, *Religion in America* (Princeton, N.J.: The Gallup Poll, 1987), 39.

friends came from their local church.[11] Thus, for the older person in America, the church represents a vital source of informal support, both providing companionship and fulfilling practical needs.[12]

Does Religion Become More Important As We Grow Older?

Why are religious beliefs and behaviors so common among older adults? One reason may be that persons become more religious as they age. Another possibility is that older persons in America have always been religious, because they were raised during a time when religion was a more important part of society than it is today. The rapid spread of technology, communication, and education has been used to explain the decreasing importance and credibility of religion in America. At the age of 70, Sigmund Freud wrote a book called *The Future of an Illusion*. In it he claimed that as humankind evolved, religious beliefs would be replaced by "the rational operation of the intellect."[13] To what extent has his prophecy come true over the next sixty-five years? Thanks to the Gallup polls, which have been conducted yearly since the end of World War II, and the Barna surveys, there is now information to help answer this question.

When the importance of religious belief is measured by church attendance and the stated importance of religion in the United States over a period of fifty-two years (1939 to 1991), research shows that, contrary to what Freud predicted, the picture is one of stability rather than decline. In fact, interest in religion may be on the increase among young and middle-aged Americans. Social science researcher David Roozen and his colleagues reported that as the baby boomers are growing older, many are seeking meaning and purpose for their lives in religion.[14] Part of the impetus toward religion by baby boomers has been their felt need to instill moral values in their children at a time when the secular value system appears to be collapsing.

Conventional wisdom would suggest that as persons grow older and face changes in financial stability, social roles, and physical health, religion (which is largely independent of such changes) would take on greater and greater value as a coping behavior. The ability to "put it all in God's hands," as one disabled elder put it, becomes increasingly important

11. H. G. Koenig, D. O. Moberg, and J. N. Kvale, "Religious Activities and Attitudes of Older Adults in a Geriatric Assessment Clinic," *Journal of the American Geriatrics Society* 36 (1988): 362-74.
12. R. J. Taylor, "Religious Participation Among Elderly Blacks," *Gerontologist* 26 (1986): 630-36; R. J. Taylor and L. M. Chatters, "Church Members As a Source of Informal Social Support," *Review of Religious Research* 30, no. 2 (1988): 193-203; S. S. Tobin, J. W. Ellor, and S. M. Anderson-Ray, *Enabling the Elderly: Religious Institutions Within the Community Service System* (Albany: State University of New York Press, 1986).
13. S. Freud, "The Future of an Illusion" (1927), in *The Standard Edition of the Complete Psychological Works of Sigmund Freud*, ed. J. Strachey (London: Hogarth, 1962), 43-44.
14. D. A. Roozen, W. McKinney, and W. Thompson, "The 'Big Chill' Generation Warms to Worship: A Research Note," *Review of Religious Research* 31 (1990): 314-22.

as persons lose control over their lives. In a study of nearly five hundred hospitalized chronically ill adults (68 percent over age 70), we asked patients whether religion had become more important, less important, or remained the same as they had grown older. The majority (60 percent) reported that religion had increased in importance with age, whereas 35 percent indicated that it had stayed the same, and only 5 percent that it had decreased.[15] While people's growing more religious with age may not be the entire explanation for the high rates of religiosity in later life, it certainly plays a significant role.

The Powerful Role of the Pastor

Given that older Americans in general are a highly religious people in terms of belief, personal religious activity, and involvement in their faith communities, the pastor plays a key role in affecting the quality of life that this segment of our population seeks. This quality of life depends on finding purpose, meaning, and usefulness in these later years. How does the pastor assist this process? First, by proclaiming a message that challenges and deepens congregants' faith and relationship with God ("You shall love the Lord your God with all your heart, and with all your soul, and with all your mind"). This relationship and commitment to God can be the source that energizes people to lead the highest possible quality of life imbued with meaning, purpose, and usefulness. Second, by proclaiming the love of God and providing an example of the second great commandment ("You shall love your neighbor as yourself"). In this step, the pastor directs, inspires, and commissions congregants to identify their gifts or talents and then use those gifts or talents to serve others.

While some older adults may have gifts or talents that they can readily identify, others may have more difficulty with this task.[16] Let us return to the older woman with chronic pain and severe disability from crippling arthritis. What is her gift? Indeed, she may say that her illness prevents her from actively helping others, volunteering, or other acts of Christian service. Yes, but can she smile and be pleasant to her caretakers? Can she put forth her maximum effort to care for herself and make the job of her caretakers easier? Can she be grateful and express thanks for things done for her? Can she pray for her caretakers that God would be with them and make their burdens easier to carry? Can she pray for the person in the bed next to her or down the hall that is in worse shape than she is? Can she decide to love everyone in her environment to the fullest extent that she can at any given moment? The answer to all these questions is yes, and in this way, the person may express her love and devotion to God by serving

15. H. G. Koenig, *Aging and God* (Binghamton, N.Y.: Haworth Press, 1994).
16. See H. G. Koenig, T. Lamar, and B. Lamar, *A Gospel for the Mature Years: Finding Fulfillment by Knowing and Using Your Gift* (Binghamton, N.Y.: Haworth Press, 1997).

others. Carrying out this service, then, will dissolve feelings of depression, loneliness, anxiety, and fear, and return meaning, purpose, hope, and a sense of being useful and important in this life.

It is an old message, but one that works. As healthy older adults use their buried talents to serve others in greater need, and as the disabled elders serve the healthy elders in the ways described above, the whole community begins to find more fulfillment, and indeed, the kingdom of God becomes a little bit more of a reality.

PART TWO

Case Studies

Case 1

Normal Grief and Complicated Bereavement

The Grieving Widow

Richard and Julia had been planning for an extended vacation, a lifelong dream, to begin shortly after Richard's retirement at age 68. Two weeks before his retirement Richard collapsed at his office desk and died on the way to the hospital. The large congregation at Richard and Julia's church came together to worship, grieve, and celebrate Richard's life within their community. He and his family had been deeply loved in the church. His death was a shock to the congregation. He was a generous, outgoing spirit who had a strong faith in God and a longtime, close relationship with you, his pastor. Julia was a reserved, quiet person who probably depended on her husband too much. She appeared to be in a daze during the funeral. Over the three months following Richard's death, you, her family, and her fellow church members visited Julia on a regular basis. During this three-month period Julia made little progress in her ability to accept the unexpected death of her husband. She remained in a state of disbelief and melancholy. She continued to be preoccupied with thoughts of her deceased spouse, indicating she felt worthless without him around. She had difficulty sleeping and cried during much of the day while yearning to see her husband again. She was taking prescription medications for severe headaches. She had recently become more morbid in her thinking and had said, "I wish I had died with him."

People who grieve may experience many reactions to their loss as they work toward resolution. Strong, sometimes conflicting feelings such as sadness, helplessness, loneliness, guilt, or anger can emerge. Experiencing and accepting these feelings as natural is an essential part of the recovery process. Julia appears unable at present to accept the sudden and unex-

Pastoral Care Assessment

pected death of her husband and remains "stuck" in denial. Denial is not all bad. It can help one cope with overwhelming emotional pain by buffering its intensity. However, when denial becomes prolonged and intractable, you need to consider that the person may be suffering from something other than normal grief referred to as "complicated bereavement."

You can be of assistance to the mourner by seeking the answer to several questions. How serious are her morbid thoughts? What does she mean by her comment "I wish I had died with him"? Is she thinking of taking her life, or is this comment a more benign expression of her pining? She is also complaining of severe headaches. Is she somatizing her distress, that is, presenting her psychological anguish in the form of physical symptoms? What are the prescription medications she is taking for her headaches? Are these medications limiting her ability to work through the mourning process? Are these medications potentially lethal? Could they be used to commit suicide? (See case 6 for a detailed assessment of suicide potential.) A consultation with the physician who prescribed the medication, after obtaining the permission of the parishioner, would be important.

In making a pastoral assessment, it is important to also recognize the individual's strength and resources. Julia clearly has the important support of family, church friends, and you, her pastor. She has the sustaining memories of a lifetime together with her deceased spouse. She is not isolated, and although she now is experiencing "the valley of the shadow of death" through deep and painful loss, her faith can become a strong source of renewal.

Relevant History

Julia had suffered multiple losses over the past two years, including the death of her mother and her closest friend in the church to cancer and her only grandchild to AIDS. She had relied heavily on her husband of forty-two years for emotional support to weather these severe losses.

Diagnostic Criteria

Normal Bereavement

Grieving is a natural psychological process that involves working through the pain of loss. Generally, experts agree that *normal bereavement* (grieving the loss of a significant other) has three stages, although not always in the same sequence.

Stage one: The first reaction is marked by shock, disbelief, numbness, and denial. These reactions are a way to distance oneself from the loss, thereby providing protection from overwhelming emotions. Each person and situation is unique but this "shock phase" will usually last no more than a few weeks, although it may be more intense if the death is sudden and unexpected.

Stage two: The second phase involves feeling and releasing the pain of the loss. This process may take several forms. Natural feelings of sadness, loneliness, isolation, hopelessness, and helplessness emerge as the person clearly recognizes the extent of the loss. Some reactive depression is part of the necessary internal processing of loss that is expected before one can reorganize one's life. The depression may disturb sleep and appetite, decrease energy and pleasure, and be expressed through weeping. Sometimes grieving persons will become preoccupied with thoughts of how they could have acted differently to prevent the loss. A significant loss can also threaten the grieving person's fundamental beliefs about life, resulting in anger at God and life or sometimes anger at the deceased for leaving him or her behind. Many aspects of the past relationship with the lost loved one are examined through telling stories and sharing memories, sometimes over and over with many different people.

Stage three: The final phase is characterized by acceptance and resolution of the loss. This may be a process of one or two years or longer, depending upon the emotional resources of the individual and the circumstances of the death. Characteristically, depressive feelings no longer predominate in the resolution phase, although anniversaries of the death, wedding anniversaries, birthdays, and special holidays may be difficult reminders of the absence of the loved one. During the final phase, the bereaved elder begins reintegrating her or his life without the loved one by developing new social contacts and interests. During the last phase, the mourning person can come to accept the reality of the loss and the realization that, in some ways, he or she is changed by the death from that time forward.

Complicated Bereavement

Although there is no universally accepted definition of *complicated bereavement*, it generally involves being "stuck" in the early stages of grief and not moving through the natural grieving process from denial to acceptance and resolution. The *DSM IV* criteria focus on the need to assess for major depression (see case 2) after two months, particularly when the depression is characterized by morbid preoccupation with worthlessness, excessive guilt, and prolonged and marked functional impairment. Research suggests that several other symptoms are associated with complicated bereavement: yearning and searching for the lost loved one, preoccupation with thoughts of the deceased, crying, disbelief regarding the death, feeling stunned by the death, and lack of acceptance of the death.[1] In a study of elderly persons who had lost a spouse, 25 of 138 were coping poorly two years after the death, and low self-esteem was associated with difficult adaptation.[2]

1. H. G. Prigerson, E. Frank, S. V. Kasl, C. F. Reynolds, B. Anderson, G. S. Zubenko, P. R. Houck, C. J. George, and D. J. Kupfer, "Complicated Grief and Bereavement-Related Depression As Distinct Disorders: Preliminary Empirical Validation in Elderly Bereaved Spouses," *American Journal of Psychiatry* 152, no. 1 (1995): 22-30.
2. D. A. Lund, M. F. Dimond, M. S. Caserta, R. J. Johnson, J. L. Poulton, and J. Connelly, "Identifying Elderly with Coping Difficulties After Two Years of Bereavement," *Omega* 16, no. 3 (1985): 213-24.

Response to Vignette

Human beings experience grief throughout their lives. It is a universal human experience. It is what we feel when we lose someone or something to which we are emotionally attached. However, elders like Julia, who experience cumulative, frequent and negative losses, are more apt to suffer complicated grief. Losses through death come more often as one ages, and they more intensely foreshadow one's own death. Healing lies in passing through the pain, not avoiding it. Julia is having a very difficult time moving through the emotional pain of losing her lifelong partner. She has spent most of her life married, and her loss is among the most painful a person can experience. The adjustment to her loss is massive, affecting every aspect of her life, requiring her to reassess and reintegrate her personal and social identity.

Be a good listener. Encourage her to express her feelings about her husband's unexpected death as well as organize her story into a coherent whole so that she and you can have a clearer conception of the issues. Avoid being judgmental or telling her what she should feel. Don't minimize her loss or offer easy answers. Encourage the mourner to care for herself. She needs to postpone major decisions and allow herself to grieve and recover.

Supporting a mourning elder can be stressful. Acknowledge and accept your limitations. Seek help from books, workshops, support groups, and colleagues. Recognize your need to grieve the loss of your friend, Richard. Give yourself the opportunity to express your own emotions to trusted friends and colleagues.

Treatment Within the Faith Community

It is estimated that almost 1 million Americans annually suffer the loss of a spouse, and more than 50 percent of women and 13 percent of men over the age of 65 are widowed at least once.[3] Addressing spousal bereavement offers a significant opportunity for ministry. The St. Mary's Catholic Parish in Colts Neck, New Jersey, has mobilized its congregation to meet the needs of grieving persons through its Lazarus Ministry. Teams of laypersons in the parish are trained to respond to families who have lost a loved one. They are taught to understand the dynamics of normal and complicated grief and how to provide spiritual, emotional, and practical support to the mourning families.[4] Research indicates that having a strong faith commitment may ease spousal bereavement and promote more rapid adaptation.[5]

Indications for Referral

Bereavement is an area in which clergy and members of the faith community can bring invaluable resources. A living faith offers a balm for the

3. A. LaRue, C. Dessonville, and L. F. Jarvik, "Aging and Mental Disorders," in *Handbook of the Psychology of Aging*, 2nd ed., eds. J. E. Birren and K. W. Schaie (New York: Van Nostrand Reinhold, 1985), 664-702.
4. D. Dewey, "When a Congregation Cares: Organizing Ministry to the Bereaved," *Death Studies* 12 (1988): 123-35.
5. M. L. S. Vachon, J. Rogers, W. A. L. Lyall, W. J. Lancee, A. R. Sheldon, and S. J. J. Freeman, "Predictors and Correlates of Adaptation to Conjugal Bereavement," *American Journal of Psychiatry* 138, no. 8 (1982): 998-1002.

sorrowful that mental health care does not. However, Julia is in need of being evaluated by a mental health professional who has expertise in working with severe grief reactions. It is of concern that she is so morbid, takes medications, which may complicate her recovery, for possible somatic complaints, remains preoccupied with thoughts of the deceased after three months, and has significant signs of depression (problems with sleep, feelings of worthlessness, weeping, and morbid thinking).

Treatment by Mental Health Specialist

The therapist would focus on resolution of Julia's current crisis and work with her to restore her previous level of functioning. An assessment for major depression (see case 2) and suicidal risk (see case 6) is important. The therapist takes an active role while at the same time encouraging Julia to do as much as possible to resolve the crisis. This means that the therapist would work with her to enhance her strengths, including her support system (family, friends, and faith community). The therapist would also actively educate her on the dynamics of bereavement and her role in moving forward. The therapist would assist her in modifying her psychological defenses, particularly denial, that interfere with successful coping.

Actively listening to Julia's story of her husband's sudden and unexpected death and her resulting changing life circumstances could establish a working alliance and a therapeutic focus. Group therapy with other grieving persons can also be a useful resource; it can provide her with an atmosphere of support, a recognition that she is not alone in dealing with bereavement, and a setting in which to practice more adaptive means of coping.

Local Resources

Resources

Bereavement support groups are located throughout the United States. Many can be found as a part of a hospice program. The great majority (80 percent) of hospice programs provide support groups for family members as well as for the community-at-large. According to the Hospice Facts Sheet distributed by the National Hospice Organization (August 1995), most (63 percent) of hospices work with churches. You can locate a hospice in your area by calling the Hospice Helpline at 1-800-658-8898 or by writing to the National Hospice Organization, 1901 North Moore Street, Suite 901, Arlington, VA 22209. Bereavement support can also be found locally through widow-to-widow programs sponsored by Widowed Person's Services—American Association of Retired Persons (AARP), 601 E Street, NW, Washington, DC 20049 (phone 202-434-2277). In these programs, widows of at least two years are paired with new widows to offer volunteer support and practical advice. Outcome research indicates that emotional and practical support given to grieving mourners in widow-to-widow programs can speed recovery.[6]

6. Ibid.

National Resources

There are several computer accessible Internet addresses and World Wide Web sites that provide information on grief and bereavement resources. *GriefNet* is a directory of resources of value to those who are experiencing loss and grief, sponsored by the nonprofit Rivendell Resources based in Ann Arbor, Michigan (griefnet@rivendell.org, or phone 313-761-1960). GriefNet has an e-mail discussion group for widows that can be subscribed to via majordomo@falcon.ic.net. *WidowNet* is a second information and support resource for widows and widowers (goshorn@fortnet.org), which includes listings of grief-related resources offered by the American Association of Retired Persons, 601 E Street, NW, Washington, DC 20049 (phone 202-434-2277).

The Minister As Crisis Counselor, by David Switzer (revised edition, Nashville: Abingdon Press, 1985), offers a very informative chapter on pastoral responses to persons with normal and complicated grief reactions. *Clinical Management of Bereavement*, by George M. Burnell and Adrienne L. Burnell (New York: Human Sciences Press, 1989), and *Helping the Bereaved*, by Alicia S. Cook and Daniel S. Dworkin (New York: Basic Books, 1992), are instructive books written from a mental health professional point of view.

Self-Help Resources

Losses in Later Life: A New Way of Walking with God, by R. Scott Sullender (New York: Paulist Press, 1989), is a sensitive and thoughtful text on the dynamics of grief among older persons, written from a faith perspective.

Cross-Cultural Issues

Each culture defines the processes of bereavement in ways unique to its experience. *Grief As a Family Process*, by Ester R. Shapiro (New York: The Guilford Press, 1994), offers a superbly written chapter ("The Sociocultural Context of Grief") on the need to appreciate the interacting effects of cultural, familial, and personal factors when promoting healing in grieving families.

Major Depression

I'm Just Sick

Seventy-year-old Wilson has been irregular in his attendance at church this month. After church one Sunday, you ask Wilson's wife, Sarah, how her husband is doing. She replies that for the past month her husband has had little energy or motivation to do anything. He spends a good deal of time in bed during the day, but cannot sleep at night; he wakes up around 4:00 A.M. and is unable to get back to sleep. Over the past three weeks, he has been skipping meals and has lost about ten pounds. You make a home visit to talk with Wilson and find out if there is anything you can do to help. Wilson greets you at the door with a handshake but avoids eye contact and shows little expression in his face. When you ask how he's been doing lately, Wilson says "lousy" and tells you that he's been under a great deal of stress. Hospital bills have gone unpaid; his breathing is more difficult; and his sister with whom he was very close died last month. When asked why he hasn't been to church lately, Wilson indicates in a defensive tone that he hasn't felt much like socializing; people make him irritable and he just doesn't want to hassle with them. While he has stopped going to church to avoid having to interact with others, Wilson admits to feeling guilty about this. He's also been feeling worthless and a burden on his wife because of his inability to help around the house or work in the yard. Despite the fact that you are warm, supportive and empathetic, Wilson responds only briefly to these gestures of concern.

Besides meeting with Wilson and talking with him about his life and troubles, you should also pay special attention to the way he appears, behaves, and talks. Wilson is a tired appearing elderly man who talks and moves about slowly. His facial expression is flat and he spends much time looking at the floor. He provides little initiation in the conversation (minimal spontaneous speech) and tends to respond to questions with monosyllables (yes, no, etc.); after a while, he begins to talk more fluently, although with an irritable tone. Wilson denies feeling depressed. "Pastor,

Pastoral Care Assessment

I'm just sick," he barks. Wilson admits, however, that he feels tired and under a lot of stress, and his conversation is dominated by negative ruminations about loss, feelings of worthlessness, and being a burden on others. He denies having any strange experiences lately (i.e., auditory or visual hallucinations) and does not feel that people are trying to harm him or steal from him (paranoia). Wilson does, however, admit that he doesn't care whether he lives or dies, although he has no specific plans of ending his life. His concentration is poor, and during your conversation he has difficulty remembering dates of important events.

Relevant History

In addition to talking with Wilson, you should also get further information from his wife that he might not be as willing to share. Sarah tells you that Wilson had a problem with drinking ten years ago (*substance abuse*). Although claiming to have the problem "under control," he still takes three shots or more of bourbon each night to help him sleep. As far as his *psychiatric history* is concerned, he has never had any contact with mental health professionals and has never been treated for depression or other mental health problems in the past. Recently, however, Sarah recalls that his medical doctor placed him on Valium for his "nerves." Further inquiry about any *family history* of emotional problems reveals that Wilson's mother had periods of depression, but never sought treatment. His father died in a nursing home at the age of 75 from multiple strokes and had memory problems.

You also learn that Wilson has struggled with severe congestive heart failure. He had coronary artery bypass surgery five years ago and a repeat operation three years ago. He takes one medication for high blood pressure (Inderal), a heart pill (Digoxin), and a water pill (Lasix); he also takes thyroid pills because he was diagnosed with hypothyroidism one year ago. He gets short of breath when he exerts himself and sometimes experiences pains in his chest, for which he takes nitroglycerin. Remember to always ask about any *concurrent medical problems* and any *medicines*, since these, rather than an emotional illness, may actually be the primary cause for a person's symptoms.

Diagnostic Criteria

Wilson has a *major depressive disorder*, a condition diagnosed when a person has experienced two weeks or more of feeling sad, depressed, or irritable or of losing interest, motivation, or pleasure in usual activities.[1] Along with depressed mood or loss of interest, the diagnosis also requires the experience of two weeks or more of at least four of the following eight symptoms: fatigue or loss of energy; physical slowing down (retardation) or increased restlessness (agitation); loss of or excessive gain in appetite and weight; difficulty sleeping or sleeping too much; loss of social or

1. *DSM IV*, 320-27.

sexual interest; feelings of worthlessness, being a burden, or guilt; diffi-culty concentrating; feeling that life is not worth living, wanting to die, or feeling suicidal. Wilson has had at least four of these symptoms as well.

Wilson has a particularly serious form of major depression called *melan-cholic subtype*. Melancholic features that define this type of depression (which is particularly responsive to antidepressant medication) include early morning awakening (waking at least two hours before usual), loss of interest and pleasure in activities once enjoyed (anhedonia), a slowing up of physical movements or speech (psychomotor retardation), a loss of mood reactivity (the person's mood does not improve much even when he or she is talking to a friend or hearing good news), weight loss (10 pounds or more within a one-month period), excessive guilt (thoughts focus on real or imagined acts for which forgiveness cannot be obtained), and a depressed mood that is worse in the morning but improves later in the day (diurnal variation).

Wilson also has a secondary diagnosis of alcohol abuse, given his heavy intake of bourbon, which is clearly excessive for anyone his age and may be contributing to his depressive symptoms and his memory loss.

Response to Vignette

Wilson has a number of risk factors for depression that make him par-ticularly vulnerable to this disorder. First, he has a family history of depression and therefore a genetic predisposition for the disorder. Second, he has a history of alcohol abuse and currently drinks heavily. Third, he has multiple medical problems that are not well-controlled and cause him considerable disability and physical discomfort. Fourth, he is taking med-ications that may predispose him to depression (Valium, a tranquilizer, and Inderal, an antihypertensive). While the rate of major depression in healthy elderly people is well under 1 percent, it exceeds 10 percent in those with chronic health problems.[2] Wilson's case of depression is a seri-ous one, and he is at high risk for suicide. Elderly men with depression, alcohol use, multiple physical health problems, and increasing disability have a higher rate of suicide than any other group in the United States.

Religion has been shown to be a major coping strategy that either pre-vents depression or helps to resolve it more quickly in men with physical health problems.[3] When older persons with health problems are asked what enables them to cope with the stress of illness and disability, one out of four will spontaneously report (without prompting) that religion (faith, God, prayer, etc.) is the primary factor. On the other hand, severe depres-sion may make it more difficult for a person to pray, read the Bible, or

2. H. G. Koenig and D. G. Blazer, "Epidemiology of Geriatric Affective Disorders," *Clinics in Geri-atric Medicine* 8 (1992): 235-51.
3. H. G. Koenig, H. J. Cohen, D. G. Blazer, C. Pieper, K. G. Meador, F. Shelp, V. Goli, and R. DiPasquale, "Religious Coping and Depression in Elderly Hospitalized Medically Ill Men," *American Journal of Psychiatry* 149 (1992): 1693-1700.

attend church because of the loss of energy and motivation and the decreased concentration that accompany the illness. Antidepressant treatments can often restore a person's interest, motivation, and concentration, so that the person can once again involve himself or herself in the church community and in private religious activities that may bring comfort.

Treatment Within the Faith Community

Along with referral for professional treatment, Wilson would benefit from supportive listening and counseling; this may be done by the pastor, clergy staff, or a sensitive, trained layperson within the congregation. Use of Scriptures can be very helpful in such treatment. Biblical figures (Job, David, Jeremiah) present excellent role models whom the person can readily identify with. The book of Psalms, in particular, provides a message of comfort, love, and hope that these persons so desperately need. More information on how to integrate religious and secular techniques in psychotherapy with older adults can be found in *Aging and God*.[4] Finally, if Wilson allows, his wife should be included in at least some of the sessions, since his depression will certainly affect their marital relationship (and vice-versa in some cases). Family members often need to be involved in the person's treatment both to monitor the depressed person (for suicidal risk) and to ensure compliance with treatments (antidepressants or psychotherapy homework assignments). Confidentiality is essential.

Indications for Referral

Indications for referral are the following:

- physical symptoms such as weight loss, insomnia, or fatigue that cause excessive social or occupational dysfunction
- suicidal thoughts
- psychotic symptoms such as auditory or visual hallucinations, or paranoid delusions (fixed false beliefs that rational discourse cannot dissuade the person of)
- melancholic symptoms (discussed above)
- no improvement after three or four weeks of supportive counseling within the church

Studies have shown that once the organic or biological symptoms of depression have set in (weight loss, insomnia, decreased concentration, severe fatigue, and loss of energy), religious forms of supportive therapy may not be effective in reversing the illness.[5]

4. H. G. Koenig, "Use of Religion in Psychotherapy," in *Aging and God* (Binghamton, N.Y.: Haworth Press, 1994), 323-46.

5. H. G. Koenig, H. J. Cohen, D. G. Blazer, K. R. R. Krishnan, and T. E. Sibert, "Cognitive Symptoms of Depression and Religious Coping in Elderly Medical Patients," *Psychosomatics* 36 (1995), 369-75.

Wilson needs immediate referral to have his medications reviewed, to have his danger of congestive heart failure evaluated, possibly to undergo detoxification from alcohol, and most likely, to receive treatment with anti-depressant medication. A general medical physician could initiate evaluation and treatment and then refer the patient to a psychiatrist or psychologist for further treatment if necessary. There are several new anti-depressants that relieve depressive symptoms quickly and with only mild side-effects; these drugs give the depressed person enough energy and motivation to work on their problems. A combination of both medication and psychotherapy has been shown to effectively treat depression in 80 percent of cases;[6] for many of the remaining 20 percent, electroconvulsive therapy (ECT) can rapidly reverse depression and sometimes be lifesaving. While ECT has received a lot of bad press over the years, it is a remarkably safe form of treatment for serious depression in later life. At Duke Hospital, over 70 percent of the more than 1,500 ECT treatments given each year are administered to persons aged 60 or over. The major side-effect is mild *temporary* loss of memory, which usually returns to normal within a few days to a few months after treatment; in fact, ECT treatments may improve memory in some depressed persons who have difficulty concentrating because of their depressive illness.

Local Resources

If the condition is life-threatening (the person is suicidal or has medical complications), the person should be taken to the local emergency room. If the condition is less urgent, an appointment should be made, first with the person's medical physician, and then, if need be, with a psychiatrist or psychologist who has interests and skills in geriatric issues. If the person has limited funds, the county mental health center may be quite helpful.

National Resources

The National Institute of Mental Health's "Fact Sheet" on depression can be obtained by writing the Mental Disorders of Aging Research Branch, NIMH, 5600 Fishers Lane, Room 7-103, Rockville, MD 20857; for a free publication entitled "If You're Over 65 and Feeling Depressed . . . Treatment Brings New Hope," contact D/ART Public Inquiries, NIMH, 5600 Fishers Lane, Room 15C-05, Rockville, MD 20857. The National Depressive and Manic-Depressive Association (NDMDA) has more than two hundred chapters in the United States and Canada that offer support

6. C. F. Reynolds et al., "Combined Pharmacotherapy and Psychotherapy in the Acute and Continuation Treatment of Elderly Patients with Recurrent Major Depression: A Preliminary Report," *American Journal of Psychiatry* 149 (1992): 1687-92.

to people with depression and their families; this group sponsors education and research programs and distributes brochures, videotapes, and audiotapes about depression; write NDMDA, PO Box 1939, Chicago, IL 60690, or call 1-800-826-3632. The National Alliance for the Mentally Ill (NAMI) has groups in all states that provide emotional support and can help people find local services; for more information, write NAMI, 2101 Wilson Boulevard, Suite 302, Arlington, VA 22201, or call 1-800-950-6264.

Books providing further information about depression in the elderly include *Depression in Late Life*, by Dan Blazer (St. Louis: Mosby, 1993); *To Be Old and Sad*, by Nathan Billig (Lexington, Mass.: D. C. Heath & Co., 1987); *Compassionate Care of the Aging*, by John Gillies (Nashville: Thomas Nelson, 1985); *Aging and God*, by Harold Koenig (Binghamton, N.Y.: Haworth Press, 1994).

Our "Religion, Aging, and Health" program within the Center for Aging at Duke University Medical Center, Durham, North Carolina, is devoted to doing research and educating clergy on this and other mental health topics; write to Dr. Koenig, Box 3400 DUMC, Durham, NC 27710.

Self-Help Resources

There are several books about depression that older people can read to help them break out of their cycle of negative thinking. Books from a Christian perspective include *Telling Yourself the Truth*, by William Backus and Marie Chapian (Minneapolis: Bethany House, 1980); and *How to Win over Depression PA* (large-print version available), by Tim LaHaye (Grand Rapids: Zondervan, 1976). Books from a secular perspective include *Feeling Good: The New Mood Therapy*, by David Burns (New York: Penguin, 1980); and *Overcoming Depression*, by Paul Hauck (Philadelphia: Westminster Press, 1978). These books also describe the need to develop activity schedules to maximize pleasure. Counselors should be familiar with these books so that they can monitor and encourage progress.

Cross-Cultural Issues

Older depressed African Americans are, in general, less likely than members of other ethnic groups to admit to feeling depressed, sad, or blue. Instead, they will say "I feel sick," "It's my stomach, my head, my teeth," "I have trouble," "I'm not doing well," "I feel tired," "I get along the best I can," or "I've got troubles." They may also express certain nonverbal signs of depression such as "decreased eye contact," "wrapping self up in clothing or blankets," "distancing self from interviewer by shifting away from interviewer," or "anger and irritability."[7] Blacks or Whites

7. Fran M. Baker, M.D., University of Maryland, Baltimore, personal communication, 23 June 1994.

who are uneducated and not psychologically minded may have difficulty differentiating feeling bad physically from being mentally depressed; physical and emotional pain blend into each other. In general, older persons from other countries or cultures feel more comfortable expressing physical symptoms than expressing emotional ones, because of the stigma of mental illness; the exceptions to this may be elderly Jews or Italians, who seem to have little difficulty expressing their emotions. Persons from Irish backgrounds, by contrast, may be quite stoic about their pain. Certain emotions, such as shame, are much more important in Asian cultures than among Caucasians or African Americans.

Minor Depression

I'm Getting Tired

Betty, a usually spry and active 63-year-old member of the choir, has not reported for the past two choir practices. After church, you wave her down to express your concern about her absences. "Betty, how are you doing?" you ask in a friendly, open tone. "We've missed you at choir practice." Responding to your greeting, Betty replies, "Well, Ron, not so well. There's a lot going on in our lives now." You suggest that she and her husband have lunch with you on Wednesday and talk more about it. Betty agrees, with some show of relief.

On Wednesday after lunch, Betty tells her story; her husband, Tom, chimes in periodically to provide bits of information for clarification. Their eldest son, now 32 years old, has had a difficult time finding work after separating from his wife and two children six months ago. Three months ago, he moved back into his parents' house; since then, he has disrupted their home by playing his stereo loudly during the day, not cleaning up after himself, and staying out until all hours of the night, often returning at 2:00 or 3:00 A.M. and sleeping until noon. Last week, he was arrested for driving while intoxicated and called Betty and Tom at 4:00 A.M. to come and bail him out of jail (which they did). In addition, last month Betty was asked to leave her part-time job at the library because of state budget cuts. She had originally taken this job because of trouble with their finances. Two years ago, Tom had a heart attack and then a coronary artery bypass operation; his health condition over the past 6 months has deteriorated to the point that he has been forced into early retirement, eliminating their major source of income. This, combined with the high cost of his medical bills, has caused them to deplete much of their savings. While Tom has been quite supportive of Betty, he himself is struggling to come to terms with his worsening physical health problems and increasing dependency.

Betty says in a dreary tone, "Ron, I feel stressed out. I'm getting tired and starting to feel down and discouraged about life. Even God doesn't seem to hear my prayers anymore." She goes on to explain that she has not been sleeping well at night because of all her worrying and has been eating everything in sight around the house, gaining five pounds in the past two weeks. While her overall interest and enjoyment of things has remained about the same, she doesn't have her previous motivation to become involved in activities—such as choir practice. Likewise, over the past month she has tried to avoid social events at church, since she hasn't felt much like talking anyway and doesn't want to bore others with her problems. Also, the chronic pain from her arthritis has flared recently and has made her feel more irritable than usual. Otherwise, however, Betty still enjoys doing crossword puzzles, going out to eat with her husband, and taking short drives into the country. She also continues to give piano lessons, although she hasn't taken on any new students for three months now because of her arthritis. She has mixed feelings about their vacation at the coast next month and is concerned about how they will pay for it and whether it is safe to leave their son alone in their home for that time. "Ron, what should we do? I'm not sure how much longer I can handle all this."

Pastoral Care Assessment

The first step in pastoral assessment involves careful listening to Betty's story. The second step involves careful observation of Betty's appearance and behavior as you are talking with her. In this case, Betty appears nicely groomed and well-dressed. When she talks with you, her tone is friendly, she looks you straight in the eye, and she actively contributes to the conversation. She becomes teary-eyed at appropriate times during the conversation, is able to smile and laugh on occasion, and has no difficulty concentrating; she laughs when you ask her about any suicidal thoughts, and says, "Oh, no, I'd never do that." In order to clarify and better define the problem, you may wish to obtain collateral information from close family members or friends, with her permission, of course.

Assuming that there are no correctable medical causes for Betty's symptoms, your major task is to determine whether Betty is (1) reacting appropriately to the stresses in her life, or (2) reacting in an exaggerated or neurotic fashion to experiences or circumstances that most persons would handle without difficulty. You decide that Betty is dealing with *real problems* in her life and is appropriately crying out for help. This does not mean that she has not contributed in some way to these problems because of dysfunctional attitudes or maladaptive behaviors, but only that these negative attitudes or personality traits are not the primary cause for her difficulty. This distinction is important because your intervention will depend to some extent on whether Betty's problems are primarily situational (requiring simple support) or primarily neurotic (requiring psychotherapy directed at changing attitudes and behavioral patterns).

You would also want to inquire more about Betty's feelings toward God. She has already admitted that she doesn't think God is listening to her prayers anymore. Is she feeling angry toward God for allowing these things to happen to her? And is she then feeling guilty over feeling angry at God? You want to know about these things, and she needs to discuss them with someone in a safe, noncritical atmosphere. Finding out about her religious history is also important before initiating any intervention that involves God. You want to learn about her religious experiences as a child and as an adult, and acquire an understanding of how she views God. Does she see God as angry and vengeful, distant and unconcerned, or rigid and unforgiving (perhaps like her own natural father)? A gentle exploration of these areas can uncover important information that has direct bearing on your management of her case.

Relevant History

In further conversations with Betty and her family, you find that Betty has never felt this way before and has no prior history of depression or any other emotional problems. In fact, she has usually quickly bounced back without problems from other stressors in the past two years, including the deaths of her brother and mother. She is well-liked in the church, has many longtime friends, and has actively contributed to the faith community in a number of areas. You also learn that Betty has no family or personal history of emotional problems or substance abuse. With the exception of her arthritis, her health is relatively good, and she takes no other medications except Tylenol and aspirin for her arthritis pain. She also has no history of thyroid problems (a common cause of anxiety and depression), eats a relatively balanced diet (B vitamin deficiency has been associated with depression), and exhibits no other obvious symptoms of neurological dysfunction.

Diagnostic Criteria

Betty has a *minor depressive disorder*, a mild though clinically significant depression that is diagnosed when depressive symptoms are present, but they are not severe enough or long lasting enough to meet diagnostic criteria for a major depressive disorder or dysthymia (see next case). There are several subtypes of minor depression, including *adjustment disorder with depressed mood* (in which emotional symptoms are directly related to a specific stressful experience or situation), *atypical depression* (a depressed mood that is associated with weight gain, oversleeping, hypersensitivity to criticism, and prominent anxiety features), and *depressive disorder "not otherwise specified"* (basically, a mild depression that doesn't fit into any other diagnostic category).

Betty likely has an adjustment disorder with depressed mood, since her symptoms seem clearly linked to situational stressors. Pastors are likely to encounter many elders with minor depression, since this is the most common form of depression in middle age and later life. Minor depression is present in up to 15 percent of noninstitutionalized older adults in the United States and up to 40 percent of those with significant health problems. Because of its wide prevalence, minor depression causes more disability and days lost from work than does major depression. This subtype of depression is important for clergy to know about because it is the most common type of depression that can be treated successfully within the faith community.

Response to Vignette

Compared with Wilson in the previous case, Betty has a relatively mild form of depression. With timely and appropriate treatment, Betty should return to full functioning within a month or two. Factors that predict a good prognosis for Betty and rapid response to treatment include the following:

- no prior history of significant depression or other psychiatric illness
- besides arthritis, no significant health problems
- good social support
- no history or current alcohol or drug abuse
- good interpersonal skills

Without treatment, however, there is a chance that her symptoms will worsen and eventually take on a life of their own in the form of a major depressive disorder. Rapid intervention is the key to successful treatment. The pastor's primary task is to mobilize and orchestrate (1) emotional support from trained pastoral staff, and (2) instrumental or practical support from members of the faith community (see below). Professional referral, then, becomes unnecessary.

Because of their proven usefulness in relieving symptoms of depression, religious resources should be an important part of your treatment plan for Betty. Cognitive-behavioral psychotherapy that utilizes a religious framework has been shown to be more effective in treating mild forms of depression than secular psychotherapy (even when the religious therapy is administered by secular therapists!).[1] Furthermore, religion as a coping behavior (using prayer, Bible reading, or trust and faith in God to cope with stress) has been associated with less emotional distress than has use of nonreligious coping behaviors, particularly in milder forms of depression, and in adjustment disorders in particular.[2] However, if there is unresolved conflict in a person's relationship with God (such as anger toward God or distrust of God), this often blocks the person from utilizing faith as a resource.

Treatment Within the Faith Community

First, Betty's friends and other members within her church community should be mobilized to minister to her and her family. Knowledge that fellow

1. L. R. Propst, R. Ostrom, P. Watkins, T. Dean, and D. Mashburn, "Comparative Efficacy of Religious and Nonreligious Cognitive-Behavioral Therapy for the Treatment of Clinical Depression in Religious Individuals," *Journal of Consulting and Clinical Psychology* 60 (1992): 94-103.
2. H. G. Koenig, D. B. Larson, and D. Matthews, "Religion and Psychotherapy with Older Adults," *Journal of Geriatric Psychiatry* 29, no. 2 (October 1996).

church members and friends are praying for one's health and well-being can have a direct salutary effect on both mental and physical health.[3] Of course, Betty's friends and fellow church members must be informed of her needs in a sensitive and confidential manner, with direction and permission from Betty herself.

At the next level, Betty would benefit from supportive listening, emotional support, and sensitive counseling from either her pastor, a trained member of the pastoral staff, or a trained member of the congregation. Training in sensitive, supportive care is essential, because healing support is a learned skill, and seldom comes naturally. Support must be tailored to the person's personality. If Betty were an independent, self-sufficient, controlling type of person, then support would be directed at giving her more information, practical ideas, or other help that might help her maintain independence and control over her situation; a display of concern, caring, and kindness might surprisingly be met with anger and rejection because of its implication that she is weak, needy, or out of control. On the other hand, if Betty were a dependent, submissive type of person, then support would be directed at providing caring concern that encourages temporary dependence on the supporting person; giving information or practical solutions to her problem might increase her anxiety and worsen her depression. The appropriate integration of religious beliefs and teachings into supportive care must also be carried out skillfully, tailored to Betty's personality and her previous life experiences.

Finally, members of the congregation should be mobilized to provide practical, instrumental support to Betty and her family. This might involve taking up an offering for urgent medical needs, providing transportation to or companionship at the doctor's office, preparing and bringing over meals, mowing their lawn, cleaning their house, and other necessary chores that might be difficult for Betty or her husband at this time. This objective display of love and care from one's faith community breeds a sense of security that is a powerful antidote for feelings of anxiety and isolation.

Indications for Referral

Should interventions by the faith community not succeed in breaking the vicious circle of Betty's deepening depression, then professional help will be needed. This would be the case particularly if there were more neurotic elements to Betty's character (see below). Other indications for referral are the same as for major depression (see case 2).

Treatment by Mental Health Specialist

If negative attitudes, dysfunctional behaviors, or interpersonal relationship problems were at the core of her emotional problems, making it difficult for her to adapt even to normal life stresses, then Betty would need

3. R. C. Byrd, "Positive Therapeutic Effects of Intercessory Prayer in a Coronary Care Unit Population," *Southern Medical Journal* 81 (1988): 826-29.

professional psychotherapy to help change her attitudes, alter her dysfunctional behaviors, and perhaps restructure her personality so that she could deal with situations and people in a more constructive fashion.

Antidepressant medications may not be highly effective in treating mild forms of depression and may not be worth the side effects they cause. On the other hand, if depressive symptoms persist despite other psychological interventions, then a time-limited trial of antidepressant medication (particularly bupropion or one of the new serotonin reuptake inhibitors—fluoxetine, sertraline, and paroxetine) may be attempted.

Resources

See case 2, "Major Depression," for local, national, and self-help resources.

Cross-Cultural Issues

See case 2, "Major Depression."

Chronic Dysthymia

I'm Depressed

Helen, an attractive 66-year-old woman who only recently began attending your church, comes in to see you one afternoon. After making herself comfortable on your couch, she begins by saying "I'm depressed and unhappy with my life." She then launches into a list of complaints about her previous pastor and the way members of that church treated her. You have difficulty getting a word in edgewise, so you find yourself doing a lot of nodding. Helen continues on to provide a detailed description of how deeply she was hurt six years ago when the leadership at her church asked her to step down as church secretary. "I just can't get over how they treated me," says Helen. "I gave them my life, and look what it got me." She then begins talking about her marriage of thirty-five years. "Tom has never loved me as a husband should. He's not very supportive, doesn't like the things I do, and spends most of his time at work, even though he's retired!" She also indicates that she has few friends and even feels that her two children try to avoid her. "They say I meddle too much," she explains.

Further conversation reveals that Helen has been depressed on and off since her teenage years, but nearly continuously so for the past six years. She has seen numerous therapists and doctors, none of whom have been able to help her, she says. Helen recently stopped seeing her therapist of two years because "We just weren't making any progress." Her current complaints include chronically low energy, difficulty sleeping at night, and low self-esteem. She also has a problem with God. "I've been praying to God, but he's not answering me," she declares in an irritable tone. "My life has no purpose or meaning, and I don't know why God doesn't just let me die." On further questioning, she reveals no plans of ending her life and admits to having numerous reasons to live—her grandchildren, her little poodle, and her flower garden. Yet she is still unhappy. As Helen's conversation drifts over and over again to the time six years ago when she was let go as church secretary, she obsesses about how she deserved better and how she hopes the people in this church will treat her better than the people in the last one did.

"What can I do to help?" you ask in a cautious but kindly tone. Helen reports that she needs someone to talk to, and she knows that you can help her. "You're not like my last pastor; you seem like you care," she exclaims with a pitiful, almost begging expression on her face.

Pastoral Care Assessment

Further information about Helen's history is clearly necessary, from Helen, from her husband, and also from her latest therapist (with Helen's permission, of course). You need to talk with her husband to get his side of things and collect more information about how Helen typically relates to people. Talking to her former therapist would likely reveal a wealth of information about her personality and about what counseling with Helen will be like for you (or for whomever this task falls on). Bear in mind, however, that information from either her husband or her previous therapist will be provided from their own unique viewpoints and should not necessarily be accepted as fact. You could also obtain important information by talking with Helen's former pastor, although she will likely be reluctant to give you permission to contact him. You also need to find out what, if anything, has occurred recently that may have precipitated Helen's visit to you today (as well as her decision to switch churches).

During your interview with Helen, you make the following observations about her appearance and behavior. She is expensively dressed and nicely groomed, and her speech is that of a well-educated woman who is familiar with psychological jargon (due to years of psychotherapy). She speaks in a somewhat distant tone, being engrossed with and fixated on her problems; for a moment, you get a feeling that it wouldn't matter if you were in the room or not. She does not smile much and does not joke or laugh. She is frequently cynical and even bitter at times. Her thinking is logical, though sometimes distorted, but there is no evidence that she has any delusions or frank paranoia. She also does not have any suicidal thoughts other than those mentioned above. Further history from her husband reveals that she has never attempted suicide.

After talking with Helen and obtaining collateral information from her husband and other sources, you come to the conclusion that Helen has been depressed for a long time now and that no specific life event precipitated her coming into your office, other than growing dissatisfaction and increasing boredom. Certainly, her spiritual life appears at a low ebb, and she is treating God as she is treating everyone else in her life—as someone who has disappointed her and not met her expectations. If there is to be any hope of true healing, you will need at some future time to explore and perhaps gently challenge her beliefs about God.

As noted above, Helen has a somewhat extensive history of depression and has seen numerous therapists and doctors in the past, although she has not taken medication for her problem over the past two years. She has no history of previous or current alcohol or drug abuse. Because of her long-standing problems, you want to learn more about her childhood and adult life experiences. From her last therapist, you learn that she was neglected as a small child, having grown up in a professional family that had little time for her. She was the third child and was not expected or planned for. Helen's school days were difficult for her; she was frequently made fun of by others because of her weight, and she felt rejected by her peers. After her marriage, she spent most of her time as a housewife and raising her children. After her last child left home, she took a job as church secretary, a position she held for almost five years. In this job, she felt needed and accepted for the first time in her life. But things had not gone well during her final two years in that position. Her need for control caused problems with other members on the pastoral staff, and when she was confronted by her pastor, she became angry and walked out. Although she stayed on as secretary for three more months, the atmosphere around the office was tense and she was eventually dismissed. She had not worked or performed any volunteer activity since then.

Helen's family history is significant for alcoholism in her father and depression in an aunt. Her mother, whom she describes as cold and distant, had no diagnosable psychiatric problems. Helen's past medical history is unremarkable; she has no major medical problems and takes no medications.

Helen has *dysthymia*, which is a chronic depressive disorder that has been present most of the time for the past two years or longer. She does not fulfill the severity criteria for major depression, although she may have done so in the past. Sometimes it is difficult to determine whether a person has a dysthymia or has an inadequately treated major depressive disorder that is persisting over time; the distinction is important because treatment may differ. Dysthymia has gone by a variety of different names in the past, including characterological depression, depressive personality disorder, and depressive neurosis.

Persons with dysthymia are difficult to deal with, yet their problems are very real. Frequently, these persons have deeply ingrained psychological conflicts and unresolved needs that have their origins in early life, often because of neglect or abuse. Persons with dysthymia frequently have unrealistic expectations of others, are sensitive to rejection, and focus on the negative side of life, preferring to complain about the half-empty glass rather than be thankful for the half-full glass. Situational factors or life circumstances play a less prominent role in dysthymia than in adjustment disorders; often, persons with dysthymia will focus on and obsess over one traumatic event in their distant past (which most persons would have quickly adapted to). Chronic dysthymia, at its extreme end, may be difficult to distinguish from more severe forms of personality pathology such as borderline personality disorder or narcissistic personality disorder. Persons with these character disorders are characterized by extreme self-centeredness, unstable interpersonal relationships, anger and dependency, self-abuse (frequent suicide attempts, cutting or burning themselves), and a tendency to bring havoc on any group that they belong to.

Dysthymia is much less frequent than minor depression (case 3), and is less frequent in persons over age 65 (1 percent of men and 2 to 3 percent of women) than in those under age 45 (2 percent of men and 4 percent of women). Because almost 15 percent of persons with dysthymia end up dying from suicide, this is not a benign condition.

Response to Vignette

People like Helen pose more of a challenge to pastors than do people like either Betty (with adjustment disorder) or Wilson (with major depression). Because of her long history of unsuccessful prior psychotherapy and turbulent interpersonal relationships, Helen's prognosis is not good. In fact, most pastors (as well as therapists and, especially, physicians without training in this area) would like to avoid people like Helen, if that were possible. Such people can be draining on a pastor's time and emotional reserve. Nevertheless, the call to the ministry includes loving the less than lovable. And that is precisely what people like Helen need—love, understanding, and consistent and patient concern. Because psychological techniques frequently fail, these are cases that need spiritual intervention—both for the patient and for the counselor.

On the other hand, many persons with dysthymia may not have received the correct medical therapy for their depression or may not have had adequate counseling in a safe environment where they can unload their fears, concerns, and guilt. Many of these persons need to forgive others for past hurts and forgive themselves for missed opportunities. Helen needs to resolve the hurt she feels from losing her job as church secretary. She needs to realize that losing that job meant much more than simply being laid off from work; instead, this event has become the focus for all her unmet expectations and dreams, which have their origin in wounds from her early youth. As a minister, possessing the authority of God's calling, you are in an ideal position to help persons like Helen give and obtain forgiveness, achieve healing, and make a fresh start. Because you have the tools of spiritual authority and power, you have an advantage over secular counselors and therapists, and you should not forget this or fail to use these resources.

Treatment Within the Faith Community

Helen's greatest hope for healing lies in her receiving full acceptance and integration into the faith community. She must be accepted just as she is—complaining, dissatisfied, suspicious, and constantly on guard for the slightest sign of rejection—if she is ever to move beyond that. In all likelihood, Helen, through no fault of her own, somehow missed the unconditional love that most babies and small children receive from their parents. She has spent her life unsuccessfully trying to force others to give her that love. It is only within a community, where the burden of providing unconditional love can be spread out among numerous persons, that this can be achieved. It is safe to say that no one person possesses the emotional and spiritual resources necessary to provide Helen with all that she needs. For some persons, it will take a miracle to achieve a full and permanent healing. If such a miracle cannot happen in the church, then where can it happen?

If you choose not to take on this task yourself, you should assign one person from the pastoral staff or the congregation to be the primary counselor for Helen. This person's task is to meet regularly with Helen (once a week to once a month) to allow her to talk freely about her feelings and to provide her with spiritual counsel and direction in a sensitive, gentle manner. If Helen is too demanding, the counselor must be ready and willing to set limits on her behavior. This counselor must also mobilize other people in the congregation to befriend Helen, include her in church activities, and *make her the subject of their ministry*. These people should be actively involved in praying for Helen, both with her in person and during their own private prayer time.

Indications for Referral

Should Helen's neurotic problems be so severe that efforts by the faith community fail to successfully treat her depression, or if Helen's depressive symptoms worsen to the point that they meet criteria for major depressive disorder, then professional referral becomes necessary. Recall, however, that Helen has already been in professional therapy for some time without good results. Nevertheless, a comprehensive evaluation by a trained therapist may provide direction for therapy that can take place within the local church. Because of the high risk of suicide among patients with dysthymia, counselors and those ministering to Helen in the congregation should frequently ask her about such feelings or plans that she may be developing (see case 6, "Increased Risk for Suicide"). Finally, if Helen has not previously had an adequate trial of antidepressant medication, then she should be referred for such treatment. Even if medication does not entirely reverse her symptoms, even a partial response may enhance the effectiveness of counseling and ministry within the faith community.

Treatment by Mental Health Specialist

As noted earlier, these chronic depressions are notoriously difficult to manage. Persons with dysthymia are often treated with long-term psychotherapy. Short-term cognitive-behavioral therapy or interpersonal therapy may also be helpful in some cases. Recently, success has been achieved by treating individuals with therapeutic doses of antidepressant medication. A trial of antidepressant medication, then, should be offered to all persons with dysthymia; these medicines should not be discontinued for lack of response until the person has received at least two trials of different medications at therapeutic blood levels for eight to twelve weeks each. When antidepressant medication is combined with psychotherapy, an improvement is seen in one-third to one-half of such patients. Typically, referral to a psychiatrist or geriatric psychiatrist is necessary in such cases, since primary care physicians are unlikely to possess the skill necessary to treat these individuals.

Resources

See case 2, "Major Depression," for local, national, and self-help resources.

Cross-Cultural Issues

See case 2, "Major Depression."

Bipolar Disorder or Manic-Depressive Illness

I'm on a Special Mission

Thelma is a 72-year-old woman from a very distinguished family in your congregation and is widely known in the local community. She is the heir to a large department store chain that her husband started and developed prior to his death ten years ago. She had been living independently in her own house caring for herself without difficulty until the past five years. During these past five years, she has experienced recurrent, almost cyclic episodes of depression in which she had difficulty sleeping and lacked motivation to do things around the house, bathe, or even get her mail. These periods have typically lasted about three months or so, until her family would force her to see the doctor, who would start her on antidepressants, which would make her feel better. Lately, however, when she has begun feeling better she has become overly active and involved in many things, particularly church affairs. Since she is a member of your board, you have firsthand knowledge of the situation this is creating. These periods of overactivity last for two or three weeks, after which she settles down to her normal self for a while and then starts getting depressed again.

One day, her family brings her into your office seeking advice. The daughter asks to talk with you privately and provides the following information. Thelma has been acting strangely for the past three weeks. She is staying up all hours of the night, busily rearranging things in the house, taking things in and out of drawers, making telephone calls, and generally disturbing family members and business associates. Despite her limited sleep, surprisingly, she has plenty of energy. Her daughter notes that Thelma has been very distractible, starting many projects without finishing them, leaving her house a mess. Thelma's memory has also worsened recently and she is having trouble remembering dates and times. She missed her doctor's appointment last week, and has not been paying her bills or balancing her checkbook this month. She has also refused to allow a nurse's aide into her home to help with household chores and personal care needs. Finally, Thelma has been giving extravagant gifts to people she hardly knows, and recently sent a check for $10,000 to an organization of questionable repute soliciting funds for alternative cancer treatments. When confronted about these actions, Thelma becomes very irritable, saying that she can do whatever she pleases with her money.

Pastoral Care Assessment

You end the conversation with the daughter and bring Thelma into the room. As she sits down on the couch, she comments about your pictures on the wall and then about the colors in your tie. You get her attention and begin a conversation. "How have things been going for you, Thelma?" you say in a friendly and open manner. "I'll bet my daughter has been telling you all sorts of things about me. Well, they're all true," she says with a laugh. She goes on to tell you that God has called her on a special mission to rid the government of corruption, and that she has been writing letters to the president lately. Thelma's hair is tousled and her brightly colored clothes are unkempt and wrinkled. You notice her physical overactivity and excited manner. Thelma talks rapidly without pausing, as if she cannot get her words out fast enough (pressured speech). She jumps from one topic to another (flight of ideas). She gets up off the couch and moves about the room as she talks (psychomotor agitation). When you express concern about her recent behavior and suggest that she allow her daughter to take her in for a medical evaluation, she becomes irritated and indignant, storming out of your office.

Relevant History

You ask to speak with her daughter again, and obtain the following information. Thelma has had a long history of recurrent mild depressions dating back to her mid-30s. In between depression episodes, she would return to normal, which for her was an active, highly energetic state. She never sought treatment for depression, however, until about five years ago when these episodes began to worsen in severity. Since then, she has seen her medical doctor periodically to treat her depression, but has never seen a psychiatrist or mental health professional. She responded quite rapidly to antidepressants, but as soon as her energy returned, she would stop them. She hated taking medicine because she didn't want to become dependent on anything. Six months ago she was admitted to the hospital for a spell of agitation, memory impairment, and failure to care for herself, and was discharged on a tranquilizer (haloperidol) with a diagnosis of "chronic dementia." Her family was surprised at this diagnosis, since she was usually quite alert, oriented, and was, in fact, a very intelligent person who participated actively in the operation of the family business; you recognize this to be true because of your interactions with her on the church board.

On further inquiry, you learn that Thelma has a family history of alcoholism on her father's side but does not herself drink. She has no other family members with emotional problems other than her sister, whom the daughter described as "a real character" with frequent "highs and lows . . . just like her mother." As far as Thelma's physical health is concerned, she has problems with her blood pressure and may have had a mild stroke about six years ago; the only medicine she takes is her high blood pressure pill. She has no thyroid problems and does not take any over-the-counter medicines. There have been no recent changes in her medication.

Diagnostic Criteria

Thelma has a long history of cyclothymia (mood characterized by mild depression alternating with periods of high energy and activity known as hypomania), and for the past five years has been having what sound like several episodes of recurrent major depression. Until just recently, then, her likely diagnosis was *bipolar disorder, type II*. The *DSM IV* criteria for type II bipolar disorder is a history of one or more episodes of major depression, followed or preceded by periods of hypomania, but no frank manic episode. Thelma is now, however, in the midst of a full-blown manic episode, which qualifies her for a diagnosis of *bipolar disorder, type I* (classic manic-depressive illness).

A manic episode goes beyond simple overactivity or euphoric mood, although these elements are typically present. According to *DSM IV*, a manic episode involves a distinct period lasting one week or longer of an abnormally and persistently elevated (or irritable) mood. During this period, at least three of the following symptoms must be present: inflated self-esteem or feeling of self-importance, decreased need for sleep, increased talkativeness, racing thoughts, distractibility, increased goal-directed activity or agitation, and excessive involvement in pleasurable activities that have a potential for painful consequences (buying sprees, sexual activity, foolish investments, etc.). These symptoms must be severe enough to interfere with social or occupational (self-care) functioning and cannot be due to the effects of drugs (such as cocaine or amphetamines) or medical illness (such as thyroid problems). Furthermore, before a manic episode can be diagnosed, other psychiatric conditions must be ruled out, since persons with schizophrenia (case 18), other psychotic illnesses (cases 18-21), dementia (cases 14-16), or substance abuse (cases 22-24) can have similar symptoms.

A single manic episode, with or without a history of depression, qualifies the person for a diagnosis of bipolar disorder, type I. Thelma's first manic episode probably occurred when she was hospitalized six months ago and misdiagnosed with dementia. Because during manic episodes older persons often present with atypical symptoms (distractibility, cognitive impairment, failure to care for self, and irritability), they are frequently misdiagnosed by treating physicians. Mania itself can disturb cognitive functioning and memory, which explains the confusion about Thelma's diagnosis. Thelma's second manic episode (the current one) is more classic in its presentation, making diagnosis easier. Manic patients often have psychotic symptoms, particularly delusions. For example, they might claim great powers of influence over important people such as the president; a delusional person may even come to believe that he or she is the president or is Jesus Christ. This exaggerated sense of self-importance, these feelings of profound insight or vision, and this high energy level make persons feel that they can accomplish great feats; this is called *grandiosity*. Hyper-religiosity frequently accompanies manic symptoms in persons with strong religious beliefs, and pastors should be alert for congregants who show cycles of great religious fervor alternating with periods of low interest, low energy, and discouragement. Persons with bipolar disorder do not always present with either pure mania or pure depression; they often present with a mixture of both depressive and manic symptoms, making diagnosis difficult. Although not as prevalent among older adults, alcohol and drug abuse are commonly associated with this disorder and are present in nearly two-thirds of cases.

Although bipolar disorder occurs in less than 0.5 percent of persons over age 65 living in the community, it is present in up to 10 percent of nursing home residents. Since the 1960s, when many state hospitals were closed (due to deinstitutionalization), the nursing home has become the dumping ground for older people with chronic mental illness.

Bipolar disorder and schizophrenia are the two psychiatric illnesses that show the most evidence for genetic or biological causes. Up to 24 percent of first-degree relatives of bipolar patients also have the disorder. The onset of the disorder may occur in early life (typically one's early 20s) or in later life. Those persons with late-onset mania are more likely to have structural brain changes (a stroke or other brain disease) as the cause for their mania. Recall that Thelma was diagnosed with a "light stroke" just prior to the worsening of her depression episodes and the eventual development of late-onset mania.

Response to Vignette

Having evaluated Thelma and spoken with her daughter, you make a presumptive diagnosis of bipolar disorder (manic-depressive illness). It is clear that Thelma needs to see a psychiatrist, although this is not at all clear to Thelma. For this reason, you should proceed slowly and cautiously in recommending psychiatric consultation. Recall that her daughter already failed in her attempt, and you will too if you proceed without establishing rapport with Thelma. Rapport will develop slowly as you spend time with Thelma and demonstrate a sincere interest in her plight; even most manic patients know when someone sincerely wishes to help them. At times, however, when the manic individual has absolutely no insight into his or her condition, you may have to play along with the delusional thinking and even "trick" him or her into seeking professional assistance. If neither of these maneuvers succeed, then you or a family member may need to pursue legal channels in order to force the person to have proper medical and psychiatric evaluation. You may need to involve the local department of social services. Arrange to have them visit Thelma in her home, and then they will decide whether there is sufficient cause to force her to see a doctor. If she refuses to see a doctor, the department of social services will complete commitment papers at the magistrate's office, and the sheriff will bring Thelma to the doctor's office for a medical and psychiatric evaluation. Remember that your first priority in such cases is to ensure the person's safety.

The faith community can (1) help Thelma's family obtain a proper evaluation for her, and (2) provide emotional support and reassurance for both Thelma and her family during evaluation and treatment phases. Once a diagnosis is made and other pharmacological, medical, and psychiatric causes for her symptoms are excluded, a management plan for Thelma will be devised and implemented; this typically occurs in a hospital inpatient setting. After her illness has been stabilized, she will be discharged either back to her home to continue living independently (with in-home services) or to a relative's home until she has recovered more completely.

Treatment Within the Faith Community

It is during the recuperative and maintenance phase of Thelma's illness that the faith community can be of greatest help. A supportive community can ensure that she keep her doctor appointments and take her medication, as well as monitor her for symptoms of relapse. Persons with bipolar disorder are known for their dislike of the medications necessary to control their disease. For one thing, many feel that having bipolar disorder is like having a character flaw or a mental defect; taking medication reminds them of their condition, assaulting their pride and self-esteem. Another reason is that many persons with the disease enjoy the high they experience when hypomanic and dislike taking medication that prevents this mental state. A third reason is that the medications used to treat bipolar disorder may have unpleasant side effects (especially initially). However, if medication is discontinued, the chance of relapse in the next six months is very high, and there is some evidence that once discontinued, the medications may not be as effective in controlling the next episode of illness as they were at first. Helping persons see bipolar disorder as an illness just like any other physical condition will help them accept their condition and its treatment. Indeed, evidence from family studies and genetic research suggests that this illness is no different from other physical disorders such as diabetes or high blood pressure and should be treated similarly.

Finally, because severe psychological or social stress can bring on a manic episode in a susceptible person (even when the person is taking medication), it is important that either stress levels are minimized or the person learns to cope with stress better. Again, a strong religious faith can be a very effective stress reducer, so maintaining spiritual fitness by regular involvement in private and public religious activities and by giving of oneself to others through volunteer activity (as long as it is not too stressful) can help prevent future manic episodes.

Indications for Referral

Because of the genetic causes for this disorder, the physical brain changes responsible for symptoms, the availability of effective treatments, and the devastating effects that an uncontrolled manic episode can have on a person's life, immediate psychiatric referral is needed for any person suspected of having this disorder. Likewise, persons who have already been diagnosed with the disorder and are being monitored within the religious community should be encouraged to see their doctor if any of the following symptoms of decompensation appear: increased talkativeness, abnormally increased energy or activity level, decreased need for sleep, or any of the other manic symptoms noted earlier. Studies have shown that if a person with bipolar disorder is sleep-deprived for one night, this greatly increases his or her chances of having a manic episode in the next few days; for this reason, proper sleep and rest is essential. Because persons with this disorder often do not recognize that they are having manic symptoms, friends and family members have a heavy responsibility to monitor them for early signs of relapse.

Treatment by Mental Health Specialist

All people with bipolar disorder must have their care managed by a psychiatrist, particularly older people. General medical physicians do not have the training necessary to manage these patients, from either a psychological or a pharmacological perspective. Lithium is the primary drug used to treat bipolar disorder. It improves the severity of the illness's cycles by nearly 80 percent. But lithium can have unpleasant side effects, including tremor, nausea and diarrhea, fatigue, difficulty concentrating, weight gain, and effects on the kidneys and the skin. Other newer drugs in the anticonvulsant class (carbamazepine and valproic acid) have been shown to be as effective as lithium, but with fewer side effects (although these drugs have their own side effects). During an acute manic episode, medications other than lithium or the anticonvulsants are often necessary to control symptoms. These include neuroleptic medication (such as haloperidol or risperidone) and minor tranquilizers (such as lorazepam or clonazepam). Most acute manic episodes need to be treated in the hospital.

Episodes of depression are difficult to treat in persons with bipolar disorder. While antidepressants can be used to relieve symptoms, they can also cause the person to flip into a manic episode or result in "rapid cycling," which is a severe, difficult to treat form of bipolar disorder. Nevertheless, a psychiatrist who sees large numbers of such patients becomes skilled in treating both the manic and depressive episodes of illness using medications that have tolerable side effects. With adequate treatment, most patients with bipolar disorder can lead completely normal lives and are often very intelligent and productive individuals (see Patty Duke's book below).

Local Resources

Resources

Community mental health centers provide outpatient mental health care on a "sliding scale" fee basis to persons with bipolar disorder who cannot afford a private psychiatrist. Also, most major hospitals affiliated with universities have outpatient clinics that are staffed by psychiatrists in training who provide care at a reduced rate. Severe cases require the involvement of social services and the assignment of a case manager to help coordinate care. A collaborative effort between social service agencies and the local church can maximize the quality of care that persons with this illness receive.

National Resources

The National Depressive and Manic-Depressive Association (NDMDA) has more than two hundred chapters in the United States and Canada that offer support to people with bipolar disorder and to their families. This group sponsors education and research programs and distributes brochures, videotapes, and audiotapes about depression. For more information, write to NDMDA, PO Box 1939, Chicago, IL 60690, or call 1-800-826-3632. The National Alliance for the Mentally Ill (NAMI) has groups in all states that provide emotional support to elders with bipolar disorder and to their families. They can also help people find local services. For more information, write NAMI, 2101 Wilson Boulevard, Suite 302, Arlington, VA 22201, or call 1-800-950-6264.

Self-Help Resources

Actress Patty Duke's 1992 book *A Brilliant Madness* (New York: Bantam Books) can help dispel negative attitudes about this illness and can also help persons accept their diagnosis and comply with treatment.

Cross-Cultural Issues

In some cultures, persons with mania were elected as the community shamans or priests to act as intercessors between the community and the spirit world. Their hallucinations and delusions were understood as special powers. This is generally no longer true in Western societies where treatment for this condition is available. Nevertheless, because of the frequent hyper-religiosity associated with manic episodes, the disorder may sometimes be difficult to distinguish from normative religious experience (e.g., charismatics who become filled with the Holy Spirit, or simply ordinary persons with extraordinary religious zeal).

Increased Risk for Suicide

Recently Widowed

I t is a week after Celia's funeral. Marvin and Celia had been married for forty-five years. Marvin is 68. Their only daughter was killed in an automobile accident ten years ago. This latter event marked the onset of his drinking problem. Marvin's lifelong partner had been very involved in the life of the parish, while he had attended mass irregularly over the years. This is the first pastoral visit you've made since Celia died suddenly. Marvin had put you off when you asked to visit him the day after her funeral. People in town say they have not seen much of Marvin since Celia's death; he has apparently withdrawn from both family and friends. He has recently purchased a shotgun at the local store. You knock on the front door several times. He finally comes to the door in his bedroom slippers and bathrobe. It is the middle of the afternoon. Marvin looks very tired and sad. There is the smell of alcohol in the room. You sit in the front parlor together. "Father," he says, "I just haven't been myself since she died." Tears well up in his puffy eyes. "I just can't see anything worth living for. Life feels pointless without my lovely wife."

Pastoral Care Assessment

It is essential that you recognize Marvin is faced with a crisis that needs very careful evaluation and immediate intervention. The widower is overwhelmed and does not have the emotional resources to cope. Offer empathy and listen to his story while assessing his risk of self-harm and his intent to commit suicide. It is important for you to begin your pastoral assessment for suicide with a gentle, gradual progression of remarks and questions such as the following: "I can see that you are upset." "How badly are you hurting?" "Do you feel in enough pain to harm yourself?" "Do you feel suicidal now?" Don't hesitate to ask caring questions. One of the biggest myths about suicide is that asking people if they are suicidal will encourage them to take their lives. The very opposite is true. Bringing the subject out into the open will diminish the danger. Asking a person about his or her feelings communicates that someone cares.

The most immediate concern in this case is Marvin's recent purchase of a firearm. The vast majority of elderly persons who take their lives use a gun.[1] Where is the recently purchased shotgun? Does he have a plan worked out to commit suicide with it? If Marvin tells you that he is contemplating self-harm, you will need to ask about his plan. "How do you plan to take your life?" "When will you do it?" "Where will you do it?" The more detailed and concrete the plan, the greater the risk. Do not leave a person alone who has a plan of action and a means to commit suicide. Separating the person from the means of suicide is essential. Suicidal behavior is in most instances a transitory symptom of underlying, severe emotional pain that requires a team approach to treatment (mental health specialist and pastor).

Relevant History

The widower has had a history of good health. He has a limited support system with few friends and social contacts. He had become increasingly emotionally dependent upon his spouse prior to her death. He does not have a history of suicidal or homicidal behaviors.

Diagnostic Criteria

It is important for members of the clergy to understand the warning signs of suicide. Use the pneumonic device **SADPARSONS** to assist in remembering them. See next page.

Response to Vignette

The newly widowed man presents a set of factors that place him at risk for suicide. Several days after the death of a lifelong partner, he has become withdrawn and uses alcohol in an attempt to self-medicate the emotional pain he is experiencing with her loss. He has many of the signs of a "major depression": sad mood, low energy, helpless/hopeless feelings, possible sleep disturbance, and pessimism about the future. A history of alcoholism combined with depression places him at a high risk for suicide. Of the greatest concern is that he purchased a gun since the funeral. This is a very high risk sign of suicidal potential.

It is helpful that he has good health and a relationship, although infrequent, with his church and priest. He needs treatment for danger to himself, for depression, and for alcohol abuse. Inpatient mental health care is required during the crisis. He also needs assistance in developing a more adequate support system beyond the crisis period.

Treatment Within the Faith Community

Clergy are in a particularly advantageous position to recognize suicidal lethality in older persons. Pastors are often in long-term relationships with individuals and their families, enabling them to observe changes in

---

1. M. S. Kaplan, M. E. Adamek, and S. Johnson, "Trends in Firearm Suicide Among Older American Males: 1979-1988," *The Gerontologist* 34, no. 1 (1994): 59-65.

Sex. White males have increased suicide rates with each decade of life beyond 60 years of age. By age 85 the ratio of male suicides to female suicides is twelve to one.[2]

Age. The risk of suicide increases with age for all Americans. An 80-year-old person is twice as likely to take his or her life as a 20-year-old person.[3]

Depression. Several researchers estimate that the vast majority of the elderly, perhaps 80 percent, are significantly depressed when they take their lives. Intense feelings of depression and hopelessness are strongly associated with suicide. Researchers have discovered that simply being a member of a synagogue or church is a good predictor of significantly lower levels of depression in older men who have experienced "the death of someone close."[4]

Previous Attempts. Although older persons are less likely to have made prior suicidal attempts than younger persons, a history of suicidal attempts is a strong indicator of suicide potential.

Alcohol and Drug Abuse. Approximately 15 percent of persons suffering from the disease of alcoholism take their lives. The combination of depression and alcohol or drug abuse places an older person at high risk for suicide.

Iational Thinking Loss. Suicidal individuals often develop "tunnel vision" thinking. They are usually constricted in their thought processes, unable to see alternate options to suicide, and generally exercise poor judgment.

Social Support. Older persons who are socially isolated and suffer loneliness are at greater risk for suicide. Retirement or a move to a nursing home places some older persons at greater risk for suicide. Having a social network such as a church or synagogue reduces the suicide risk.

Organized Plan. The elderly are much more likely to complete suicide than any other age group. Most fatal suicides among seniors are not impulsive acts. They are planned. The more specific the plan, the greater the danger. An organized plan with an available means places a person at very high risk and demands immediate attention.

No Life-Partner. Older persons who are living alone, divorced, or widowed are at a greater risk for suicide than the general population. Widowhood increases the risk of suicide especially among elderly males the first six months after the death of a spouse.

Sickness. Long-term, incurable illness, particularly involving intractable pain, is a high risk factor for suicide among the elderly. One study found that about half of elderly suicide attempters suffered from chronic illness.[5]

2. R. L. Frierson, "Suicide Attempts by the Old and Very Old," *Archives of Internal Medicine* 151 (1991): 141-44.
3. G. E. Vaillant and S. J. Blumenthal, "Introduction: Suicide over the Life Cycle: Risk Factors and Life-Span Development," in *Suicide over the Life Cycle: Risk Factors, Assessment, and Treatment of Suicidal Patients*, eds. S. J. Blumenthal and D. J. Kupfer (Washington, D.C.: American Psychiatric Press, 1990), 1-16.
4. J. M. Siegel and D. H. Kuykendall, "Loss, Widowhood, and Psychological Distress Among Elderly," *Journal of Consulting and Clinical Psychology* 58, no. 5 (1990): 519-24.
5. Frierson, "Suicide Attempts by the Old and Very Old."

behavior and thinking. Pastors are called upon most often in times of crisis when suicidal thoughts may occur, such as "personal illness or injury, death of spouse, death of a close family member, divorce or marital separation, change in health of a family member, death of a close friend."[6] Most important, pastors are visible and available leaders in the community, offering hope. Undoubtedly, distressed older persons go to clergy in large numbers because they have questions about meaning and purpose that are uniquely addressed by communities of faith.

An extensive study based on a survey of almost 72,000 residents of Maryland reported that those who did not attend church were over four times as likely to take their lives than those who attended church regularly.[7] Religious involvement appears to provide a buffer against the hardships of aging by lessening loneliness and isolation, decreasing levels of depression and alcoholism, and offering meaningful voluntary work and activities that lift the spirit.

Indications for Referral

A referral is in order any time a serious threat of self-harm is present based on the risk factors we have noted, such as a plan or means of action, prior attempts, significant depression, alcohol or drug abuse, impaired thinking, hopelessness, or chronic illness. A referral is always appropriate when a pastor feels in over his or her head.

Treatment by Mental Health Specialist

The primary goal with a suicidal patient is safety. Treatment may involve hospitalization or nonhospitalization (outpatient care). Inpatient or hospitalized treatment is indicated when a high risk of suicide exists, when the person is psychotic, intoxicated, or has a brain disorder, or when the person's social support system is inadequate. Voluntary hospitalization is preferable to involuntary placement, although the latter is often necessary to ensure safety. Outpatient care is indicated when the risk of suicide is determined to be low or the crisis that precipitated suicidal thinking has diminished.

Resources

Local Resources

If the person's condition is life-threatening, the person should be taken to the local emergency room. If it is less urgent, an appointment with a mental health specialist will be needed. Develop a relationship with at least one mental health specialist or crisis intervention worker before you have a suicidal crisis. There are a variety of people who can help a pastor plan for a mental health emergency, including psychiatrists, psychologists,

6. R. W. Fairchild, *Finding Hope Again: A Pastor's Guide to Counseling Depressed Persons* (New York: Harper & Row, 1980).
7. G. W. Comstock and K. B. Partridge, "Church Attendance and Health," *Journal of Chronic Disease* 25 (1972): 665-72.

marriage and family counselors, pastoral counselors, social workers, social services agencies, police and fire departments, and crisis intervention centers. The essential help clergy can offer a suicidal person is the support they need until assistance is secured.

National Resources

There are several organizations that offer assistance and information about suicide prevention programs that can be useful to congregations and clergy, including The American Association of Suicidology, 2459 South Ash, Denver, CO 80222 (phone 303-765-8485); and The Samaritans, 500 Commonwealth Avenue, Kenmore Square, Boston, MA 02215 (twenty-four-hour helpline: 617-247-0220; phone: 617-536-2460).

Self-Help Resources

The Minister as Crisis Counselor, revised edition, by David Switzer (Nashville: Abingdon Press, 1985), and *Practical Psychology for Pastors*, by William R. Miller and Kathleen A. Jackson (Englewood Cliffs, N.J.: Prentice-Hall, 1985), offer helpful sections on suicide from a faith perspective. *Suicide Across the Life Span: Premature Exits*, by Judith M. Stillion, Eugene E. McDowell, and Jacque H. May (New York: Hemisphere, 1989), and *Mental Health and the Elderly: a Social Work Perspective*, ed. Francis J. Turner (New York: Free Press, 1992), offer excellent summary chapters on elderly suicide.

Cross-Cultural Issues

African American elders have lower rates of suicide than their Caucasian counterparts. The ratio of suicides of elderly Caucasians to elderly African Americans is about three to one. Despite disproportionate socioeconomic hardships, older African American women have the lowest rate of suicide when considering race, age, and gender. Older African American women also have the highest rate of church involvement.[8] The human network and interpretative meaning of religious community offer emotional and spiritual support that probably contribute to lower rates of suicide.

8. H. G. Koenig, *Aging and God* (Binghamton, N.Y.: Haworth Press, 1994).

Generalized Anxiety Disorder

I Worry All the Time

Catherine and her husband, Sam, have been members of your congregation since you started the church twenty-five years ago. They come to church every Sunday and attend most of the major church functions. At the age of 68, Sam is a deacon and your head usher. Catherine, age 67, has taken on a number of different responsibilities in the church, but none for very long. After a while, she complains that the job or task gets on her "nerves," and then she quits. Recently, Catherine took on the task of organizing a garage sale to raise money for the church; this responsibility soon got on her nerves, and now she is asking you to put somebody else in charge. This has put you in a bind, since the garage sale is only two days away. You call Catherine and arrange to meet her and Sam in the morning.

Catherine and Sam come into your office and seat themselves comfortably on your couch. You start out with small talk, but then quickly move onto the main topic. "Catherine, tell me about why you're having difficulty managing our garage sale this year," you inquire in a serious but understanding tone.

"It's just making me too nervous," Catherine explains. "You know I'm that way, pastor. Everything makes me nervous. I worry all the time." On further gentle prompting, she tells you more about her history. Since childhood, Catherine recalls always being more anxious than other people. She was able to function pretty well, however, until her "midlife change," after which her nerves became more difficult to control. "I've tried to overcome this by taking on responsibilities at church," she says. "But I just can't seem to beat this thing." Catherine tells you that over the past couple of years she has felt restless and more irritable, has had difficulty concentrating, and has felt tense and uptight nearly all the time. Everything seems to worry her—the children, the finances, her husband's health, her own health, and other less important issues.

"Why haven't you sought help for this, Catherine?" you ask in a concerned voice.

"I feel so embarrassed," cries Catherine. "I'm afraid my doctor would think I'm crazy or something, and put me on some type of tranquilizer. I don't want to become addicted. I can handle this on my own, if I keep trying."

You tell Catherine that you will put someone else in charge of the garage sale, but you ask her if she and her husband would meet with you for a few sessions to work on her anxiety problem. She and her husband agree, and you schedule your next meeting in a week.

Pastoral Care Assessment

On your next session with the couple, you first ask to see Catherine alone for fifteen minutes, then Sam alone for fifteen minutes, and then see them as a couple for the remainder of the hour. Catherine is a thin, nervous woman who appears older than her stated age. She has a fine tremor that is most noticeable in her hands. She makes good eye contact with you, but has some difficulty relating to and understanding your questions. She is able to laugh, and does not appear to be depressed or admit to feeling down or discouraged. When you ask her if she is feeling any less anxious now that the garage sale is over, she replies that she is *not*, because now she is worrying about an upcoming visit by her sister, with whom she does not get along.

You review her history and then ask to see Sam, in order to get his perspective on things. Sam confirms his wife's story and admits that her anxiety and constant worry has affected their marriage and her relationship with their children. "I can't seem to get her to relax, pastor," Sam notes. "Even when we go on vacation, she worries about everything. I've tried to get her to go to a doctor, but she always has an excuse not to go. Anyway, do you think there is anything they can do to help her?" You avoid answering this question, for now, and redirect the conversation to their marriage. Although the marriage has been a relatively peaceful one, they have always lived somewhat separate lives; Sam involved in his sales work that took him on long trips away from home; Catherine involved in raising the children and her women's group. For the past three years, since Sam's retirement, they have been forced to spend more time together, and each has had a tendency to get on the other's nerves. Nevertheless, they are devoted to each other and committed to working things out, says Sam.

Further questioning of the couple together reveals that Catherine has never had any other psychiatric problems and has never been to see a counselor, except for a brief period after their second child was stillborn. Although she has no significant family history of psychiatric problems, her mother was also an anxious woman and her father drank heavily, but "never had a problem with it." Catherine herself has no history of alcohol abuse or dependence and does not drink now. She does, however, have a number of medical problems. A forty-year history of smoking has damaged her lungs and requires that she take pills and use an inhaler to help her breathe. She also has painful arthritis in her hips and back that requires daily medication. Finally, Catherine's diet is not particularly balanced; she enjoys sweets and breads and drinks a couple of cups of coffee to get going in the morning and sometimes has a cup in the afternoon to keep going.

Catherine has been a sensitive and anxious person since childhood, although symptoms have worsened since menopause. Her mother for many years had been a role model for her in this regard. For the past ten years, she has felt tense and anxious much of the time, and if she doesn't worry about one thing, she worries about another. Even on vacations, she has difficulty relaxing and worries over minor, irrelevant details. When any pressure is placed on her, such as that involved with organizing the garage sale, her anxiety escalates to the point that it interferes with her ability to complete the task. Despite the disability this causes, Catherine has not sought medical attention. She is embarrassed about her problem and fearful of being labeled "crazy." She and her husband are having some marital problems due to his retirement and her anxiety. Marital problems can and often do contribute to tension that family members experience. Catherine's diet of concentrated sweets could lead to excess insulin production and hypoglycemic spells that will worsen anxiety. Her habit of three cups of caffeinated coffee per day is adding fuel to her already over-stimulated nervous system and is probably adding to her shakiness and hand tremor. Her medical illnesses may also adversely affect her anxiety, and her breathing medications (both stimulants) are likely to contribute to symptoms as well. Anxiety is common in persons with chronic lung disease; shortness of breath is a terrifying sensation and can worsen anxiety, just as anxiety can worsen breathing by inducing bronchospasm (spasm of the breathing tubes). Chronic pain from arthritis may also worsen muscle tension and induce spasm as well. Thus, Catherine has both internal (psychological) and external (environmental) contributors that maintain her chronic anxiety.

Relevant History

Catherine has *generalized anxiety disorder* (GAD), a common cause for chronic, disabling excessive worry and anxiety. To have this diagnosis, a person must meet the following criteria:

Diagnostic Criteria

1. Have experienced excessive anxiety and worry occurring on more days than not for a period of six months or longer.
2. Find it difficult to control his or her worry.
3. Have at least three of the following six symptoms: restlessness, easy fatigability, impaired concentration, irritability, muscle tension, and disturbed sleep.

4. Have anxiety that is not primarily due to another anxiety disorder such as panic disorder (see case 8) or social phobia.
5. *Not* have symptoms that are primarily due to the direct physiological effects of a substance (caffeine, amphetamines, cocaine) or prescription medications (e.g., breathing medicines that contain xanthenes, thyroid preparations).

While Catherine's symptoms may be exacerbated by her coffee intake and breathing medications, these are unlikely to be the major underlying cause for her anxiety. Likewise, while she may have some degree of social phobia or fear of being embarrassed in public (hence her decision to step down as the garage sale coordinator), this occurs on a background of much more widespread, constant worry and anxiety, as typically seen in GAD.

Generalized anxiety disorder is one of the most common anxiety disorders seen among older adults, particularly those with chronic health problems. Nearly one in twenty adults (5 percent) will at some time in their lives meet the diagnostic criteria for GAD. Catherine, then, far from having a strange or unusual disorder, has plenty of company from the other 10 million Americans with the problem.

Response to Vignette

After two sessions with Catherine and Sam to further define the problem and help resolve the stress their marital relationship contributes to the picture, you begin individual counseling sessions with Catherine. Your goals with her during these sessions are education, support, and preparation. First, you educate her about how her diet might be worsening her anxiety symptoms. You encourage her to avoid all caffeinated beverages (coffee, tea, colas) and to eat a more balanced diet rich in complex carbohydrates and proteins (which will help maintain a more constant blood sugar level). Likewise, you encourage her to see her doctor to be sure that her medical problems are being treated adequately and that she is not being either overmedicated or undermedicated. Second, you educate her about how common her anxiety problem is (occurring in 3 to 5 percent of the population) and the different medical treatments that are available (see below). During this time, you are also *working toward getting her to seek medical treatment for her anxiety disorder*. Simply advising her to see a psychiatrist and take medication, without adequate preparation, will probably fail as did her husband's efforts to get her to see a doctor. Catherine's long history of anxiety problems makes hers a complex case in need of specialized treatment beyond that likely to be obtained from her general medical doctor. You also want to assess and provide treatment for any component of depression that might be worsening her anxiety (see case 11, "Mixed Anxiety-Depression").

Catherine needs personal counseling, either by yourself or by trained pastoral staff, and then needs referral to a psychiatrist. However, general support and prayer from her faith community (with confidentiality maintained) will make it easier for her to make the difficult changes in lifestyle and attitude that she needs to make. Referral to Bible passages that describe God's promises of protection, peace, and care for those who are fearful or anxious (Psalm 4:8, Psalm 91:1-2, Proverbs 3:24, Isaiah 26:3, Matthew 6:25-34, John 14:27, Philippians 4:6-7, 1 Peter 5:7) can be of great comfort to her. Memorizing these verses and repeating them over and over again during times of anxiety or stress can often bring relief to those who have not been helped by other remedies.

Some effort within the local faith community to relieve symptoms through counseling and spiritual interventions should be attempted. Nevertheless, if there is no improvement within two to four weeks, persons who fulfill the diagnostic criteria for generalized anxiety disorder (symptoms of excessive worry and anxiety lasting six months or longer that interfere with work or social functioning) should be referred for specialized treatment.

Assuming that physical health conditions and medication regimens have been optimized and disorders such as hyperthyroidism have been ruled out by her medical doctor, a mental health professional will focus on education, cognitive-behavioral therapy, and drug treatments. First, he or she will reinforce the importance of the dietary changes discussed above. Second, he or she will provide cognitive therapy to help Catherine deal with the psychological component of her anxiety, as well as teach her some general relaxation and breathing exercises to help relieve chronic muscle tension. (Biofeedback can also be helpful.) Third, the mental health professional may prescribe medication to relieve anxiety. There is some evidence that persons with GAD have certain areas of the brain that are overactive, suggesting a biological component to their disease. There are medications such as buspirone (Buspar) that are nonaddictive that may help normalize brain function and relieve anxiety. Antidepressants may also be helpful in this regard and will also treat any component of depression that may be worsening anxiety. Antihistamines such as hydroxyzine (Vistaril or Atarax) can be used to relieve mild anxiety, although they produce more general sedation and may interfere with memory or induce confusion because of their anticholinergic effects.

Finally, benzodiazepines or minor tranquilizers such as lorazepam (Ativan), clonazepam (Klonopin), or alprazolam (Xanax) may be used to temporarily relieve anxiety to enhance functioning for specific events (garage sales, appearances in court, etc.). Minor tranquilizers, however, can be habit-forming and their use should usually be time-limited (prescribed for a specific time period and then tapered off and stopped). Some older

Treatment Within the Faith Community

Indications for Referral

Treatment by Mental Health Specialist

adults with GAD require lifelong treatment with these drugs, and research has shown that these individuals do not usually increase their dose or abuse these medications. Nevertheless, minor tranquilizers do have side effects that may worsen memory, lead to falls and hip fractures, or cause oversedation, and therefore must be used cautiously under strict regulation by a physician. Older tranquilizers such as diazepam (Valium), chlordiazepoxide (Librium), or meprobamate (PMB) should probably be avoided by older adults.

Resources

Local Resources

For psychological or behavioral treatments, find a psychiatric social worker or psychologist with an interest in geriatric issues. For medical treatments, a psychiatrist or geropsychiatrist should be sought. Community mental health clinics often have persons who specialize in treating anxiety disorder and can provide treatment or referral information; fees for treatment are usually based on a sliding scale depending on income. If you live in a city where there is a major medical center or university hospital, they are likely to have an anxiety disorder clinic that specializes in the treatment of these problems and may be conducting research studies (in which participation earns free treatment).

National Resources

You can call the Anxiety Disorders Association of America at 301-231-9350 for more information on anxiety problems. The Council on Anxiety Disorders, located in Winston-Salem, North Carolina, deals with education, advocacy, and mutual support for people with anxiety disorders; they mail out information packets that include articles about specific anxiety disorders (including GAD), treatments, a resource list, a newsletter, and personal stories published in newspapers. They can be reached at 910-722-7760. Finally, the National Institute of Mental Health has a panic disorder information line that will send you a resource list for further information, treatment, and referral; call 1-800-647-2642 (although there may be a wait and they deal mostly with panic disorder problems, not GAD). Other national organizations that provide information about anxiety disorders include the Obsessive-Compulsive (OC) Foundation, Inc., PO Box 70, Milford, CT 06460 (phone 203-878-5669), and the Obsessive-Compulsive Information Center, Department of Psychiatry at University of Wisconsin, 600 Highland Avenue, Madison WI 53792 (phone 608-836-8070).

Self-Help Resources

Every state has anxiety support groups; for example, North Carolina has twelve such groups. For information about the location of support groups in your state (i.e., names and phone numbers of contact persons) call the Council on Anxiety Disorders (910-722-7760). The Anxiety Disorders Association of America (301-231-9350) can be contacted for a catalogue of self-help books. Their guide on how to organize a self-help group, entitled "Help Yourself: A Guide to Organizing a Phobia Self-Help Group" (also applicable to GAD), gives the basic tools to form a self-help group, including how support groups work and how to run the first meeting.

Self-help books that provide information about anxiety disorders include David Sheehan's *The Anxiety Disease* (New York: Bantam Books, 1986); Mark Gold's *The Good News About Panic, Anxiety, and Phobias: Cures, Treatments, and Solutions in the New Age of Biopsychiatry* (New York: Random House, 1989); Greist and colleagues' *Anxiety and Its Treatment: Help Is Available* (New York, Warner Books, 1987); Isaac Marks's *Living with Fear: Understanding and Coping with Anxiety* (New York: McGraw-Hill, 1980); and Claire Weekes's *Peace from Nervous Suffering* (New York: Bantam Books, 1983). For more information about anxiety disorders in older persons with medical problems, see our article entitled "Anxiety in Medically Ill Older Adults" in the *International Journal of Psychiatry in Medicine* 25 (1995): 215-32. Also, if you desire more information from a medical perspective, see Robert Abrams's chapter on "Anxiety and Personality Disorders" in *Comprehensive Review of Geriatric Psychiatry*, editors J. Sadavoy, L. Lazarus, and L. Jarvik (Washington, D.C.: American Psychiatric Press, 1991), 369-76.

Cross-Cultural Issues

Anxiety is expressed differently in different cultures. Anxiety has both somatic (physical) and cognitive (psychological) components. Physical expressions of anxiety include shakiness, tremor, cold or clammy hands, dry mouth, lump in the throat, difficulty swallowing, rapid heartbeat, shortness of breath, dizziness, diarrhea, and urge to urinate. Psychological symptoms include worry, dread, fear, nervousness, and the like. In some cultures anxiety is expressed more in terms of physical symptoms; in others, it is expressed more in terms of psychological symptoms. One must also consider the cultural context when trying to decide whether anxiety in certain situations is excessive.

Panic Disorder and Agoraphobia

I'm Going Crazy

Ruth is a reserved, 60-year-old, lifetime member of her parish church. Because she has attended church infrequently in the past several months, you make a pastoral visit to check on her welfare. She has been married forty-one years and has five grown children. A devoted parent, she was at a bit of a loss when the last of her children moved out of the area two years prior. Ruth's husband is a sales manager who travels extensively as part of his work. His employment requires that he frequently be away from home for weeks at a time.

She greets you at the door, "Good morning, Father. I am glad to see you. I have been meaning to come to your office but I haven't been out much lately." With encouragement, Ruth is able to tell you she has been increasingly fear-ridden after a series of panic attacks over the past several months. At the time of the first attack, she was driving her car on a freeway. She states, "Father, it came out of the blue. My heart began to pound and my chest ached. I could hardly breathe. I became dizzy and thought I was going to die. I prayed the Our Father, and after a few minutes the panic went away." She indicates the panic attacks have happened several times subsequently, the last one occurring at Mass "two weeks ago." She says with sadness, "I'm scared to go to church or drive my car or leave my neighborhood for fear one of these attacks will overwhelm me again." Ruth is shaking as she tells her story. Up to this point in time, she has not told her family about her problem.

It is important to direct Ruth to seek a medical examination to rule out physical causes for these concerning symptoms. Excessive levels of thyroid hormone, certain types of epilepsy, or disturbances in heartbeat rhythm can cause symptoms similar to those found during a panic attack. Once a

Pastoral Care Assessment

physical condition is ruled out, encourage Ruth to seek specialized psychological care. Persons with panic disorder can go from one medical specialist to the next, seeking a physical diagnosis to explain the attacks. Ruth has a passive personality that can be found among some who have panic disorder. She will need more than a referral for help; she will need you or friends to take her to her first appointments and to encourage continued therapy. If she has late-onset panic disorder with agoraphobia, it can be a very disabling condition that will be highly stressful to Ruth and her family; they will need support and encouragement from you and her friends within the parish.

It is important when making your assessment to remember that Ruth has strengths as well as weaknesses. In Ruth's case, it is helpful that the attacks have only recently begun and she has not accepted her condition as being a permanent disability. Ruth also has a living faith. She used the Our Father prayer as a creative resource to reassure and calm her when she had a panic attack. Encourage her to utilize her faith. It is also very positive that she trusts you enough to tell you about her secret painful problem. Social isolation coupled with a fear of stigmatization are common among persons with mental illnesses and are strongly counterproductive to recovery. It is important to ask her if she has had thoughts of hurting herself, as repeated panic attacks can be so frightening that the risk of suicide is significant.[1]

Relevant History

Ruth has a problem being assertive or speaking up for herself. She tends to want to please others rather than be herself. This has been her pattern of coping since early childhood within her family of origin and now with her spouse. There is no history of panic disorder or agoraphobia within Ruth's family of origin. She does not drink alcohol, which is important to know because 30 percent of the people who have panic attacks abuse alcohol.[2]

Diagnostic Criteria

A panic attack is a discrete period in which a sudden onset of intense apprehension, fear, or terror occurs unexpectedly, often associated with a sense of impending doom and an urge to escape. (The word *panic* comes from the name of the Greek god *Pan*, who frightened sojourners by springing at them unexpectedly.) At least four of thirteen symptoms develop abruptly and reach a peak within ten minutes: dizziness, shortness of breath or a smothering sensation, pounding heart, sweating, trembling, choking, nausea, chest pain, chills or hot flashes, numbness, a fear of dying, a fear of going crazy, and derealization (feeling of unreality) or depersonalization (feeling detached from oneself).

1. B. J. Cox, D. M. Direnfeld, R. P. Swinson, and G. R. Norton, "Suicidal Ideation and Suicide Attempters in Panic Disorders and Social Phobia," *American Journal of Psychiatry* 151, no. 6 (1994): 882-87.
2. H. I. Kaplan and B. J. Sadock, *Synopsis of Psychiatry*, 5th ed. (Baltimore: Williams & Wilkins, 1988), 319.

The word *agoraphobia* comes from the Greek words *agora* (marketplace) and *phobos* (fear). The disorder involves anxiety about being in situations or places from which escape might be difficult (or embarrassing) or in which help might not be available if a panic attack or paniclike symptoms were to develop (e.g., a sudden attack of chest pains or a heavily pounding heart). Agoraphobia fears typically involve being outside the home alone, being in a crowd or standing in line, traveling in a vehicle, or being on a bridge or elevator. By definition, agoraphobia results in avoidance of fearful situations (e.g., travel restrictions or avoiding a crowded church) or endurance of those situations either with marked distress or with a companion present. Often persons with this malady restrict themselves to a "zone of safety" that may include their home or neighborhood. Typically they lead lives of extreme dependency as well as great discomfort.

Panic disorder may occur with or without agoraphobia. In panic disorder, panic attacks recur, and the person develops an intense apprehension of having another attack. It becomes a "fear of fear." The sufferer may have a persistent concern about having another attack, worry about the implications of the attack or its consequences, or display a significant change in behavior related to the attacks. Agoraphobia affects about a third of all people with panic disorder, and women with panic disorder are affected by agoraphobia twice as frequently as men with panic disorder.

Response to Vignette

Ruth has symptoms that strongly indicate she is suffering from late-onset panic disorder with agoraphobia. When physical causes are ruled out, studies indicate that 2 to 5 percent of the general population suffer from panic disorder at some period in their lives. Although this disorder has typically been thought of as a problem among young adults, recent findings suggest that panic disorder has a much more frequent onset among the elderly than was previously recognized.[3]

Ruth's panic attacks are repeated and unpredictable. She has discussed several symptoms characteristic of panic attacks: rapid heartbeat, chest pains, dizziness, and fear of dying. Ruth also lives in apprehension that the attacks will happen again and has become fearful of leaving the safety of her neighborhood (agoraphobia). Her isolation in not being able to tell others about the attacks needs to be addressed, as it amplifies her fears. One wonders about communication issues in her family. Why has she not been able to talk to her spouse about her problems? Is poor communication in the marital relationship part of the problem? A meeting with Ruth's spouse and other family members could help you gain a better picture of the family dynamics and provide an opportunity to model for Ruth a more open and direct style of communicating her needs and feelings.

3. B. A. Raj, M. H. Corvea, and E. M. Dagon, "The Clinical Characteristics of Panic Disorder in the Elderly: A Retrospective Study," *Journal of Clinical Psychiatry* 54, no. 4 (1993): 150-55.

There is research evidence that suggests that those whose spouses accompany them into treatment for agoraphobia show longer-lasting improvement.

Treatment Within the Faith Community

Parish caregivers who offer supportive help to Ruth need to find the positive in even small changes and not enable Ruth's tendency to avoid her problems. People who help her should not panic when she panics. Be patient and accepting without giving her the message that she has a permanent condition. Also, don't say, "Relax," or "Calm down," or "Don't be anxious," which can set up a test that may trigger greater anxiety.

Teach the facts about anxiety disorders, including panic disorder, as a minister to your community of faith. Only about one in four persons with anxiety disorders receives adequate treatment. Much of the resistance to treatment results from the fear of stigmatization. Myths about mental illness can be dispelled best through open, frank, and informed dialogue. Visitation, supportive counseling, tangible practical help, and prayer by members of the parish can provide nurturing and care to Ruth and her family.

Indications for Referral

Those who suffer from panic disorder need to see a medical doctor to rule out a physical condition and need specialized cognitive-behavioral therapy to treat the condition. Recent research suggests that religious clients respond better to cognitive-behavioral therapy that is adapted to their religious values and concerns.[4] Shared religious values may be a consideration when making a referral.

Treatment by Mental Health Specialist

Treatments for panic disorder and agoraphobia most often involve the use of medications and cognitive-behavioral therapy. These treatments have been shown to be helpful in the great majority of cases. Cognitive-behavioral approaches reduce anxiety while teaching Ruth how to view the panic situations differently. This treatment approach helps Ruth to think logically about her nonreality-based dread, and helps her to see she has nothing to fear. By modifying her thought patterns, Ruth can gain more control over her problem. Behavioral-based breathing exercises will most likely be used in conjunction with cognitive therapy. With this intervention and the slow breathing and relaxation training, Ruth will learn to control one of the most frightening symptoms of panic attacks, hyperventilation.

To address Ruth's agoraphobia with real-life exposure therapy can be beneficial. This is a treatment modality in which she is very slowly exposed to the fearful situation until she becomes desensitized to it. In this way Ruth begins to see that, as frightful as her feelings are, they are

4. L. Propst, R. Ostrom, P. Watkins, P. Dean, and D. Marshburn, "Comparative Efficacy of Religious and Nonreligious Cognitive-Behavioral Therapy for Treatment of Clinical Depression in Religious Individuals," *Journal of Consulting and Clinical Psychology* 60 (1992): 94-103.

not dangerous and will pass. Ruth may find that this step-by-step process can gradually assist her in mastering her fears. Some therapists, who specialize in treatment of agoraphobia, might go to Ruth's home to conduct initial sessions. They would accompany Ruth on shopping outings or go driving with her to help her overcome her fears. Marital therapy can be used as an adjunct treatment modality if it appears that Ruth's marital relationship is part of the dynamic of the problem.

Ruth may find the greatest relief from panic disorder symptoms when using certain prescription medications. Medications are used to prevent panic attacks and reduce their severity. The two most common medications are benzodiazepines and antidepressants. Benzodiazepines are high-potency tranquilizers that have a calming effect and act rapidly. Some common trade names for these medications are Xanax, Librium, Valium, and Ativan. Benzodiazepines can be addictive and cause withdrawal symptoms when stopping or reducing the dose after prolonged use. Several of the benzodiazepines (e.g., Valium, Librium) are not commonly prescribed to seniors because of increased side effects such as falls and confusion.

The most widely used antidepressant medication that has a beneficial effect on panic disorders is imipramine (trade name Tofranil). Imipramine is slowly introduced to minimize side effects such as dry mouth, constipation, and blurred vision. The antidepressant can also be beneficial to the almost 50 percent of panic disorder patients who have a depression sometime during their life.

Local Resources

Resources

It can be difficult to locate persons who have training and experience in the therapy modalities that are most effective for patients with panic disorder and agoraphobia. The Anxiety Disorders Association of America provides a list of professionals in your area who provide specialized treatments for anxiety disorders. You can call the association at 301-231-9350 or write Department A, 6000 Executive Boulevard, Rockville, MD 20852. You may also contact the Association for the Advancement of Behavioral Therapy, 305 Seventh Avenue, New York, NY 10001 (phone 212-647-1890); or the American Psychological Association, 750 First Street, NE, Washington, DC 20002 (phone 202-336-5500).

National Resources

The National Institute of Mental Health has a Panic Disorder Education Program that provides helpful educational materials. For more information call 1-800-64-PANIC or write NIMH, Publications List, Room 7C-02, 5600 Fishers Lane, Rockville, MD 20857. You can also obtain helpful information about panic disorder from the National Alliance for the Mentally Ill, 200 North Glebe Road, Suite 1015, Arlington, VA 22203-3754 (phone 1-800-950-6264); or Phobics Anonymous, PO Box 1180, Palm Springs, CA 92263 (phone 619-322-2673); or the National Anxiety Foundation, 3135 Custer Drive, Lexington, KY 40517 (phone 606-272-7166).

Self-Help Resources

The American Psychiatric Association (APA) has a pamphlet written for the lay audience, entitled, "Let's Talk Facts About Panic Disorder." Free samples are available, as well as a booklet entitled, "A Mental Illness Awareness Guide for the Clergy," compiled by the Rev. Walter S. Hill, a theologically trained clergyman who works for the APA Department of Public Affairs. These resources and other educational materials can be obtained by calling 1-800-368-5777 or writing 1400 K Street, NW, Suite 1011, Washington, DC 20005. The National Mental Health Consumers' Self-Help Clearinghouse, 1211 Chestnut Street, tenth floor, Philadelphia, PA 19107 (phone 1-800-553-4539), provides material on organizing self-help groups for anxiety disorders and other mental health problems.

Agoraphobia and Panic: A Guide to Psychological Treatment, by Jeffrey E. Hecker and Geoffery L. Thorpe (Boston: Allyn and Bacon, 1992), is a comprehensive guide to the treatment of panic disorder and agoraphobia. *A Minister's Handbook of Mental Disorders*, by Joseph W. Ciarrocchi (New York: Paulist Press, 1993), has an informative chapter on anxiety disorders. *Handbook of Cognitive Therapy Techniques*, by Rian E. McMullin (New York: W. W. Norton, 1986), and *Anxiety Disorders and Phobias: A Cognitive Perspective*, by Aaron T. Beck and Gary Emery (New York: Basic Books, 1985), both provide a theoretical and practical guide to anxiety disorder treatment, useful for advanced students in pastoral counseling.

Cross-Cultural Issues

While people of all races and social groups can have panic disorder, there appear to be cultural differences in how individual symptoms are manifested. Cross-national studies indicate that similar symptom profiles for panic disorder have been found in the United States, Western Europe, Canada, South America, and Mexico. Whether panic disorders exist in Asian or African cultures remains understudied.[5]

---

5. M. Amering and H. Katschnig, "Panic Attacks and Panic Disorder in Cross-Cultural Perspective," *Psychiatric Annals* 20 (1990): 511-16.

Post-Traumatic Stress Disorder

The Overwhelmed Grandfather

> *The essence of psychological trauma is the loss of faith that there is order and continuity in life. Trauma occurs when one loses the sense of having a safe place to retreat within or outside oneself to deal with frightening emotions or experiences. This results in a state of helplessness, a feeling that one's actions have no bearing on the outcome of one's life. Since human life seems to be incompatible with a sense of meaninglessness and lack of control, people will attempt to avoid this experience at just about any price. . . . Much of human endeavor, in religion, art, and science, is centrally concerned with exactly these grand questions of meaning and control over one's destiny.*
>
> *—Bessel A. van der Kolk,* Psychological Trauma

Jim, a 64-year-old parishioner, left his granddaughter's birthday party to buy some extra ice cream and cake for the children. He felt a slight bump when he backed his truck out of the driveway. His 4-year-old grandson had hidden under the rear tire of the truck while playing hide-and-seek. The child was crushed to death.

For months after the funeral, Jim was unable to work and spent most of his time detached and withdrawn. He is still plagued with terrifying nightmares of the crushed child. He has outbursts of rage and remains inconsolable. Prior to the accident he had been very active; since the accident he has lost interest in all activities, including the church. Jim constantly blames himself for his grandson's death. He takes no comfort in family, friends, or faith. Jim is frozen in time at the moment of the trauma, re-living the traumatic accident over and over again.

Pastoral Care Assessment

The grandfather suffers from post-traumatic stress disorder, or PTSD. Weeks or months after a traumatic event, survivors, like Jim, often live the traumatic experience over and over again, avoiding situations associated with the event. Some survivors become detached and numbed to all feeling, while others become agitated and are unable to sleep. Many survivors are plagued with excessive guilt for remaining alive when others died or were injured.

Your assessment of the grandfather suffering from PTSD should include a detailed account of the traumatic event and a careful summary of current symptoms. You need to evaluate his present level of coping skills and the strength of his social support network. In this case it is essential to refer Jim to a mental health specialist for more extensive evaluation and treatment. Only if you have had specialized training and experience should you be the primary counselor treating a person suffering from PTSD.

Relevant History

Jim had no significant medical or mental health problems prior to the catastrophic accident. He had and continues to have a supportive family as well as supportive friends and fellow church members. Post-traumatic stress disorder symptoms can result as a "normal" response to extreme stress. Anyone confronted with a similar horrific experience might react similarly.

Diagnostic Criteria

In order to meet the criteria for the diagnosis of PTSD, a person must experience, witness, or be confronted with an event that involves actual or threatened death or serious injury to self or another that results in intense fear, helplessness, and horror. We may understand PTSD by grouping the symptoms into three types: reexperiencing (intrusive), avoiding, and physical hyperarousal. An individual must have one reexperience symptom, three avoidant symptoms, and two physical hyperarousal symptoms to meet the diagnostic criteria. These symptoms must be present for a minimum of one month and impair normal life activities. In some cases, PTSD can be delayed and becomes manifest six months or more after the traumatic stressor.[1]

Reexperiencing takes the following forms:

- recurrent and intrusive, distressing recollections of events
- recurrent distressing dreams of the events
- suddenly acting or feeling as if the traumatic event were recurring

1. *DSM IV*, 424-29.

- intense psychological distress at exposure to events that symbolize or resemble an aspect of the trauma, including anniversaries of the experience (e.g., an elderly man reexperiences the trauma of the accidental shooting of his grandchild in his home when he hears a passing car's engine backfire)
- physiological reactivity upon exposure to events that symbolize or resemble an aspect of the traumatic event (e.g., an elderly woman who was raped in a church breaks out in a cold sweat when entering any church)

Avoiding may take the following forms:

- efforts to avoid thoughts or feelings associated with the trauma
- efforts to avoid activities or situations that arouse recollection of the trauma
- inability to recall an important aspect of the trauma (psychogenic amnesia)
- markedly diminished interest or participation in significant activities
- a feeling of detachment or estrangement from others
- a restricted range of affect (commonly the loss of feelings associated with intimacy, tenderness, and sexuality)
- a sense of a foreshortened future (e.g., persons do not expect to have a normal life span)

Physical hyperarousal not present before trauma may appear in the following forms:

- difficulty falling or staying asleep
- irritability or outbursts of anger
- difficulty concentrating
- hypervigilance/hyperalertness (always "on guard")
- exaggerated startle response ("very jumpy" behavior)

Response to Vignette

Jim has suffered a severe psychological trauma caused by his involvement in the accidental death of his grandson and is at high risk for PTSD. The severity of the traumatic experience is the single strongest predictor of PTSD.[2] Jim has disturbing nightmares (reexperiencing intrusively), detachment and loss of all interest in activities (avoiding), outbursts of anger, and lack of concentration (physical hyperarousal). It appears Jim is suffering from excessive guilt for remaining alive after the accidental death of his grandchild (survivor's guilt). In treatment, it would be important to assist the grandfather in releasing his self-blame. At this point, it

2. D. W. Foy, "Introduction and Description of the Disorder," in *Treating Post-Traumatic Stress Disorder: Cognitive-Behavioral Stategies*, ed. D. Foy (New York: Guilford Press, 1992), 1-12.

may be easier for the survivor to blame himself for the accident than to feel the massive grief his grandson's death should arouse. Healing will require that he process his loss and find an end to excessive self-blame.

Of particular concern is Jim's degree of withdrawal from his social network of family and friends. He has not been able to work, and his faith appears to be of little help as a coping resource. He needs a very careful assessment for depression and suicide and immediate referral to a mental health specialist who works with persons who have had severe psychological trauma. He may need hospitalization until he has gained emotional strength to cope with his life. You, as an informed and caring pastor, can be an invaluable member of the treatment team, helping Jim struggle with questions of life, death, meaning, and purpose.

Treatment Within the Faith Community

With psychological trauma, an individual's sense of order and continuity of life is shattered. Questions of meaning and purpose predominate as a person experiences a loss of control over his or her destiny. There is no more difficult question than that of why terrible things happen to good people. It is a question that will be asked in many forms by survivors, family, friends, and members of the congregation. Modeling the caring presence of a tender God, who does not abandon us in our horror and helplessness, is more healing than quick, pat answers. Be a good, empathic listener who gently reassures and supports. Acceptance of rage at life and God can be healing.

Since church members will be affected by the trauma, the use of groups to process emotions and to gather the collective wisdom of the faithful is important. Pastors are in a unique position of trust, in which they can assist persons in reconnecting to support systems available through their faith communities. Research indicates that religion is a primary coping strategy for persons suffering severe psychological trauma.[3] It is essential that clergy who give pastoral care to the traumatized have a supportive network of colleagues to avoid isolation and burnout.

Indications for Referral

Education about treatment options for PTSD will assist you in making an informed referral. Seek out mental health professionals who are open to having a collegial relationship and are willing to answer specific questions regarding their treatment plan and your pastoral role in the treatment process. Referring a person suffering PTSD to a mental health professional does not mean you cannot continue a collaborative role during the treatment process. A traumatized person often feels fearful, suspicious, and threatened. Jim can be very resistant to entering and continuing therapy. You, as a knowledgeable pastor, can be very helpful in guiding Jim to treatment as well as supporting the ongoing process.

3. S. Weinrich, S. B. Hardin, and M. Johnson, "Nurses' Response to Hurricane Hugo Victims' Disaster Stress," *Archives of Psychiatric Nursing* 4, no. 3 (1990): 195-205.

The overall treatment strategy is to facilitate Jim's understanding and integrating of the traumatic experience into the ongoing context of his life, so that he is no longer stuck in the continual reexperiencing of the trauma. Most mental health professionals will work individually with Jim. They will focus on the current situation in the aftermath of the trauma by exploring the immediate effects on Jim. The therapist is less likely to probe earlier life conflicts, concentrating rather on the here and now. The therapist will assess and support the survivor's coping skills, including appropriate religious expression. The therapist will facilitate the natural grieving process and will assist the person in formulating concrete, realistic plans to restart her or his life.

Often, individual therapy is utilized in conjunction with group therapy. Group therapy can assist the survivor to "normalize" her or his experience by providing an environment for working through the healing process with others who can empathize with and understand the painful impact of the traumatic event. Such a group can be a natural bridge in the process of reconnecting with community when survivors are tempted to withdraw and isolate themselves.

Increasing numbers of mental health specialists are utilizing behavioral treatment, particularly with more severe cases of chronic and delayed PTSD. Several methods of behavioral therapy have been employed: implosive/imaginal flooding, systematic desensitization, behavioral rehearsal, and stress inoculation training. The goal of behavioral treatment is to reduce avoidance of the traumatic memories and the anxiety caused by recalling the trauma.

Medications are often employed in conjunction with psychotherapy. Antidepressant and antianxiety medications are used to decrease anxiety and hyperarousal, improve depressive mood, promote sleep, control nightmares, and enhance control of aggressive and violent impulses.

Where the trauma has been less severe and the person has effective coping skills and a strong support system, the prognosis is good for brief therapy of three to four months. In more severe, chronic cases—especially those in which the treatment did not begin soon after the trauma, the coping skills are weak, and the support network is absent—the treatment may be much longer. The most important clinical help you can offer Jim is an early, accurate assessment with appropriate support to facilitate entrance into and continuation of treatment.

Treatment by Mental Health Specialist

Local Resources

Resources

If the person's condition is life-threatening (suicidal), the person should be taken to the local emergency room. If it is less urgent, an appointment with a mental health specialist who has skills in PTSD and geriatric issues is very helpful. If the person has limited resources, the local county mental health center may be quite helpful.

National Resources

The American Psychiatric Association (APA) offers a free booklet on PTSD and other materials (some specifically designed for clergy) on mental health issues; phone 202-682-6000 or write 1400 K Street, NW, Washington, DC 20005. The Society for Traumatic Stress Studies, 60 Revere Drive, Suite 500, Northbrook, IL 60062 (phone 708-480-9080), and the Anxiety Disorders Association of America, Department A, 6000 Executive Boulevard, Rockville, MD 20852 (phone 301-231-9350), provide educational materials on PTSD and other anxiety disorders.

Self-Help Resources

The Gift from Within is a nonprofit organization dedicated to helping those who suffer from PTSD. It maintains a roster of trauma survivors who participate in a national network for peer support. Call the organization's toll free number, 1-800-888-5236, or write #1 Lily Pond Drive, Camden, ME 04843.

In the pastoral care literature a comprehensive chapter with very useful material for pastors on PTSD can be found in "Posttraumatic Stress Disorder," by D. W. Foy, K. D. Drescher, A. G. Fitz, and K. R. Kennedy, in *Clinical Handbook of Pastoral Counseling*, volume 2, edited by R. J. Wicks and R. D. Parsons (New York: Paulist Press, 1993), 621-637. One of the most creative approaches to treatment of PTSD has been the "family therapy" model found in *Helping the Traumatized Family*, by Charles Figley (San Francisco: Jossey-Bass, 1989). The family therapy modality utilizes the primary support group of the family to assist in coping with, integrating, and healing the traumatic experience. It also acknowledges that a psychological trauma affects family members as well as the survivor. *Trauma and Recovery*, by Judith Lewis Herman (New York: Basic Books, 1992); *Post-Traumatic Therapy and the Victims of Violence*, edited by Frank Ochberg (New York: Brunner/Mazel, 1990); and *Post-Traumatic Stress Disorder: A Clinician's Guide*, by K. C. Peterson, M. F. Prout, and R. A. Schwarz (New York: Plenum, 1990), are well researched and highly readable texts.

Cross-Cultural Issues

Although PTSD is most prevalent among young adults because of the higher incident rate of precipitating stressors, older adults have more difficulty coping with traumatic stress. Older people may be physically frail and less able to maintain coping strategies. A lack of adequate social support will make an older person more vulnerable to PTSD. Religious involvement reduces the adverse effects of stressors on older persons, particularly African American and Hispanic elders.[4]

4. C. Manfredi and M. Pickett, "Perceived Stressful Situations and Coping Strategies Utilized by the Elderly," *Journal of Community Health Nursing* 4, no. 2 (1987): 99-110.

Obsessive-Compulsive Disorder

The Woman Who Washed Her Hands

The young man comes into your office concerned over his 75-year-old aunt, Ruby, who recently has recovered from major surgery. He begins, "I have always been very fond of my Aunt Ruby, but lately I have become very concerned for her welfare, and I am not sure how to help her. Aunt Ruby has always had perfectionistic habits, but they recently have become much worse." He describes his aunt as obsessed with cleanliness and dirtiness, spending hours either washing her hands or checking that the faucets in her apartment are turned off. She wears gloves or uses paper towels to touch various "dirty objects." At times Ruby will watch a water faucet in her house for fifteen or twenty minutes to make sure it is shut off. She is now doing these unusual behaviors several dozen times a day. She is also becoming increasingly socially isolated and unable to function. Recently, when her nephew tried to engage her in a conversation about her condition, Ruby said, "I know it's stupid. I feel like a crazy person, but I know I'm not crazy!"

It would be helpful in this instance for you to work with the nephew to gain a clearer picture of Ruby's situation. How long have these unusual behaviors been occurring, and how much have they increased lately? Is she open to treatment? Who might she most trust to help intervene in the situation? A complete history could be developed, with the nephew and other family members, to help guide the decision process. From the information the nephew has already shared with you, Ruby appears to have symptoms associated with obsessive-compulsive disorder, or OCD. The disorder requires specialized professional care. The good news is that most people (60 to 80 percent) who comply with some combination of treatment, behavior

Pastoral Assessment

therapy, and medications have moderate to significant improvement in their symptoms.[1] Your central role in this case is to guide the nephew in how to best find specialized help to assist his aunt, and to provide support and encouragement to Ruby and her family during the treatment process.

Relevant History

While working with Ruby's nephew and several other family members to gain a more complete history of her problem, it becomes clear to you that Ruby is experiencing several signs of significant depression: difficulty sleeping, fatigue, and feelings of helplessness. This is not unusual for persons with OCD; about 30 percent of those with the disorder have a coexisting major depression.[2]

Diagnostic Criteria

Obsessive-compulsive disorder (OCD) is characterized by patterns of repetitive thoughts or impulses (obsessions) and behaviors (compulsions) that are persistent and distressing enough to result in significant interference in one's usual functioning at work, in social activities, or in interpersonal relationships. The obsessions and compulsions are typically extremely difficult to overcome and when left untreated can be disabling. Common examples of these unwanted, obsessive thoughts involve contamination, repeated doubts, a need to have things in an exact order, or aggressive and sexual impulses. Compulsions are aimed at reducing distress or preventing a dreaded event; however, they are not connected in a logical way to this purpose. The most common of these are washing and checking. For example, a person who is obsessed with the thought of having left an appliance on may have the compulsion to repeatedly and excessively check all appliances before leaving home.

Response to Vignette

Although the onset of OCD after the age of 50 is unusual, OCD is not uncommon among the elderly, primarily because the disorder often goes undiagnosed and therefore untreated for years or decades.[3] Obsessive-compulsive disorder is a chronic disorder that can have symptoms that wax and wane through a lifetime and may only be finally diagnosed in old age. In some cases OCD becomes known in the elderly person because the strategies the person has used to conceal or cope with the symptoms no longer work. This appears to be the case for Ruby. It well may be that the crisis of her surgery exacerbated her condition to the point that she could no longer conceal her symptoms.

Ruby has two of the most common compulsions: cleaning rituals and checking rituals. She is repeatedly washing her hands as well as checking

1. H. I. Kaplan and B. J. Sadock, *Synopsis of Psychiatry*, 5th ed. (Baltimore: Williams & Wilkins, 1988), 328.
2. S. A. Rasmussen and J. L. Eisen, "Clinical Features and Phenomenology of Obsessive-Compulsive Disorder," *Psychiatric Annals* 19 (1989): 67-73.
3. M. A. Jenki, "Obsessive-Compulsive Disorders in the Elderly," in *Geriatric Psychiatry and Psychopharmacology*, ed. M. A. Jenike (St. Louis: Year Book Medical Publishers, 1989), 339-62.

to see whether the water faucet is turned off. Ruby, like most OCD sufferers, may appear bizarre while almost always retaining full insight and recognizing that her thoughts and impulses are unreasonable and alien. Persons who see their behaviors as nonrational, as Ruby does, are more apt to respond well to treatment. Moreover, neither the duration nor the severity of the symptoms is associated with an unsuccessful treatment. Treatment compliance is the strongest predictor of a successful outcome. Older persons with a long history of OCD, like Ruby, can have as much success as younger persons if they find specialized care and are willing to follow through with treatment.[4] Ruby's depression will also need to be addressed (see case 2, "Major Depression").

For a long time it was thought that OCD was a relatively rare disorder. However, recent studies have led experts to recognize that a surprisingly high estimated 2 percent of the population are affected by the disorder. One of the reasons that OCD remains a hidden problem is that sufferers often feel shameful and try to conceal their obsessive-compulsive symptoms. Unfortunately, their secrecy means they do not find professional care that will improve their symptoms. Faith communities can play a critical role by providing people with accurate information about OCD. One important point that needs to be emphasized is the increasing evidence that biological factors are a primary contributor to the disorder. The fact that persons with OCD respond well to specific medications that affect the neurotransmitter serotonin suggests a biological basis to the disorder not unlike that associated with diabetes. Unfortunately, persons suffering from serious mental health problems such as OCD are regarded with more distaste and less sympathy than virtually any other disabled group in our society.

Treatment Within the Faith Community

Obsessive-compulsive disorder is a mental health disorder that will need a referral for specialized treatment. Ruby's situation has deteriorated to the point where she is virtually disabled by OCD and needs immediate professional help.

Indications for Referral

Psychotherapy aimed at helping the person gain insight into his or her problem is generally not helpful with OCD. However, a specialized behavior therapy called "exposure with response prevention" has proved to be effective for the majority of sufferers and is considered to be the behavioral treatment of choice. This procedure involves exposing the patient to situations that evoke discomfort while blocking the obsessions or compulsions that usually occur in those situations. For example, a compulsive hand washer like Ruby may be instructed to touch an object

Treatment by Mental Health Specialist

4. E. B. Foa, J. B. Grayson, G. Stektee, H. G. Doppelt, R. M. Turner, and P. R. Latimer, "Success and Failure in Behavioral Treatment of Obsessive Compulsives," *Journal of Consulting and Clinical Psychology* 51 (1983): 287-97.

believed to be contaminated and then denied the opportunity to wash her hands. A second procedure is called "systematic desensitization." This involves exposure to a graded hierarchy of anxiety-evoking situations with simultaneous training in relaxation techniques. Behavioral therapists often use "homework assignments" to increase the effectiveness of the treatment. These behavioral therapies are most effective if the patient initially has a moderate level of anxiety and is highly motivated; if the therapist is well-trained in the techniques and is respectful, understanding, and encouraging; and if the family is supportive.

In recent years, medications that affect the neurotransmitter serotonin have been shown to significantly reduce OCD symptoms. Two of the most commonly prescribed selective serotonin reuptake inhibitors (SSRIs) are clomipramine (Anafrail) and fluoxetine (Prozac). In the elderly, Prozac may be the drug of choice because it often has no side effects. Medications are helpful in reducing symptoms of OCD, but often, when the medications are discontinued, the symptoms return. Seniors with OCD can benefit from a combination of medications and behavioral therapy.

Resources

Local and National Resources

The Obsessive Compulsive Foundation, PO Box 70, Milford, CT 06460 (phone 203-878-5669), offers free or low cost brochures for individuals with obsessive-compulsive disorder and their families. They also have videotapes and books available as well as a nationwide listing of 250 support groups. The Dean Foundation Obsessive Compulsive Disorder Information Center, 8000 Excelsior Drive, Suite 302, Madison, WI 53717-1914 (phone 608-836-8070), has an information computer database with detailed information about OCD, its diagnosis, its treatment, and research on the disorder, along with listings of mental health referrals and support groups working with OCD issues.

Self-Help Resources

Obsessive Compulsive Disorder: A Guide, a pamphlet by John H. Greist (Madison, Wisc.: Obsessive Compulsive Disorder Information Center, 1992), has a useful discussion of medication and behavioral therapy treatment options for the disorder. *Learning to Live with Obsessive Compulsive Disorder*, a pamphlet by B. Livingston (Milford, Conn.: OCD Foundation, 1989), provides information for family members of those suffering from OCD. Michael A. Jenike's article "Obsessional Disorders," in *The Principles and Practice of Geriatric Psychiatry*, edited by J. R. M. Copeland, M. T. Abou-Saleh, and D. G. Blazer (New York: John Wiley and Sons, 1993), gives a good summary of the disorder and treatment options for the elderly.

Obsessive-compulsive disorder strikes all ethnic groups and affects both genders at about the same rate. Researchers have found that about 6 percent of persons with OCD have religious obsessions.[5] Persons from overly strict religious backgrounds may be at greater risk than the general population for having obsessive thoughts about religion.[6]

Cross-Cultural Issues

5. E. B. Foa and M. J. Kozak, "DSM-IV Field Trial: Obsessive-Compulsive Disorder," *American Journal of Psychiatry* 152, no. 1 (1995): 90-96.
6. S. A. Rasmussen and J. L. Eisen, "The Epidemiology and Clinical Features of Obsessive-Compulsive Disorder," *Psychiatric Clinics of North America* 15, no. 1 (1992): 743-58.

Mixed Anxiety-Depression

I Can't Stand It

Three months ago, Martha received from her doctors the distressing news that she had colon cancer. After several weeks of diagnostic tests, radiation treatments, and chemotherapy as an inpatient in the hospital, she was discharged home two weeks ago. Martha, aged 74, is now recuperating at home having suffered weeks of nausea, vomiting, and diarrhea from treatments. During this time, she lost nearly thirty pounds, and much of her hair fell out. Prior to this illness Martha had been one of your most faithful churchgoers and volunteer workers. You visited her several times when she was in the hospital, and now you are making a home visit to see how her recovery is coming along.

"Good morning, Martha," you say, as she meets you at the door. "Come in, pastor, and make yourself at home," she responds timidly in a shaky voice, and motions toward the kitchen. You follow her as she moves slowly and carefully toward the kitchen table with her walker. She offers you something to drink, but you decline (seeing her obvious difficulty in getting about). You assist her as she sits down at the table, and then initiate the conversation after giving her a couple of moments to catch her breath. "Well, you're finally home, Martha. It must be good to get out of the hospital after all that time."

Martha acknowledges your comment, and responds "It is good to be home, pastor, but I don't think I'm doing so well. I feel tired all the time, and I don't feel like doing anything around here. I'm really worried about my daughter and the burden I've become on her. She has to come over every day to cook, clean, and even do the laundry, since I'm having trouble holding my urine and bowels. You know, I used to be so independent and active. Now look at me. They say that the cancer has responded to treatment, but I'm not sure if I should have had this chemotherapy at my age. Maybe it was my time to go and I should have let God take me." You listen attentively without saying a word but nod your head to let her know that you are trying to understand.

She continues. "I feel so discouraged about all this. I feel much worse than I did before going into the hospital. My nerves are really bad. I can't sleep at night and feel restless all the time. I worry about everything—the medical bills, my daughter, the grandchildren. Sometimes I start shaking all over, my heart races, I have difficulty breathing, and I think to myself, 'This is it. It's my time to go.' I'm afraid to leave the house even to get the mail because I might fall down in the driveway. I feel so helpless and alone. Pastor, I can't stand it," she blurts out, and begins to sob. You take her hand in both your hands and sit quietly with her.

Pastoral Care Assessment

Martha is dressed in a wrinkled nightgown covered with a robe. She appears frail and tremulous, and has lost weight recently. She looks sad and is obviously distressed now. Her thinking appears rational, however, and there is no evidence for significant memory impairment, delirium, or psychotic symptoms (hallucinations or delusions). To assure her safety, you need to ask her about suicidal thoughts or plans and what would keep her from harming herself (she says that while she doesn't feel life is worth living like this, she would never harm herself because of her strong religious faith).

During your previous visits with Martha in the hospital and talks with her daughter, you learned a lot about her psychiatric, medical, and social history, which makes detailed questioning less necessary at this time. Martha has always been a somewhat nervous person, but she has been more nervous since her husband died three years ago. She was treated for depression once in her 30s when she was raising three small children, and then again briefly after her husband's death. She has not taken any nerve medicine for at least two years now. Martha has never had an alcohol or drug use problem, although her father and two brothers were heavy drinkers. She was raised in a troubled home situation, and her father would frequently beat her mother and the children when he was drunk. Until her recent diagnosis of bowel cancer, Martha was in good physical health. She enjoyed working in her yard and garden, and had no difficulty maintaining a large, two-story, brick home. She took no medications and only infrequently saw the doctor. Martha has numerous friends in the church, although she has mostly kept to herself since her cancer diagnosis and treatments (she's ashamed of her appearance). Martha has one daughter who lives just down the block from her and is supportive but quite busy with a part-time job and a family of her own to take care of. Martha also has two sons, but they live outside the state and visit only once or twice a year.

Relevant History

Martha has felt emotionally distressed for at least a month now. Although some of her symptoms might be side effects from chemotherapy (loss of weight, decreased energy), others are clearly of psychological origin. She has a family history of alcoholism and a personal history of several episodes of mild depression and nerves, which make her vulnerable to more serious emotional problems after major stress. Previously an active and independent woman, Martha's recent health problems have forced her to become more dependent on others, which is disturbing and threatening to her. Martha's strengths include her social skills, her previous active involvement in her church community, her numerous long-standing friendships, her supportive family (daughter who lives nearby), her lack of alcohol or substance abuse problems, her intact memory and cognitive function, and her willingness to seek treatment. She is also a devoutly religious person with a strong faith.

Because of her anxiety symptoms, you would also want to ask her about her dietary habits (coffee, tea, and cola use) and explore in detail any over-the-counter medications that she may be taking (and certainly any prescription drugs, if she is taking any). Martha has been a nervous person much of her life. In other cases, however, when an older adult begins to experience significant anxiety for the first time, a general rule is that the anxiety should be assumed to be due to medical causes or medications until proved otherwise (see case 7, "Generalized Anxiety Disorder").

Diagnostic Criteria

Martha has a mixture of anxiety and depressive symptoms (*mixed anxiety-depression*). She may fulfill criteria for several different psychiatric disorders. If her depression is severe enough (which it appears to be), she may fulfill criteria for major depression (see case 2); in addition, she may also be experiencing panic attacks (episodes of severe anxiety with racing heart, difficulty breathing, and sense of doom), mild agoraphobic symptoms (fearful of leaving her house), and symptoms of more generalized anxiety (worrying about everything) (see case 7, "Generalized Anxiety Disorder," and case 8, "Panic Disorder and Agoraphobia"). Diagnostic assessment is made more difficult by the heavy overlap of symptoms in anxiety and depressive disorders. While only 2 percent of older psychiatric inpatients have isolated anxiety disorders, nearly 40 percent with major depression fulfill criteria for anxiety disorders, suggesting that a primary underlying depressive disorder often accounts for anxiety symptoms in older adults (and should be the focus of treatment).

Alternatively, if Martha's symptoms are not severe enough to warrant a diagnosis of major depression or any other specific anxiety disorder, then she would likely fulfill criteria for an *adjustment disorder with mixed anxiety and depressed mood*. DSM IV devotes an entire chapter to adjustment disorders, which are defined as "clinically significant emotional or behavioral symptoms in response to an identifiable psychosocial stressor or stressors." Symptoms must begin within three months of the onset of the stressor, have a clinically significant effect on the person's life, and not last longer than six months after the stressful event. *Clinical significance* depends on whether the emotional response is characterized "by marked distress that is in excess of what would be expected given the nature of the stressor, or by significant impairment in social or occupational functioning."[1] Adjustment disorders are subcategorized depending on type of accompanying symptoms. When depressive symptoms predominate, then adjustment disorder with depressed mood is the diagnosis; when anxiety symptoms predominate, then adjustment disorder with anxiety is the diagnosis; when symptoms of both anxiety and depression are present (as in Martha's case), the diagnosis is adjustment disorder with mixed anxiety and depressed mood.

Adjustment disorders are very common among older persons with physical health conditions (particularly recent onset disability), and are frequently associated with symptoms of both anxiety and depression. In a study of over two hundred patients with cancer, the most frequent psychiatric diagnosis (13 percent) was adjustment disorder with mixed anxiety and depressed mood, and the next most common diagnoses were adjustment disorder with depressed mood (12 percent) and adjustment disorder with anxiety (6 percent).[2] Thus, almost one-third of patients experienced an adjustment disorder of some type or another.

Panic attacks frequently occur during the course of major depression (in one-quarter to one-third of depressed persons). These persons do not have panic disorder; instead, their panic attacks are due to their depression. Treatment of the underlying depression, then, becomes essential.

Response to Vignette

Older persons with mixed anxiety-depression syndromes, particularly men with physical health problems, are at high risk for suicide. Restlessness and impulsiveness, combined with discouragement and hopelessness, create an almost intolerable emotional state that can quickly precipitate a suicide attempt. For this reason, such persons need immediate psychiatric evaluation and treatment (even those with only adjustment disorder, in some cases). In Martha's case, although she probably needs psychiatric treatment, her gender and strong religious faith reduce the level of concern for suicide.

Your first intervention, after completing your assessment and appraising Martha's potential for committing suicide, is just what you are doing—spending time with Martha and seriously, attentively, and empathetically listening to her talk about her distress. Mild forms of major depression and most adjustment disorders respond very well to such supportive interventions. Either you or a trained member of your staff should see Martha twice

1. *DSM IV*, 623-27.
2. L. R. Derogatis, G. R. Morrow, J. Fetting, D. Penman, S. Piasetsky, A. M. Schmate, M. Henrichs, and C. L. M. Carnicke, "The Prevalence of Psychiatric Disorders Among Cancer Patients," *Journal of the American Medical Association* 249 (1983): 751-57.

a week for thirty minutes to an hour for the first two or three weeks; this may be all the treatment she needs to reverse her downhill course. This is particularly true if you use religious interventions to support and bolster her religious faith, which may be the most important way that she is coping with her situation. Religious coping has been shown to be particularly helpful for older adults with adjustment disorders.[3] This includes (1) praying with her (prayer that is positive, reassuring, and hopeful), (2) discussing stories in the Bible that deal with people suffering and overcoming their problems, and (3) helping her conquer any barriers interfering with her ability to utilize her faith (e.g., allowing her to express and resolve her anger at God, helping her to forgive herself and others, and clearing up any excess guilt over real or imagined sins or past mistakes). Finally, encouraging her friends in the church to visit her may help combat her loneliness and isolation; as always, however, confidentiality must be respected and permission obtained from Martha herself.

Treatment Within the Faith Community

Important contributions the faith community can make include identifying persons with mixed anxiety-depressions (i.e., facilitating diagnosis), providing emotional support and practical help (transportation, in-home services, home repairs, yard work), encouraging compliance with treatment plans (taking medications or keeping doctor visits), and monitoring response to treatment. In Martha's case, these interventions should be directed at helping her resume self-care activities to regain and maintain her independence; if maximal independence has already been achieved and she still requires ongoing assistance, then she will need help accepting her level of dependency on others, and help both feeling and expressing gratefulness for the assistance she receives. (Also see this section in cases 2, 3, and 7.)

Indications for Referral

As noted before, much can be done within the faith community before involving health professionals. However, the threshold for referring patients should be lower for those with mixed anxiety-depressions than for those with either pure depression or pure anxiety. This is largely because of the increased suicide risk and because of the extremely effective medical treatments that are available for this problem. In any case, if there is no improvement after two to three weeks, if symptoms worsen, or if there is any chance that symptoms might be due to medical causes, then immediate referral is necessary.

Treatment by Mental Health Specialist

If the diagnosis is confirmed and evaluation rules out dietary habits, drugs, or treatable physical illness as the cause for anxiety and depressive symptoms, then medical treatments or psychotherapy or both will be

3. H. G. Koenig, H. J. Cohen, D. G. Blazer, H. S. Kudler, K. R. R. Krishnan, and T. E. Sibert, "Cognitive Symptoms of Depression and Religious Coping in Elderly Medical Patients," *Psychosomatics* 36 (1995): 369-75.

instituted. Medical treatments usually involve either a sedating antidepressant (nortriptyline, trazodone, doxepine) or a combination of an antidepressant (sertraline, paroxetine, bupropion) and a minor tranquilizer (clonazepam, lorazepam). These medications are usually quite effective in relieving symptoms of anxiety and depression. If immediate relief from symptoms is necessary in order to reduce the risk of suicide or other impulsive activity, then alprazolam (Xanax) is rapidly effective; however, persons may become very attached to this medication, and it may require weeks or months to taper them off the drug. Psychotherapy usually involves a combination of support and cognitive-behavioral therapy, although if psychodynamic issues play a dominant role (this is relatively uncommon), psychodynamic psychotherapy may help.

Resources

See case 3, "Minor Depression," and case 7, "Generalized Anxiety Disorder," for local, national, and self-help resources.

Cross-Cultural Issues

See case 3, "Minor Depression," and case 7, "Generalized Anxiety Disorder."

Case 12

Age-Related Cognitive Decline

Where Did I Put That?

You go out for breakfast one morning with a group of men from the church. On leaving the café, one of the men, Dick, grabs your arm and asks if you've got a moment to discuss something. As the two of you stroll along the sidewalk, Dick reveals his concerns. "Pastor, there's been something on my mind for some time now, and I've just got to talk with someone about it. It's really not that important, but I've got myself worked up over it." Dick, a sharply dressed 79-year-old retired bank executive, goes on to tell you that he's worried about his memory. "I used to be able to remember every customer by name, and we had literally hundreds of clients. Recently, though, I've been having trouble remembering names of the guys at church. Pastor, I've known these fellows for thirty years or more. And that's not all," he continues. "I've been misplacing things too. The other day, I was looking for my favorite coffee mug and it was gone! 'Where did I put that?' I thought. When I asked my wife about it, she found it right off, and said it was right where it usually is. Sometimes I go into the kitchen for something and just stand there, forgetting why I went in there in the first place. I feel so stupid, but it's starting to scare me, Pastor. Do you think I've got Alzheimer's disease?"

You listen carefully to Dick, noticing how worried and frightened he is. You learn that these problems have been going on for the past year and have not gotten much worse or much better during this time. You set up an appointment with Dick so that you can talk with him at length about his problem.

Pastoral Care Assessment

Dick comes into your office and sits down. He is nicely dressed, friendly, and outgoing, as usual. "Besides these memory problems, tell me about what else is going on in your life," you ask. Dick tells you with some hesitation that about a year ago, his only son got involved in drugs and has been in and out of jail since. He's just sick about this, he says, and worries all the time about where his son is and what he might be doing. Furthermore, Dick confesses that his marriage of forty-five years is on the rocks, and he doesn't know what to do about it. "And now this memory thing. I'm about ready to go over the edge," Dick exclaims. On further questioning, you learn that Dick's 75-year-old brother-in-law was diagnosed with Alzheimer's disease about nine months ago.

You ask Dick if he has any physical health problems or takes any medications. He says he's in pretty good health for his age, but has chronic allergies, for which he takes an over-the-counter decongestant; he also admits that since all these other problems started, he's been taking one or two Sominex nightly to help him to sleep (note that both of these drugs have anticholinergic side effects that may interfere with memory). You encourage Dick to talk more about his son and his marriage, and after about thirty minutes of blowing off steam, he seems relieved. "I feel much better after talking with you, Pastor," Dick says with a sigh. You reassure him about his memory problems, but encourage him to make an appointment with his medical doctor for a thorough physical and mental examination.

Relevant History

Dick has never had any emotional or memory problems in the past and has never been to see a psychiatrist or had any type of counseling. He's always prided himself in having a "strong mind." Dick admits to drinking alcohol socially, but not more than one or two drinks at a time and not every day; he has never been a heavy drinker. There is no family history of Alzheimer's disease among his blood relatives, and most of those who have died lived into their late 80s. Dick himself has never become disoriented while driving or gotten lost. He still plays golf "with the best of them," and keeps score for his partners without difficulty. He continues to balance the checkbook and pay all the bills, and he never misses an appointment or a church function.

Diagnostic Criteria

In all likelihood, Dick's minor memory lapses are due to his getting older, combined with a number of other factors that can affect his concentration. It is hard to say what effect stress is having on Dick's memory, but his preoccupation with family problems could certainly cause him to be less attentive to the outside world. The medications he is taking for allergies and sleep, as well as his periodic social drinking, could also contribute to Dick's memory problems. The most likely cause, however, is his age. When his brother-in-law was diagnosed with Alzheimer's, it made him start worrying about his memory to the point that he became preoccupied with and focused on it, magnifying his minor memory deficits out of proportion. *DSM IV* defines this problem, *age-related cognitive decline*, as "an objectively identified decline in cognitive functioning consequent to the aging process that is within normal limits given the person's age."[1]

You have done a fine job in handling Dick's case. First of all, you took his complaints seriously and listened attentively to them, and did not simply dispel them outright. Second, sensing his level of worry, you arranged a meeting when you could at greater length discuss his problems. Third, you inquired about what else was going on in his life, thus uncovering his other worries. Fourth, you allowed him to talk about his family problems and voice his concerns about having Alzheimer's disease, like his brother-in-law. Fifth, you acquired important clues from his past medical history about medication and alcohol use that may be affecting his memory, and have appropriately referred him for professional evaluation. Finally, you will stand by Dick, whatever the outcome of his medical visit, and will assist him in dealing with his family problems.

You and Dick's friends in the faith community (if he wishes) can provide him with emotional support to deal with his son's problems and his own marital difficulties (in confidentiality, of course). After his memory concerns have been addressed, you might want to set up a session with Dick and his wife.

Any memory complaints that seriously worry an older member of the congregation or his or her family, deserve referral for professional evaluation.

Dick's physician will likely review his past medical history and his prescription and over-the-counter medications, perform a physical examination, and perhaps obtain some routine screening labs (B vitamin levels, thyroid function, and blood count). He will also likely administer a brief memory screening test such as the *Folstein Mini-Mental State Examination*, a test of orientation, concentration, language, and constructional abilities. If Dick scores poorly on this test (which is unlikely), he will be referred for more detailed psychological testing by a trained psychologist using a battery of different neuropsychiatric tests.

Local Resources

An older adult who appears to be suffering from age-related cognitive decline should be referred to his or her regular medical physician, geriatric

Response to Vignette

Treatment Within the Faith Community

Indications for Referral

Treatment by Mental Health Specialist

Resources

1. *DSM IV*, 684.

medicine specialist, or a geriatric psychiatrist or psychologist. Some larger cities with medical centers have memory disorder clinics that specialize in the evaluation of these problems.

National Resources

For more information about age-related cognitive decline write to the National Institute on Aging Information Center, PO Box 8057, Gaithersburg, MD 20898-8057.

Self-Help Resources

For persons wanting more information from a medical viewpoint on how to distinguish "normal aging" from dementia (see cases 14-16, 21), we suggest a review article by R. Jutagir, entitled "Psychological Aspects of Aging: When Does Memory Loss Signal Dementia?" published in *Geriatrics* 49, no. 3 (1994): 45-46, 49-51 (available at any medical library).

Cross-Cultural Issues

Because dementia is a biological illness, a brain disease, cross-cultural factors play less of a role in its diagnosis and its differentiation from age-related cognitive decline. Educational level, of course, must be considered when assessing cognitive functioning, and this may vary by culture.

Delirium

Where Am I?

Mary, a 75-year-old member of your congregation, arrives at around 5:00 P.M. for a Thursday-night church supper being held in the rectory building. One of her friends brought her today, since Mary does not drive anymore and has no remaining family alive in the area to provide transportation. Food preparations are underway, and you are wandering about in the crowd socializing and laughing with friends. Frances, the person who drove Mary to the church, touches your shoulder and asks you to come over for a minute. You break free from your conversation and go to where Frances is standing. "Isn't this a big crowd! We've got a lot of food to eat before we can go home tonight," you say with a laugh. Frances responds in a serious tone, "Pastor, I'm worried about Mary. She's not herself tonight. She's got a glazed look in her eyes and is talking about all kinds of silly things. I think she's confused. It's really embarrassing. Mary is calling people by the wrong names, and I'm not even sure she knows where she is. She's talking about needing to care for her children. What children? They've all grown up and moved away. I've never seen her like this."

Going over to Mary, you greet her pleasantly. "Hello, Mary. How are you tonight?" you say, not letting on that you suspect anything is wrong. "Is that you, Pastor? Oh, thank God you're here," Mary exclaims. "Where am I? Is this a marketplace or some type of fair? I think I've lost the children. Please help me." Mary is trembling and looks scared. You gently reassure her, take her by the hand, and slowly walk her over to your office, with Frances following closely behind.

In your office, you have Mary take a seat and continue with your assessment. She is obviously confused, rattling on about her children and jumping from subject to subject. She calls you "Doctor" on several occasions, and at one point, looks over at Frances and asks "Who is she?" You ask her where she thinks she is now. Mary responds that she thinks this is some type of clinic, and wants you to call her husband (who has been

Pastoral Care Assessment

deceased for five years now). She insists on leaving to search for her children and at one point raises her voice impatiently. You calm her down and then obtain the following information from her friend. Frances, a retired nurse, has been taking Mary to her doctor's appointments and knows a good deal about her condition. Mary has no history of emotional problems or psychiatric illness, and she has never been a drinker of alcohol. You find out that she has a history of high blood pressure, suffered a stroke about two years ago, and has been having some mild memory problems, but nothing that has interfered with her life in any way. She also suffers from mild congestive heart failure (for which she takes a water pill), diabetes (requiring insulin injections), and depression (for which she takes an antidepressant). Over the past week, she's been having trouble with dizziness and is taking meclizine (Antivert) for this; in fact, she just took two of these before leaving her home so that she wouldn't get dizzy at the church supper. Frances reports that Mary was just fine when they left home, but over the past hour or two things have changed noticeably.

Mary is clean and nicely dressed, suggesting that her confusion is of more recent onset. You notice that Mary is becoming sleepy and is fading in and out during your conversation. When you speak to her, she arouses herself momentarily but cannot focus on what you are saying for long; she is quite distractible, and her attention span appears short. She can tell you her name but is disoriented to time and cannot give the date or the year; likewise, she is disoriented to place and cannot recall the name of the town or the type of building she is in (i.e., a church). She periodically becomes mildly agitated and tries to get up from the chair; Frances and you try to discourage her, fearing that she might fall. "Just sit here for a while, Mary, everything's going to be all right," you reassure her. You have Frances watch Mary carefully as you get on the telephone and call her medical physician.

Relevant History

Mary's disorientation and strange behavior are both of relatively recent onset. Two hours ago, according to Frances, she was behaving normally. You have already learned that Mary has no prior psychiatric or drinking problems, suggesting that what is going on now is probably a medical problem. She has a history of high blood pressure and stroke. Could her current behavior be the result of another stroke? She has a history of diabetes and is taking insulin. It's getting close to supper time and she has not eaten. Could she be hypoglycemic (have low blood sugar)? She takes a number of medications, including two medications (an antidepressant and Antivert) that have anticholinergic side effects that could cause or worsen confusion. You already know that Mary has a history of "mild memory problems" from her previous stroke that could increase her vulnerability to medication side effects. Mary also has a history of congestive heart failure and takes a pill that makes her urinate more to remove the fluid from her lungs. Could she have become dehydrated from this medicine (as well as from poor fluid intake or excessive sweating on a hot day)? The time of day is also relevant, because many older persons with mild memory problems experience a worsening of symptoms in the early evening (called "sun-downing").

You are fortunate that Frances is a retired nurse and knows about Mary's medical history. If this were not the case, you would have to track down a close family member who might have access to this type of information, since Mary is in no condition to provide it herself.

Mary has signs and symptoms of *delirium*. Among older persons hospitalized with acute medical illness, from 10 to 25 percent experience some degree of delirium. According to *DSM IV*, delirium is "a disturbance of consciousness that is accompanied by a change in cognition that cannot be better accounted for by a preexisting or evolving dementia (see cases 14-16). The disturbance develops over a short period of time, usually hours to days, and tends to fluctuate during the course of the day."[1] There must also be some evidence from the history or physical examination that the condition is a direct physiological consequence of a medical condition, alcohol intoxication or withdrawal, use of a medication, or toxin exposure.

Mary demonstrates a "disturbance of consciousness" in that her level of alertness is decreased; she is sleepy, fading in and out, mildly agitated, and distractible. This feature distinguishes persons with delirium from those with dementia (chronic impairment of memory and orientation), the condition that delirium is most likely to be confused with. Older persons with dementia do not usually have impaired alertness, which is the hallmark of delirium. Furthermore, Mary's symptoms came on relatively quickly (over a matter of hours), as opposed to dementia, which develops slowly and progressively (over months or years). Mary demonstrates other characteristics of delirium, including an inability to focus, sustain, or shift attention; in fact, carrying on a conversation with her is almost impossible because her attention wanders and she is easily distracted. Finally, persons with delirium experience a change in cognition (memory impairment, disorientation, language disturbance), and in some cases, disturbances of perception (misinterpretations, illusions, hallucinations). In Mary's case, identifying the cause of her delirium is of utmost importance. If she has had another stroke or is experiencing severe low blood sugar, immediate treatment is necessary.

Besides dementia, a number of psychiatric conditions can mimic delirium in an older person. These include a mania (case 5), a psychotic depression

Diagnostic Criteria

1. *DSM IV*, 124.

(case 19), another acute psychosis, or an episode of severe anxiety (panic attack, case 8). Mary's history provides little evidence for any of these conditions.

Response to Vignette

Your first concern is to ensure Mary's safety. You need to get her to a safe place where she will not hurt herself, particularly by falling. Your next task is to quickly obtain a medical history and list of medications from a relative or knowledgeable friend. Learning that she has diabetes and takes insulin, you would immediately get her some orange juice or other concentrated source of sugar to treat low blood sugar, in the event that this might be the cause for her symptoms. At the same time, you would try to contact her physician or call 911, if her condition is deteriorating. If her condition is less emergent, her physician can tell you what to do at the scene and arrange transportation to get Mary to her doctor's office or the emergency room, if necessary.

Treatment Within the Faith Community

Your primary responsibility is to ensure Mary's safety and help provide emergency treatment at the scene under the direction of a physician, nurse, or paramedic. You can also help by providing transportation to and from her doctor's office and by supplying emotional support and reassurance to Mary during the ride; having familiar faces around her will reduce Mary's anxiety and help her to remain as oriented as possible, given her condition.

Indications for Referral

Any person with a change in mental state that has a relatively sudden onset should immediately be referred for medical evaluation.

Treatment by Mental Health Specialists

Her medical doctor will quickly draw blood for testing, start an intravenous line to administer fluids or drugs if necessary, review her medical history, and conduct a careful physical and neurological examination. As noted above, it is essential to rapidly determine the cause of Mary's delirium; if her condition is left untreated, there is a chance of permanent damage or even death.

Resources

For detailed information about delirium, consult any general medical text.

Cross-Cultural Issues

As with any other psychiatric condition in which mental state is being evaluated, one must consider the person's cultural background. What may seem to be delirium may be a ritual trance. See this section in cases 18-21.

Early-Stage Alzheimer's Dementia

I Can't Remember

You and Jim are talking one day after church. He expresses concern about his wife and her failing memory. "Pastor, Jennie had a birthday last week. She just turned 73. I'm worried about her and don't know where to go for help. Maybe you'll have some ideas." Jim goes on to explain that his wife is beginning to have problems forgetting the names of friends they have known for years. She often goes into a room and just stands there. When asked what she is doing, she says she doesn't recall why she went into the room or what she needed there. Jennie frequently misplaces things, often forgets items when she goes to the grocery store, and has recently forgotten appointments with her dentist and her hairdresser. Jim reports that last month he had to take over balancing the checkbook, a task that his wife has handled without difficulty throughout their forty years of marriage. These problems with memory seem to have come on very gradually, almost imperceptibly, over the past year. In many other areas of life, however, she is functioning well. She has never gotten lost while driving the car, has no difficulty maintaining the house, and continues to enjoy social gatherings with family and friends. Most of their acquaintances and family haven't noticed anything different about her behavior. Jim asks, "Is there something wrong with my wife, or is this to be expected as we grow older? Jennie had a sister who had memory problems like this when she turned 75, and she ended up in a nursing home with 'no mind.' Should I be worried? Is there somewhere I can go to learn more about what's happening, if anything, to my wife?"

Jennie is having mild memory problems that may represent either the normal memory changes associated with aging (age-related cognitive decline) or the memory changes due to an underlying depressive disorder (major depression); or she may have an early stage of a progressive dementia, such as Alzheimer's disease. Alternatively, she may have a chronic infection of her central nervous system, a tumor or other expanding mass in her brain, a B vitamin deficiency, multiple small strokes, or the effects of chronic alcohol use; or she may simply be experiencing side effects of medicines taken for other health problems. Thus, there are many possible reasons for her forgetfulness, ranging from a normal decline in memory with age, to a readily treatable vitamin deficiency, to a severe, life-threatening brain disorder. Many persons in their 70s and 80s develop minor problems with forgetting names or misplacing objects; these changes are commonplace. Among persons aged 85 or older, nearly 50 percent of those living in the community have significant memory problems that could fulfill criteria for the diagnosis of Alzheimer's disease.[1] Jennie needs a comprehensive medical, neurological, and psychiatric evaluation to determine the cause of her symptoms.

Pastoral Care Assessment

Your assessment of Jennie would involve setting up a formal meeting with her husband to acquire further details about his wife's behavior and his causes for concern. Then you would meet with Jennie to determine why she thinks her husband is worried about her, assess her level of concern about the problem, and get a sense of what might be going on. Is there a reasonable explanation for the problems Jennie has been experiencing? Is she overconcerned or underconcerned? Many elderly patients cope with increasing memory problems by denying that any changes are taking place and become offended or more anxious when challenged on this point. Is she depressed? Does she appear drugged or oversedated? You must carefully weigh both the information you receive from the family and the information from the patient. Sometimes it is the spouse, not the identified patient, who has a problem.

Relevant History

Jennie has never used alcohol excessively and has no past history of depression or other psychiatric illness. She does have a history of high blood pressure and sinus problems. She is taking medications for these problems. The blood pressure pill could cause either depression or other mental changes that interfere with memory; alternatively, her blood pressure might not be adequately controlled with the medicine and she may be having frequent, small strokes affecting her memory. Her sinus medication may also have anticholinergic side effects that could interfere with her memory. Further history from Jim indicates that his wife has not recently experienced head trauma and has no other history of neurological illness;

---

1. D. A. Evans, H. H. Funkenstein, M. S. Albert, P. A. Scherr, N. R. Cook, M. J. Chown, L. E. Hebert, C. H. Hennekens, and J. O. Taylor, "Prevalence of Alzheimer's Disease in a Community Population of Older Persons: Higher Than Previously Reported," *Journal of the American Medical Association* 262 (1989): 2551-56.

he also reports that she eats well and has not been losing weight recently (and thus is unlikely to have a vitamin deficiency). She does, however, have a family history of memory problems in both a sister and her mother.

Diagnostic Criteria

Jennie has symptoms and signs of an early dementing illness. *Alzheimer's disease* and related *dementias* (disorders of memory) come on gradually and slowly over a period of months or years; the total disease course may last from two years to fifteen years. They are often hereditary. Symptoms and signs of these disorders involve a slow decline of "higher brain functions" such as memory or concentration; verbal, language, and math skills; and the ability to perform complex and coordinated physical activities. Alzheimer's disease is a clinical diagnosis. In other words, there are no blood tests or medical procedures (except for brain biopsy, which is seldom done) that can determine for certain whether the disease is present. Instead, the diagnosis depends on the history gathered from the patient or relatives and on the mental status examination. Alzheimer's disease is the diagnosis in about 50 to 60 percent of irreversible cases of dementia; other causes include multiple strokes (multi-infarct dementia, or vascular dementia, 10 to 20 percent of cases), chronic alcohol abuse (alcoholic dementia, 6 to 11 percent of cases), and other, more rare disorders (Pick's disease or Creutzfeldt-Jakob disease, less than 5 percent of cases). Tests are indicated only to rule out treatable causes for the memory disturbance—B vitamin deficiency, thyroid deficiency, central nervous system infections, or brain tumors. Other easily treatable disorders that mimic dementia are depression or delirium due to medications or medical conditions. In the early stages of Alzheimer's disease or other dementing illnesses, insight is often preserved. In other words, patients recognize that something is wrong with them. This itself may cause a serious depressive reaction, resulting in the co-occurrence of two disorders—depression and dementia.

Response to Vignette

Jim and Jennie are both likely to be experiencing great stress, even if it is unacknowledged. They are confronting an unknown enemy in their lives, over which they have little control. As their minister, you are in a key position to make a quick assessment of the problem and direct them to appropriate help, as well as relieve their undue anxiety through education. Timely assessment and referral may avoid problems in the future, particularly if a treatable disease can be identified early and reversed. You must proceed cautiously in counseling such patients and their families. Either an underestimation or an overestimation of the seriousness of the problem can worsen the situation. You must convince the spouse that his or her loved one needs professional evaluation and ensure that such evaluation is sought. At the same time, you should always be calming and reassuring to the patient to allay anxiety. It is best to say that many persons normally experience memory problems as they get older, and that if there is a problem, there is often safe and effective treatment to help improve memory or prevent further memory loss. Remember that if a true dementing illness is present, insight may be lost and the person may vigorously deny having a problem; furthermore, denial is a way that some persons cope with the fears and anxieties associated with this disease. Problems arise when family members also deny a problem and delay seeking evaluation.

Treatment Within the Faith Community

At this early stage in the disease process, the most important intervention is to obtain professional evaluation. The faith community may help by providing transportation to the doctor's office or otherwise removing barriers to evaluation. You or members of your staff can provide support and understanding to both the patient and his or her spouse, allowing them to ventilate their fears and frustrations. Active listening, validation of feelings, and sincere display of empathy are most important. Neither simple dismissal of fears as unfounded nor superficial reassurance is appropriate, and both can make matters worse by discouraging discussion and fostering isolation. On the other hand, overconcern by the helper and exaggeration of the problem may generate unnecessary fear and anxiety in the person, which will paralyze further action.

Indications for Referral

Persons who complain of memory problems (or whose families complain of their memory problems) should almost always be immediately referred for medical assessment. This is because most persons usually do not display concern or seek help until the process is advanced and causing problems with functioning. Minor problems with memory, such as name forgetting, missing of appointments, misplacing of objects, or easy distractibility, are common in later life, particularly when they occur only sporadically. However, any consistent pattern of forgetfulness that represents a significant change from prior functioning requires careful evaluation.

Treatment by Mental Health Specialist

Making an accurate diagnosis is the first step. Most family physicians, general internists, geriatric psychiatrists, and neurologists are trained to evaluate older persons for memory problems. Formal psychological testing may be helpful in distinguishing different causes for the memory disturbance. Repeated observation over time (every three to six months) is often necessary to determine the rate of memory decline and ascertain whether it is abnormal. Once a diagnosis of significant memory impairment is made, the doctor will try to identify treatable causes. If a B-12 vitamin deficiency is present, then giving monthly B-12 shots may take care of the problem. If low thyroid is detected, then administration of thyroid medication will help restore memory and function. Treatment of depression with antidepressant medication may completely reverse problems with concentration and memory. Removal of unnecessary medication, reduction of dose, or switching to other medications without adverse side effects may quickly help clear up the mental state. Cessation of alcohol intake will often prevent further memory loss. Treatment of high blood pressure and administration of a daily aspirin tablet may prevent small strokes. If early Alzheimer's dementia is present, then treatment with the drug Tacrine may help some patients; however, this medication does have significant side effects, and its overall benefits have been questioned. New anti-Alzheimer's drugs are currently under development (see below for more information).

Also see case 17, "Caregiver Stress."

Resources

Local Resources

After the diagnosis is confirmed, educating the person's family about the condition becomes important. A knowledgeable social worker can provide information about local and national resources. Family members need to know about the disease's course, treatments, financial planning, legal issues (e.g., power of attorney, guardianship, living wills), and sources of emotional support. Information can be obtained from the local chapter of the Alzheimer's Disease and Related Disorders Association (ADRDA). This group often coordinates support groups for spouses and other family members. University medical centers may also have clinics that specialize in memory disorders and can provide the comprehensive evaluation necessary to make the diagnosis, as well as be a source of information for families.

National Resources

The ADRDA is a national organization devoted to helping families of persons with dementing illnesses. Write to 919 North Michigan Avenue, Chicago, IL 60611 (phone 1-800-621-0379, or if in Illinois, 1-800-572-6037). It has local chapters in most medium- and large-sized cities in the United States. The Alzheimer's Disease Education and Referral Center (ADEAR) is a clearinghouse supported by the National Institute on Aging; it provides information on Alzheimer's disease and vascular dementias. Write to PO Box 8250, Silver Spring, MD 20907-8250. The American Association of Retired Persons (AARP, 601 E Street, NW, Washington, DC 20049, phone 202-434-2277) and the National Institute of Mental Health (Barry Liebowitz, Mental Disorders of Aging Research Branch, 5600 Fishers Lane, Room 7-103, Rockville, MD 20857) may also be contacted for information and referral sources.

For families wanting information about the latest drug trials for the treatment of Alzheimer's disease or the agitation associated with it, contact the Alzheimer's Association (ADRDA, above) for copies of its "drug fact sheets." These fact sheets provide a wealth of information about the different drugs, why they are being studied, how many patients will be studied, who is eligible to participate, information about the study design, and location of places where the studies are taking place. As of July 1995, there are ten different drugs being tested in cities all over the United States; none of these drugs is curative, but all are meant to slow the progression of the disease. To request the most up-to-date set of fact sheets, call 1-800-272-3900. The ADRDA also has a fact sheet on Tacrine, currently the only approved drug for the treatment of Alzheimer's disease.

Self-Help Resources

By far the best source of information for families is *The 36-Hour Day*, by Nancy L. Mace and Peter V. Rabins (Baltimore: Johns Hopkins University Press, 1981). This 250-page book addresses such questions and topics as "What is dementia?" "Getting medical help for the impaired person," "Characteristic problems of dementia," "Problems in independent living," "Problems arising in daily care," "Medical problems," "Problems of behavior," "Problems of mood," "Special arrangements if you become ill," "Getting outside help," "You and the impaired person as parts of a family," "How caring for an impaired person affects you," "Caring for yourself," "For children and teenagers," "Financial and legal issues," "Nursing homes and other living arrangements," "Brain disorders and the causes of dementia," and "Research in dementia." Robert Davis, a Presbyterian pastor, has written a fascinating book entitled *My Journey into Alzheimer's Disease* (Wheaton, Ill.: Tyndale House, 1989), which provides important firsthand insights on how Alzheimer's disease can affect one's religious faith.

Cross-Cultural Issues

African American and minority families frequently develop elaborate social support systems in the community that help compensate for problems in functioning encountered by elders with dementing illnesses. These elders may shy away from the medical establishment, not presenting for professional evaluation until late in the course of their disease. Many cases of treatable memory loss could be detected and reversed if such elders sought help early for these conditions; this is particularly true for African American elders who have high rates of hypertension (often untreated) or for those with a history of substance abuse. Ministers of African American congregations, then, have a particularly crucial role in detecting and motivating such elders to seek evaluation and treatment.

Legal Issues

Relatives of persons with dementing illnesses such as Alzheimer's disease should be familiar with the following three legal documents: power of attorney, durable power of attorney, and living will. Many problems later on can be prevented by obtaining *power of attorney* before the person becomes severely impaired. This involves having the ill person willingly sign a written statement that gives another person the power to make decisions regarding the ill person's finances or health care (or both), in the event that the ill person is not able to make these decisions for himself or herself. *Durable power of attorney* is best, because when a person's disease progresses to the point that he or she can no longer make decisions, this allows the designated person to make the appropriate financial or health care decisions for the patient. If durable power of attorney has not been obtained beforehand, and the impaired person refuses to cooperate, then court proceedings will be necessary in order to have the person declared incompetent (after medical evaluation) and a guardian appointed.

Power of attorney and guardianship can be obtained separately for decisions regarding financial matters and for those concerning health care matters. As far as financial decisions are concerned, if Jim and Jennie's assets are in both of their names, then power of attorney and guardianship concerns are less pressing; but if much of the assets are in Jim's or Jennie's name only, then these legal procedures become important and sometimes complex. When there is no spouse available, then it is particularly necessary for children or next of kin to pursue these legal actions early in the course of illness.

A *living will* is an "advanced directive" that provides written instructions by the patient concerning health care in the event of terminal illness (whether he or she wants cardiopulmonary resuscitation, artificial nutrition or hydration, and so forth). This makes it easier for loved ones to make difficult health care decisions and can help avoid family conflict over these matters. The best time to have these documents drawn up is when a family member is in the early stages of dementia.

Always have your church members consult a lawyer before setting up power of attorney, joint account, trust, or guardianship (and ask about the consultation fee). For help in locating a lawyer, write to the American Bar Association's Lawyer Referral and Information Service, 750 North Lake Shore Drive, Chicago, IL 60611. Free legal and financial assistance may be available from your local agency on aging or may be obtained by contacting the National Association of Area Agencies on Aging (1112 Sixteenth Street, NW, Suite 100, Washington, DC 20036) or the Legal Counsel for the Elderly (601 E Street, NW, fourth floor, Washington, DC 20049). For tips on how to prepare personal and financial records that minimize confusion during times of crisis, write the National Institute on Aging Information Center, PO Box 8057,

Gaithersburg, MD 20898-8057, and ask for the AgePage entitled "Getting Your Affairs in Order."

Obtaining a power of attorney (durable) and a living will should be among the highest and earliest priorities for family members after the diagnosis is established. Too often, a family waits to initiate these documents until the disease advances to its middle stage, often too late for the demented loved one to have any meaningful input.

Middle-Stage Alzheimer's Dementia

What Should I Do with Bob?

You notice that Helen, your church secretary, has not been herself over the past week. She has made more typing errors in reports than usual and has misfiled a number of important documents that you've needed for meetings. You come into her office and sit down. "Helen, you're not yourself lately. Is there anything you'd like to talk about?" you ask, with a concerned tone in your voice.

"Yes, pastor, there is," she responds, after a long sigh. "My husband, as you know, has Alzheimer's, and over the past month he has been just impossible to live with." Sixty-eight-year-old Bob was diagnosed with Alzheimer's disease about five years ago. You know him and his wife well, since they have been actively involved in the church for years and Helen has been your secretary for the past ten years.

Helen goes on to tell you that Bob had been functioning rather well until the past six months. Since then, he has become increasingly difficult to manage. He sits around most of the time and refuses to help around the house or even maintain the yard. When Helen tries to get him to do things, he becomes angry and yells threateningly. She is not worried that he would ever be violent toward her, but she doesn't know what might happen if things continue as they are. Because of worsening memory, Bob sometimes forgets to take his pills and even forgets to eat lunch, unless she reminds him. She has become concerned about leaving him at home alone even for the four hours each day that she works at the church. He apparently got lost the other day after leaving the house to go for a walk; he became disoriented and began walking away from the house. Luckily, a friend saw him wandering about and helped him back home. She is also afraid that Bob might get in an accident with the car. He has already run a couple of red lights, and the other day he backed up into a light pole, causing serious damage to their car. "What if he ran over a child crossing the street because he can't stop quick enough?" she cries. Bob is insistent, however, on continuing to drive. Even more disturbing to Helen is that he has become increasingly jealous of her, accusing her of cheating on him when she goes off to work. "Should I quit my job at the church and stay with him at home?" Helen asks. "I'm not sure if I could handle that emotionally. You know, getting out of the house for just a few hours each day has been such a blessing. I promised him I'd never put him in a nursing home, but I don't know now. Pastor, what should I do with Bob?"

Pastoral Care Assessment

You arrange a meeting with Helen and Bob in order to further assess her husband's condition. The best place to make this assessment is in Helen and Bob's home. If this is not feasible, then an office visit will have to suffice. In talking with Bob, you want to do three things:

1. Assess his memory and orientation to get some sense of how severely impaired he is. (Does he know how long they've been married? Their wedding date? How many children they have, and where the children are living now?)
2. Assess his mood state. (Is he depressed, anxious, or irritable?)
3. Assess his insight into his condition and the effects that it is having on his wife. (Does he think he has memory problems? Is he aware that his memory problems are causing her stress?)

His appearance and behavior during your meeting are important. Does he appear to be drugged or oversedated? He does not. (If he did, you would need a list of the medications he is taking and why he is taking them). Is he clean and neatly dressed? No, he smells as if he has not bathed recently, and his clothes are wrinkled and unkempt. Is he restless and agitated, or are his actions slow and unconcerned? He is restless and has difficulty sitting still but is not agitated. Does he become angry and impatient with you? Yes, he doesn't understand why you are having this meeting with him today and wishes to leave. Is he paranoid and suspicious? Somewhat—he avoids eye contact and keeps his distance. During your conversation with Bob, you learn that his memory is very poor; he even has difficulty remembering his age and how many children he has. He adamantly denies feeling sad, discouraged, or hopeless. In fact, he claims that there is nothing wrong with him. He clearly does not appreciate the burden that he is currently placing on his wife.

Assessment of Bob's functional level is also important in determining his care needs. You learn later from Helen during a private session that Bob still dresses himself, bathes himself, and only infrequently has episodes of urinary incontinence (wets himself). His sleep-wake cycle has shifted, though, and though he sleeps on and off during the day, he gets up in the middle of the night and rummages about the house. This behavior is disturbing Helen's sleep and may be contributing to her sense of exhaustion. This assessment of Bob will give you some sense of what Helen is dealing with, the resources Bob needs, and how you might be able to help both of them.

Other information relevant to Bob's case includes any medical illnesses that he might have. You find out that other than having memory problems, he is quite healthy. He takes no medications and has never been admitted to the hospital, except once for hernia surgery. Untreated medical illness or excess medications can worsen dementia and lead to agitation or temporary disorientation (see case 13, "Delirium"). You also learn from Helen that Bob does not drink alcohol, smoke, or use any over-the-counter medications. There is no family history of any type of mental problem like manic-depression or schizophrenia, although his father died in his 70s with dementia. An important fact you learn is that Bob's mother took care of his father for years in their home before he died, and Bob expects his wife to do the same for him.

Relevant History

The course of Alzheimer's disease varies in length from two to fifteen years. Bob has had the diagnosis of dementia for five years now. Over the past few months, he has entered into the middle stage of the disease. The middle stage of Alzheimer's dementia (as well as other dementing disorders), as described by Kaufman, is characterized by "overt memory loss accompanied by impairment in other intellectual functions. Language impairments . . . are followed by a decline in comprehension of written and verbal communications. . . . In addition, patients commonly suffer depression, hallucinations, and in 20 to 40 percent of cases, prominent paranoid ideation that sometimes reaches psychotic proportions."[1] Bob has a number of symptoms that mark him in the middle stage of the disease, including significant impairment of memory and language, increasing disorientation, periodic agitation, paranoid thinking that is almost delusional, an altered sleep-wake cycle, decreased motivation to care for himself or his surroundings, and increasing limitations in his ability to perform activities of daily living. See case 14, "Early-Stage Alzheimer's Dementia," for a discussion of the mental and physical conditions that can cause or worsen dementia. Although these are not factors for Bob, the most common offenders are untreated medical illnesses and doctor-prescribed or over-the-counter drugs that affect mental status.

Diagnostic Criteria

Bob is beginning to demonstrate a number of behaviors that are making his care increasingly difficult. This commonly occurs during the second

Response to Vignette

1. D. M. Kaufman, *Clinical Neurology for Psychiatrists* (Philadelphia: W. B. Saunders, 1990), 116-17.

stage of the disease, and is associated with increasing caregiver stress and the need to make decisions that will both ensure patient safety and guarantee the meeting of basic care needs. This is a particularly important time, when the caregiver's burden must be addressed, and efforts must be made to reduce it to a tolerable level.

If he has not had one recently, Bob needs a comprehensive medical assessment to rule out any new physical health problems that may be causing his dementia symptoms to worsen and to determine whether a depressive disorder is contributing to his lack of motivation, irritability, sleeplessness at night, and paranoia. You or your pastoral staff can help Helen find a physician to provide this comprehensive assessment, help Bob get to and from the appointment, and support the physician's recommendations and treatment plan (if it is reasonable). Helen needs counseling about what she can do to relieve the stress of caregiving, how she can ensure Bob's safety, and how she can meet his current care needs. She must acquire knowledge about resources available in the community that can provide respite for her (time away from Bob) and provide care for Bob's special needs. She also needs advice about long-term planning, including the possibility down the road of nursing home placement.

Legal issues must also be addressed, including decisions about whether to obtain power of attorney or guardianship and how to go about this. The input of a good lawyer may be helpful. See the "Legal Issues" section, below.

Treatment Within the Faith Community

Interventions by the faith community include (1) facilitating Bob's medical and psychiatric reevaluation, (2) providing information to Helen, (3) offering practical assistance in Bob's care, and (4) providing emotional support to both Helen and Bob.

We have already discussed how pastoral staff can help Helen find medical specialists to reevaluate Bob and help her get him to and from his appointments. We suggest that pastoral staff develop a list of geriatric medicine specialists and geriatric psychiatrists in their area and information about the quality of care that these practitioners deliver. Such information includes how quickly an appointment can be obtained, how much time the physician spends with patients, whether he or she is competent and knowledgeable about the latest advances in the field, whether he or she is responsive to patients' telephone calls, and the friendliness and competency of his or her office staff (receptionists, nurses, social workers). You can acquire such information by accompanying patients to their office visits and seeking feedback from members of the congregation treated by these physicians.

We also recommend that pastoral staff develop a list of other resource persons (social workers, nurses, knowledgeable laypersons) in the community who can provide information about local caregiver support groups, inexpensive (but responsible) in-home services, yard and home upkeep services, and the like. Alternatively, pastoral staff can obtain such information themselves and develop a library or central information resource that members of the congregation can utilize when necessary. Included here, for instance, would be updated information about the quality of local adult day care programs, board and care homes, rest homes, and skilled nursing facilities, as well as information about the quality and costs of retirement communities in the area.

Several churches might combine their resources and volunteer personnel to help establish and operate programs that meet the special needs of cognitively impaired or severely disabled older adults in their community. For example, volunteers might be organized to make up teams of workers to help provide in-home services and yard services or deliver meals-on-wheels. Alternatively, an adult day care program might be developed within a church to provide structured activities for cognitively impaired older adults for four to six hours each day (just what Bob needs). The Shepherds' Center concept, developed by Dr. Elbert Cole (a Methodist minister in Kansas City, Misssouri), involves churches banding together to enlist elderly volunteers to utilize their special skills and talents to meet the needs of their less fortunate peers living in the community. Over the past fifteen years, Shepherd's Centers have sprung up rapidly throughout America, with over 1,800 congregations affiliated with ninety centers nationwide in 1994. For more information, write to Shepherd's Centers of America, 6700 Troost, Suite 616, Kansas City, MO 64131 (or call 816-523-1080).

Besides providing information and practical assistance, the faith community can offer emotional and spiritual support to Helen and Bob. Calling them on the telephone, visiting and spending time with them, and making the extra effort to include them in activities and social functions are sure ways of demonstrating that the members of your faith community take seriously their charge to love one another and bear one another's burdens. These duties require relatively little training, but much sensitivity, compassion, and common sense. Many Protestant churches have developed "Stephen's ministries," in which laypersons are trained to provide supportive counseling to suffering members in their congregation. Persons who take it upon themselves to minister to persons with Alzheimer's disease or dementia must realize that, depending on the stage of the person's disease, the task may be a difficult one with few external rewards. Thus, one's motivation must often be that of service and storing up treasures in heaven. The pastor's role is to inspire his or her faith community into action while clarifying the difficulty of the task and the necessary attitude that helpers take.

Whenever there is a significant change in the demented person's functioning or in the functioning of the caregiver, professional help is needed.

Indications for Referral

Referral is also indicated when special problems arise that threaten the safety of the individual, the caregiver, or the community. For example, Bob is continuing to drive despite the danger to himself and to those around him. Likewise, if Bob were unable to care for his needs or would not allow others to do so, he should be referred for evaluation. Finally, significant caregiver stress that does not respond to interventions within the faith community should prompt professional involvement.

Treatment by Mental Health Specialist

The first responsibility of health care professionals is to ensure the patient's safety. The second is to diagnose and treat medical and psychiatric conditions that are contributing to worsening dementia. The third is to provide information to facilitate caregiving. Repeated cognitive assessment can determine the rate of cognitive decline (or worsening of dementia), which can help predict immediate and future care needs (e.g., how soon the person will need placement in a nursing home). Likewise, assessing the person's emotional state may help identify a depressive disorder, which increases the risk of suicide (a not infrequent cause of death for elderly men with dementia). Assessing whether the demented person is receiving adequate care and supervision within the home is another important aspect of ensuring patient safety. In Bob's case, the physician should also recommend he stop driving and notify the state department of motor vehicles if he does not follow through on the recommendation. Finally, medications can be prescribed that reduce agitation, facilitate sleep, and reduce paranoia and suspiciousness; these medications, however, have numerous side effects and must be used with caution.

Resources

See case 14, "Early-Stage Alzheimer's Dementia," and case 17, "Caregiver Stress," for local, national, and self-help resources.

Legal Issues

See case 14, "Early-Stage Alzheimer's Dementia," for information about establishing durable power of attorney and creating a living will.

Information About Nursing Homes

If placement becomes necessary in the future, Helen will need information about how to choose a nursing home that best meets the needs of her spouse. Again, you or your pastoral staff can be an invaluable resource to Helen if you have ready access to this type of information. Also see this section in case 16, "Late-Stage Alzheimer's Dementia."

Cross-Cultural Issues

See this section in case 14, "Early Stage Alzheimer's Dementia."

Late-Stage Alzheimer's Dementia

Leave Me Alone

Laura is an 83-year-old member of your congregation who has been living for the past year at Restwell Nursing Home. She was placed there by her daughter Teresa after she became too much to handle at home. Teresa, also a member of your church, had valiantly tried to care for her at home for two years, but she has three children and a husband who need attention, and she works part-time outside the home to help make ends meet. Just prior to moving to the nursing home, Laura required in-home nursing assistance seven days a week, and this was draining her financial reserves rapidly. Also, Teresa was quickly becoming exhausted by her mother's nighttime activities. Laura was diagnosed with Alzheimer's dementia about ten years ago, and had gradually worsened to the point that she stayed in bed most of the time, was incontinent of urine and stool, and had to be fed, bathed, and turned every two hours to avoid bed sores.

This had continued for the past year, since her placement at Restwell, but her condition has worsened over the past several months. She is now totally bed-bound and lies most of the day in a fetal position with her knees tucked up to her chest and surrounded by her arms. She is able to sit up in a chair briefly each day, but when the nurses try to get her up or to turn her from side to side, she cries out, "Leave me alone!" and strikes at them. Teresa faithfully visits her mother every day after work, keeping fresh flowers in her room and feeding Laura her supper (which she also fights over). At times, it seems as if Laura can recognize Teresa and is glad to see her; at other times, however, the blank stare on Laura's face gives away that Teresa is just another stranger.

Her mother's deteriorating condition has been bothering Teresa. One day, Teresa calls you for an appointment to talk. As her pastor, you have also been visiting Laura every couple of months at the home, but are not too sure why you are doing this or if it is doing Laura any good. Teresa sits down in the chair across from your desk. After some small talk, she gets to the point. "Pastor, I'm worried about Mother. She's going downhill fast, and I don't know what to do. At times, she seems as if she recognizes me, and I know that she still has feelings. The other day, tears came to her eyes when I played a favorite hymn of hers on a cassette player. The nurses are so busy, and don't seem to care. I've often found her wet and soiled when I arrive to feed her. Maybe I never should have placed her in that nursing home after all." Teresa is sobbing now. You reach out and place your hand on her arm, trying to console her. "I need some advice," she says. "It's killing me watching her suffer like this and not being able to do a thing about it."

Pastoral Care Assessment

Given the concerns of her daughter, you decide to pay Laura a visit early this month to perform a more complete assessment of the situation. When you arrive, Laura is sitting up in a chair, restrained so that she cannot wiggle herself free and fall on the floor. Her head is drooped over and resting on her chest, but her eyes are open. "Hello, Laura, this is Pastor Jim," you greet her in a friendly tone. She looks up at you, straining to see who you are, but soon drops her head back to her chest and mumbles, "Leave me alone."

Laura is thin and gaunt in appearance: her hair is tousled and unkempt and her gown is soiled in places. The smell of urine pervades the room. Her glasses and hearing aide are neatly packed away in her nightstand drawer. You get her glasses and gently place them on her forehead. Now she can see you, and a look of recognition comes across her face. You catch the attention of a nurse's aide passing by the room and ask her to place Laura's hearing aide in. Now, Laura is actually looking at you and has her head raised slightly off her chest. "Please, get me out of here," she begs you. "I want to go back to bed."

You tell Laura that you will tell the nurses about her request, but you would like to talk with her a bit. Her head falls back on her chest, and she quits talking. You are at a loss as to what to do next, so you gently take her hand and just sit there. Laura does not resist you, and in fact tightens her grip on your hand. You offer to say a prayer, and since she does not protest, you go ahead and do this. When you finish, you notice that she is more relaxed, but still says nothing to you and stares downward. You then read a passage out of Psalms from your Bible. After sitting quietly with her for another fifteen minutes, you give her a hug, get up, and leave the room.

Relevant History

It is important for you to obtain Laura's social history from Teresa, so that you can assess the types of supportive relationships that may still exist in the community. You learn that Laura's husband died seven years ago and all her brothers and sisters have likewise passed on. In her earlier life, she had worked as a secretary to the mayor for many years. When she was 28 years old, she married her husband, a promising lawyer. They had three children, of whom Teresa was the oldest and now the only relative who lives in the same town. Her other two children live in distant cities, and they visit only infrequently. Until about eight years ago, Laura had been an active church attender and had many friends in the congregation; only a few of these friends, however, are still alive now.

Also important is Laura's past medical and psychiatric history. Does she have any physical illnesses that might be contributing to her disability or causing discomfort? Has she been examined by a physician recently? What about her medications? Elderly, agitated patients in nursing homes are difficult to care for, so nursing staff will sometimes call the patients' doctors and ask for medication to sedate them. Chronic oversedation can worsen cognitive impairment and lead to sensory deprivation as well as other side effects that might lead to worsening function. Does Laura have a history of depression or any other psychiatric illness? Is she now depressed? If Laura even periodically has any insight into her condition, then she is likely to become depressed. Alzheimer's disease is a *cortical dementia* and usually does not involve the emotion centers of the brain. Thus, Alzheimer's patients even in advanced stages retain the capacity for emotions. Treatment with antidepressants may help reduce Laura's agitation and at times may even increase her alertness and motivation.

Diagnostic Criteria

Laura is in the late stages of Alzheimer's dementia. According to Kaufman, "In the late stage, physical as well as cognitive deficits become profound. Patients tend to be mute, unresponsive to verbal requests, and bedridden in a decorticate (fetal) posture."[1] Diagnosis, however, should still be questioned, since other illnesses can mimic this stage of the disease. Severe depression can cause a person to take to bed and retard his or her movements, as well as cause negativism, agitation, and even muteness—symptoms that resemble those of late Alzheimer's disease. Other psychiatric illnesses, such as schizophrenia, catatonic variety, can mimic this condition as well. Finally, certain neurological conditions (e.g., strokes or head injuries) result in a "locked-in" syndrome, in which the person is fully alert but cannot express himself or herself in any meaningful way except by the blinking of eyelids in some cases. More common, as noted above, are the many treatable medical conditions that can worsen early- or middle-stage dementia to make it appear like late-stage dementia.

1. D. M. Kaufman, *Clinical Neurology for Psychiatrists* (Philadelphia: W. B. Saunders, 1990), 177.

Response to Vignette

Even though Laura's condition may seem somewhat hopeless, there are still a number of things that you and Teresa can do to help make her last months or years of life as painless as possible. First, you or your pastoral staff must work with Teresa to ensure that Laura is in a nursing home where she is likely to get good care. Second, you and Teresa must ensure that Laura receives a complete medical and psychiatric evaluation to rule out treatable causes for her deterioration. Third, you must remember (and also remind Teresa) that Laura still has the capacity to experience a wide range of emotions and even spiritual experiences.

Not all nursing homes are alike. The type of care given often depends on the philosophy and the priorities of the home's administrators. These priorities and philosophies determine the quality and training of staff, as well as the number of aides and nurses on duty to attend to patients' needs. This will affect the attitudes that nursing staff have toward patients; do they see patients' requests for help as burdensome distractions in their already hectic schedules, or do they see these as opportunities to minister to the needs of people who are suffering? Laura was left sitting up in her chair without her glasses on or her hearing aide in; this shows little concern for her personal need for stimulation from her environment. For more information on choosing a nursing home, see below.

If care at the nursing home is adequate, and a patient's condition continues to deteriorate, then some attempt to rule out treatable medical or psychiatric conditions becomes necessary. Optimally, the types of treatments patients in Laura's condition receive or don't receive should be guided by their living will (see the discussion of "Legal Issues" in case 14). Treatments that reduce pain, anxiety, or other unpleasant physical or emotional symptoms should receive the highest priority. Certainly, reexamination of Laura's medical regimen is necessary to ensure that she is not being over- or undermedicated.

Finally, patients in the later stages of Alzheimer's disease still retain the capacity to experience emotions and communicate at some rudimentary level.[2] Even though they have difficulty expressing emotion, these patients can tell when someone is kind to them, is concerned about their feelings, and cares about them. Likewise, many such patients become more peaceful and less agitated following spiritual activities in their presence such as prayer, scripture reading, the singing of well-known hymns, and various religious rituals. Thus, time spent with Laura by Teresa and yourself is not wasted time, and there are a number of things that you can do to bring comfort and combat isolation.

Treatment Within the Faith Community

You, your pastoral staff, or a sensitive, knowledgeable, and committed member of your congregation can do much to minister to the needs of patients like Laura. Visits should be regular (weekly), but can be short

2. L. Jansson, A. Norberg, P. Sandman, E. Athlin, and K. Asplund, "Interpreting Facial Expressions in Patients in the Terminal Stage of the Alzheimer Disease," *Omega* 26, no. 4 (1992–1993): 309-24.

(fifteen to thirty minutes). When working with cognitively impaired adults, the following suggestions are helpful:

1. Know as much about the person's religious background as possible. This will enable you to select religious activities that have been important to the person. For Catholics, taking Communion or saying the Rosary may be particularly meaningful.
2. Approach the person using a conversational tone, taking hearing or visual impairments into consideration.
3. Prayer with patients is vital, but keep it short, supportive, and familiar.
4. Recite familiar scripture passages with patients (start them off and keep them short).
5. Visual cues such as a cross, a rosary, or a Bible should be used to help communication.
6. Provide weekly sacraments, such as Communion, to those accustomed to receiving them.
7. Sing, whistle, or play old familiar hymns.
8. Involve the family when possible. For example, even if the patient's family cannot be physically present, you can play a tape recording of the patient's grandchildren singing hymns or reading scriptures.

You should persist in these activities even if the patient shows no visible reactions of pleasure or recognition; but if the patient gets upset or agitated, you should stop. Sometimes, just spending time with Alzheimer's patients, holding their hands or stroking their brows with a wet wash cloth, can provide them with the sense that they are cared about.

As always, family members like Teresa need the support and concern of their faith community. At times like these, it is common for family to feel guilty and second-guess their decisions to institutionalize their loved ones. Helping them talk about these concerns in an atmosphere that is reassuring and supportive will enable them to work through these painful emotions. Also, instructing family members about the emotional and spiritual needs of severely demented persons and ways that they can meet those needs helps counteract a sense of helplessness.

Indications for Referral

Most patients in the latter stages of Alzheimer's disease will be institutionalized because of their need for twenty-four-hour care. Any sudden deterioration in functioning or well-being should prompt examination by a physician. Any sign of abuse or neglect by nursing home staff or by family caregivers is another indication for referral (see case 28, "Elder Abuse").

Treatment by Mental Health Specialist

Symptoms that cause discomfort or impair quality of life (pain, difficulty breathing, bed sores, anxiety, hallucinations, restlessness and agitation, depression, and so forth) should in most cases be treated by health care professionals. Interventions to reverse treatable illness in a person with late-stage Alzheimer's disease will depend on the wishes of the patient or his or her designated health care agent. Health care professionals are also required to report any signs of abuse or neglect to Adult Protective Services.

Resources

See case 14, "Early-Stage Alzheimer's Dementia," and case 17, "Caregiver Stress," for local, national, and self-help resources.

Information About Nursing Homes

There are over 1.5 million nursing home residents in the United States, and 50 to 66 percent of these have moderate to severe dementia. Although only about 5 percent of the older adult population is in a nursing home at any one time, nearly 30 percent of older adults can expect to spend some time in a nursing home setting. When family can no longer care for a loved one at home, there are several options for placement: residential care or adult foster care facilities (which provide room and board along with some activity programs), continuing care communities (which provide room and board in addition to health care and other needs including skilled nursing if required), assisted living facilities (retirement or rest homes that offer meals, recreation, and assistance with basic activities of daily living), and skilled nursing facilities (for persons requiring twenty-four-hour medical care and supervision).

When choosing a nursing home or other care facility, ask the following questions: Does the home have a good reputation in the community? (Ask the families of current residents.) Is the home close to the resident's family, friends, and community activities? What types of services are offered and carried out? What are the staffing requirements? Are there private or semiprivate rooms, and if the rooms are semiprivate, how are roommates selected? Does the home have a resident council, and what influence does it have on home procedures and policies? The most important consideration is how near the nursing home is to relatives and friends who are likely to visit. It is our experience that if residents have frequent visitors who monitor their care regularly, the quality of care delivered by nursing home staff to those residents increases.

The best nursing homes usually have long waiting lists, so the search should occur well in advance of the time when admission is actually needed. Good sources of information about nursing homes include the yellow pages of the telephone directory, personal physicians, local area agencies on aging, the department of social services of a local hospital, and the local or state health department. Things to find out about include whether the home participates in Medicare and Medicaid programs (suggesting that minimum standards of care have been met), whether it has an up-to-date state license, whether the administrator has an up-to-date license, whether state fire regulations have been met, what access there is to medical and nursing services, what arrangements have been made for medical emergencies, what types of rehabilitation and social programs are offered, and the quality of the food service. It may be helpful to drop in once or twice unannounced during the evening to assess staffing levels and activities provided during nonregular hours. Once a decision has been made, it is essential to obtain a thorough understanding of the nursing home's contract or financial agreement; it is best to have a lawyer review the agreement before signing.

For more information about how to choose a nursing home write the National Institute on Aging Information Center, PO Box 8057, Gaithersburg, MD 20898-8057, and ask for the AgePage entitled "When You Need a Nursing Home." The Nursing Home Information Service provides information on nursing homes, including a free guide on how to choose a nursing home; for more information write to the National Council of Senior Citizens, Nursing Home Information Service, 925 Fifteenth Street, NW, Washington, DC 20005. The National Citizens Coalition for Nursing Home Reform helps local persons work for nursing home reform and improvements in long-term care; you may contact them by writing NCCNHR, 1424 Sixteenth Street, NW, Suite L-2, Washington, DC 20036. Finally, information on long-term care can be obtained from AARP Health Advocacy Services, 1909 K Street, NW, Washington, DC 20049. To obtain information about "continuing care communities," write AARP Housing Activities, 1129 Twentieth Street, NW, Suite 400, Washington, DC 20036-3489.

Cross-Cultural Issues

African Americans, Mexican Americans, and Asian Americans are likely to try to care for older relatives in their homes. There is strong community support for this, with neighbors and extended family often pitching in to help out. At times, however, when the care burden becomes excessive, these persons may need encouragement to place a severely demented relative in a nursing care facility to ensure that he or she receives adequate care. The family members responsible for such a decision may need counseling to help them overcome the associated guilt.

Caregiver Stress

I Feel So Alone

Elaine walks slowly into your office and slumps down into the chair across from your desk. She bursts into tears. "I feel so alone. I just can't take it anymore!" she exclaims.

Somewhat taken aback by her overt display of emotion, you compose yourself and ask in a quiet, caring voice, "What is bothering you, Elaine?"

Elaine begins her story, telling it with a mixture of sadness, fear, anger, and at times, desperation. She is now 71 years old, and she and her husband, William, have worked hard all their lives trying to accumulate a nest egg they could retire on; she, in particular, has looked forward to traveling and taking it easy in her later years. Five years ago, William was diagnosed with Alzheimer's disease. For the first couple of years, they did all right, since he remained mostly his old self except for a gradually worsening memory. In the past two years, however, things have taken a turn for the worse. Their marriage has never been a great one, and they had lived relatively separate and independent lives until recently, when her husband's deteriorating condition forced them into closer contact. As the dementia has progressed, his controlling personality traits and bad temper have gradually worsened. William has begun drinking heavily, started accusing his wife of stealing things from him and trying to poison him, and shouts and threatens her when he is drunk. His doctor told him months before to stop driving; and when he found out about William's drinking, he firmly told him to stop both. Since then, William has remained irritable around the clock—blaming his wife for the doctor's discovering his drinking and driving habits.

Elaine is not well herself, with insulin-requiring diabetes, mild heart failure, and a hip fracture suffered in a recent fall. Despite these health problems, over the past year she has been forced to take over more and more of the household and other duties—paying the bills, balancing the checkbook, doing the laundry, cooking the meals, cleaning, as well as doing the yard work and car maintenance tasks. Furthermore, in the past six months, her husband's condition has become so bad that he has stopped bathing and shaving himself, often wets the bed at night, and becomes hostile whenever she asks him to help out. At times, he even has trouble recognizing who she is and has asked her on a couple of occasions to get out of his house. Elaine is becoming increasingly fearful that he will become violent toward her.

Over the past three months, Elaine has become exhausted. Because of her heavy duties at home, she has been unable to maintain her social relationships and is increasingly feeling isolated and intensely alone. When she went to see her doctor, he suggested she put William in a nursing home to relieve herself of the burden. She has already looked into this possibility, but at a cost of $35,000 per year, this option would quickly exhaust their savings and soon force her to sell her home. No, she could not do this. She has spent nearly forty years in her home and raised her children there. Her doctor prescribed an antidepressant for her, a tranquilizer for her husband, and suggested she get someone to help her with caregiving and household chores. Unfortunately, no family members are available to help out; their two children have moved out of state in search of work and are actively involved raising their own families. Elaine has looked into hiring someone to come in two or three times a week to bathe and shave her husband as well as help out with the cleaning duties. An aide from a home health agency would cost her $15 per hour, and Medicare will not pay for this. Their medical bills, along with over $200 per month for medications, are already consuming most of their social security checks. She just cannot afford the additional expenses for in-home services. She feels trapped and desperate over her situation, and has finally come in to see her pastor, as a last resort. "Please, Pastor, what can I do?" she sobs.

Pastoral Care Assessment

After listening carefully to Elaine's story, you schedule a meeting that will include both her and her husband. You need to see Elaine and William together to complete your assessment. Perhaps the best place for this visit to occur is their home, where you can see firsthand what Elaine's situation is like. You should encourage her to show you the types of problems she is having. Your goal is to get all the facts about the situation and to try to get inside Elaine's head in order to better understand how she is perceiving things (whether or not you feel her perception is accurate). With Elaine's and William's permission, you may wish to talk with a family member, a neighbor, or a close friend to round out your assessment by seeing how others are perceiving the situation. You may also want to speak with Elaine's doctor. The more information you have about the situation, the better position you will be in to help this family, either by orchestrating support services yourself or by assigning this task to a responsible staff person or member of the congregation.

The level of Elaine's exhaustion is a concern. Without help, she probably will not last more than another month or two. She will either physically collapse, necessitating hospitalization for herself, or become more depressed (even on antidepressant medication), to the point that she may become at risk for suicide or even possibly homicide. In other circumstances, if the unwell spouse is passive or unable to defend himself or herself, he or she is at high risk for physical abuse from the caregiver. It is not uncommon for the frustrating and exhausting task of caring for an uncooperative, demented person to elicit rage and actual physical attack from a tired, worn-out caregiver.

Another concern is that there are no family members nearby to help, and concern over finances is preventing Elaine from getting needed in-home help. In this circumstance, there are really only a few options: (1) get in-home help, (2) put William in an adult day care, or (3) place him in a rest home or nursing home. Clearly, Elaine needs help in looking for the best way to use her limited resources, with the understanding that she will have to make some tough choices.

Finally, there is the concern about William's health. Is he still drinking? Is he receiving the right type of medication for his condition, and is he taking this medication correctly? A treatable depression could be contributing to his irritability, as well as his reluctance to help out with his care needs. He may be experiencing side effects to medications that further agitate him; an excessive dose of a tranquilizer can cause motor restlessness and agitation (called akathisia). He may have another medical condition that is worsening his dementia. Appropriately treating this condition could make him feel better and make his care easier. Thus, optimizing William's medical and psychiatric care is essential.

As Elaine is perceiving and reporting her situation, she appears to be experiencing caregiver stress and burnout. Although we do not have information about her sleep, appetite, concentration, guilt feelings, or other symptoms of depression, in all likelihood she is clinically depressed (suffering from either a major depression or an adjustment disorder). Although it is unlikely in this case, Elaine may have a personality disorder that interferes with her ability to perceive her situation correctly; this is why you must be sure of all the facts about the situation before deciding on what needs to be done about it. You will need to obtain collateral information about Elaine's past psychiatric history and prior interpersonal relationships. The quality of her relationships with others in the church often provides important information in this regard. There are situations in which the designated caregiver may actually be more demented than the patient himself or herself, requiring an entirely different treatment plan.

Relevant History

Diagnostic Criteria

Response to Vignette

Your response to Elaine's situation includes listening, assessment, and orchestrating the help that she needs, which includes counseling, providing of information, practical services, respite from caregiving, and referral sources for social, medical, and psychiatric care.

Treatment Within the Faith Community

Elaine needs to be able to unload her problems on a caring listener, as well as later receive counseling in order to help her see her choices more clearly and resolve whatever issues are blocking her from making the best decision for the situation. You can be that listening ear, or you can designate this task to another responsible, sensitive, and knowledgeable person. Taking antidepressant medication may help mobilize and energize Elaine so that she can begin working on her problems, but it cannot solve her problems for her; it is also not sufficient to control her depression if no changes in her environment take place. One of the most important resources that Elaine should be encouraged to utilize is her personal religious faith. While this may seem obvious to some, this resource may not be fully utilized. Studies have shown that persons with a strong religious faith, who pray frequently and read biblical scriptures for comfort are able to tolerate the rigors of caregiving better than those who do not utilize these resources.[1] Taking the time to develop one's relationship with God is well worth the effort. Caregivers face many dark hours when their relationship with God is the only relationship that will be available to sustain them.

Helping Elaine obtain in-home services, if she chooses this route, is another important task of yours. Identifying and inspiring persons in the congregation to provide Elaine with respite from her caregiving responsibilities at low or no cost is important. Having someone sit with William for a couple of hours two or three times per week while Elaine has her hair done, meets with a friend for lunch, attends church, or does some other enjoyable, restful activity, may go a long way to relieve caregiver stress. Likewise, encouraging church members to spend an afternoon twice a month cleaning Elaine's house may encourage a sense of community support as well as relieve a very real burden. Such acts of Christian service, if viewed in the correct way, can be spiritually uplifting for those willing to make this sacrifice; it may take a sermon or two from the pulpit, however, to instill such altruistic motives into the congregation. Church members can perform other, smaller acts, such as providing a meal, transportation to the doctor's office, or simply companionship, that can be immensely helpful to a lonely, isolated caregiver. If members of the faith community

1. P. V. Rabins, M. D. Fitting, J. Eastham, and J. Zabora, "Emotional Adaptation over Time in Care-Givers for Chronically Ill Elderly People," *Age and Ageing* 19 (1990): 185-90. A. M. Whitlatch, D. I. Meddaugh, and K. J. Langhout, "Religiosity Among Alzheimer's Disease Caregivers," *American Journal of Alzheimer's Disease and Related Disorders & Research* 7, no. 6 (1992): 11-20. J. B. Wood and I. A. Parham, "Coping with Perceived Burden: Ethnic and Cultural Issues in Alzheimer's Family Caregiving," *Journal of Applied Gerontology* 9 (1990): 325-29.

are unable to provide such services to needy members and family are not available or willing to help, then who will do it? It is becoming increasingly clear as cutbacks increase that it will not be government agencies.

If Elaine decides to place her husband in a nursing home, then she will need help resolving her guilt about this decision as well as advice on how to choose a nursing home that best meets their needs (see case 16). Supportive listening and time will usually help the caregiver come to terms with her or his guilt. A knowledgeable social worker, either from within the congregation or from an outside social service agency, may help with choosing a nursing home. Continued support from a loving faith community remains essential for healing to occur in the weary caregiver, even after placement has occurred. This loving support must also extend to the demented patient, who is likely to feel even more lost and isolated after moving to a nursing home. Finally, as noted above, William needs appropriate medical and psychiatric evaluation and treatment to optimize management of his other medical illnesses and the effects they have on his dementia; having a ready list of competent and caring health professionals who can provide such services in a timely manner can greatly facilitate this process and further alleviate caregiver stress.

Indications for Referral and Treatment by Mental Health Specialist

When the expertise or resources needed by an overburdened caregiver are not available within the faith community, then outside sources must be utilized. As mentioned above, both Elaine and William need to have their medical and psychiatric problems managed in a timely and appropriate fashion. If the demented loved one can no longer be reasoned with and his or her behavior is disturbing or threatening to the caregiver, then professional evaluation and treatment become necessary. If the caregiver is experiencing a depression that does not respond to compassionate support (over a two to three week period), is unable to make critical decisions in a timely and appropriate fashion, or experiences severe symptoms of caregiver stress (as Elaine has demonstrated), then referral for professional help becomes necessary (see this section under case 2). Likewise, as noted above, when expertise within the pastoral staff and congregation is lacking in the area of social services, outside referral to a knowledgeable and experienced social worker will be necessary to identify community resources such as in-home help, adult day care services, financial planning services, and information about local nursing homes.

Also see this section in case 14, "Early-Stage Alzheimer's Dementia."

Resources

Local Resources

Caregiver support groups are now located in most communities, often meeting in a local church or community center. These groups provide caregivers with peer support, sharing of information about the disease, patient management techniques, outside respite services, and medical resources. Many local university medical centers have geriatric clinics that specialize in the problems of older adults and their families; these clinics commonly have social workers who are knowledgeable and skilled in this area.

National Resources

The National Alzheimer's Association (1-800-272-3900) provides information to help caregivers and families of demented relatives. The National Association for Home Care is linked with this organization and is committed to helping relatives maintain their loved ones at home. National Eldercare Locator is an organization that provides referral information to help locate a care manager, nurse, or social worker in any community in the United States to help arrange and monitor services.

Self-Help Resources

In North Carolina, the Division of Aging for the Department of Human Resources produces a *Caregiver's Handbook* that addresses most of the important concerns that caregivers have, from explaining why caregiving is stressful, to mobilizing family and friendship support networks, to how to access community services, to explaining legal issues, to discussing financial issues related to in-home and nursing home care, living wills, power of attorney, and guardianship procedures. This handbook may be obtained from the Gerontology Program at the University of North Carolina at Charlotte (phone 704-547-2000) or from the Administration on Aging, Department of Health and Human Services, Washington, DC 20201 (ask about grant #04AM0417). This is a superb source of information and well worth the effort of obtaining a copy. Other self-help books for caregivers include *The Caregiver's Guide*, by Caroline Rob (Boston: Houghton Mifflin, 1991), and *Taking Care of Your Aging Family Members*, by N. R. Hooyman and W. Lustbader (New York: The Free Press, 1988).

Computer programs such as *ComputerLink* are now being developed that bring to caregivers who are unable to leave their homes the benefits of support groups and other service interventions, relevant information, peer advice, and professional counsel. Caregivers can simply log on from their home computers and connect to the main computer, which provides them with online information and services. Caregivers can communicate with other caregivers, sharing concerns and tips that make caring easier; there is even a nurse specialist who provides answers to caregivers' questions. For more information about *ComputerLink*, contact Patricia F. Brennan, RN, Associate Professor of Nursing and Systems Engineering, Case

Western Reserve University, Frances Payne Bolton School of Nursing, Cleveland, OH 44106 or contact the ADRDA at 919 North Michigan Avenue, Chicago, IL 60611 (phone 312-335-8700).

If nursing home placement becomes necessary, special Alzheimer's disease care units are becoming increasingly common; in theory, these units should provide an environment and array of services that conform as much as possible to the Alzheimer's Association Guidelines for Dignity (which outline the major components of good quality care for those with Alzheimer's disease). Stephen McConnell discusses the pros and cons of such units in *CARING* magazine (volume 8, number 8, pages 30-33); a copy of this article can be obtained by writing or calling Mr. McConnell, Senior Vice President of Public Policy, Alzheimer's Association, Washington, DC 20004 (phone 202-393-7737). The Alzheimer's Association can also be contacted for a copy of *A Family Guide for Alzheimer's Care in Residential Settings,* which spells out what questions families should ask when looking into the care provided in various nursing home settings; this guide is also helpful when evaluating home care and other community-based services.

As noted earlier, families and the faith community can play an instrumental role in ensuring that their loved one receives the best care possible after placement in a nursing home. For a discussion of this role, see R. J. V. Montgomery's commentary in *Alzheimer's Disease and Associated Disorders* (volume 8, supplement 1, pages S242-46; New York: Raven Press, 1994). Dr. Montgomery can be contacted for a reprint at the Gerontology Center, University of Kansas, 4089 Dole, Lawrence, KS 66045.

Cross-Cultural Issues

As noted in case 16, "Late-Stage Alzheimer's Dementia," African American families often have a wide and developed social support network within the local community (of which the church is a crucial element). Consequently, they are less likely to seek help from the medical profession or from secular social service agencies, they are less likely to admit relatives to nursing homes, and they may need to be encouraged to utilize these services. The same is true for the Hispanic community.

Legal Issues

See case 14, "Early-Stage Alzheimer's Dementia," for information about establishing durable power of attorney and creating a living will.

Schizophrenia

Somebody's Watching Me

Thomasena is a 74-year-old woman who has been in your church for years. Although you don't know her very well, her husband Bill was actively involved in the church and was a regular attender at services with his wife. When Bill died two years ago, however, his wife's attendance dropped off sharply. You were not surprised by this since she had always been a private individual who kept to herself. Nevertheless, she has been on your mind lately and you have been encouraging other church members to visit her and try to get her back to services more regularly.

After a couple of visits to her home, Sarah and Mary (trusted members of your congregation) report to you that Thomasena acted strangely when they visited her. When they first arrived, she asked in a defensive tone why they had come. After talking for awhile, Thomasena shared with them, "Somebody's been watching me." She explained that people had been driving by her house spying on her. She did not know who these people were, but guessed that they worked for some type of government undercover organization. These people, Thomasena explained in a hushed tone, had planted monitoring devices throughout her house so that they could listen in on her conversations and watch her every move. In fact, when she was asleep one night, they came into her house and planted a device inside her brain so that they could monitor her thoughts. At night she could hear them talking about her, but she could not make out much of what they were saying. On several occasions, one of these persons had spoken directly to her, which made her nervous; she was reluctant to say about what. Thomasena believed her neighbors were also involved in this scheme, and claimed that they would come into her house at night, and she could hear them rummaging through her closets. She also wondered whether some members of the congregation might also be involved, and for that reason, was staying away from church. The only place she felt safe was at home, and she only left the house for groceries. Sarah and Mary report that Thomasena looked as if she had lost considerable weight and was not caring for her appearance; furthermore, her house was a shambles and unwashed dishes were scattered everywhere.

Pastoral Care Assessment

After hearing this story, you decide to pay Thomasena a visit yourself. When you arrive, she greets you at the door in a civil but mildly suspicious manner. She invites you into her house, and you sit down together at her partially cleared off kitchen table. The smell of rotten garbage and urine pervades the house. Thomasena's clothes are wrinkled and unkempt. Her hair is uncombed, and she looks as if she has not bathed in some time. You ask her about her family and discover that she has only a few relatives still living; one is a sister who lives across town. When you ask how Thomasena has been getting along lately, she quickly responds "Oh, fine." It is not until about thirty minutes into your conversation that she begins to tell you about her situation, basically confirming Sarah's and Mary's report. On further questioning, she reports having been followed and watched for about the past six months now. She confesses that her life has been miserable during that time. "They" watch her when she goes to the bathroom, bathes, and dresses; for that reason, she has been trying to avoid bathing and changing her clothes unless absolutely necessary.

You ask, "When you hear the people talking to you at night, what do they say? Do they ever tell you to do things?" Thomasena replies that they say different things to her, sometimes just calling out her name. She admits, however, that recently they have been warning her to stay away from church and not leave her house.

You ask Thomasena her sister's name and telephone number and ask permission to call her. She somewhat reluctantly gives you this information. On contacting the sister, you learn that she has not had much contact with Thomasena since a falling-out about four months ago, when Thomasena accused her of stealing pillows and bed linen whenever she visited. The sister reports that Thomasena has been acting strangely for about a year now, ever since her discharge from the hospital last January, when the doctors thought she had had a "light stroke." The sister has tried to get Thomasena to see a doctor, but Thomasena refuses.

Relevant History

You learn from the sister that Thomasena last saw a doctor about seven months ago and takes no medication. She has never been to see a psychiatrist or taken medication for her nerves, although she has always acted a bit peculiarly and been somewhat of a loner. Her marriage had been a relatively cold one, and she had a drinking problem that worsened after her and Bill's only son died at age 35 in a car accident. As far as the sister is aware, however, Thomasena has not used any alcohol for the past ten years. You also learn that she had a brother who spent the latter part of his life in a mental institution because of "nerve problems."

The sister expresses concern about Thomasena's ability to care for herself and her increasing suspicion and reclusiveness, which has isolated her from friends and relatives. "What's wrong with my sister? Is there anything you can do to help?"

Thomasena has a psychotic disorder that is associated with bizarre delusions (fixed, false beliefs that she cannot be dissuaded from), auditory hallucinations, and paranoia, all of which are interfering with personal care and social functioning. These symptoms have persisted for at least six months and occur in the setting of a lifelong history of peculiar behavior, reclusiveness, and emotional poverty. Thomasena most likely has a diagnosis of *late-onset schizophrenia*. Schizophrenia is a chronic mental illness caused by an imbalance of chemicals in the brain (dopamine, in particular). Of all the psychiatric illnesses, this one most clearly has a biological basis, with numerous studies documenting changes in brain structure and function in this disorder. In addition, there appears to be a genetic basis for transmission, with a family history of schizophrenia present ten times more frequently in relatives of schizophrenics than in the general population. Symptoms of schizophrenia usually appear first when a person is in his or her late teens or early 20s, although they can begin at any age; 23 percent of schizophrenics have an onset of the disease after the age of 50. Late-onset schizophrenics are more likely to be women and are more likely to have been married, employed, and generally more functional than early-onset schizophrenics.

Some persons who develop schizophrenia have had a personality characterized by strange ideas or behaviors, social isolation, and emotional distance for some time before the onset of the disorder; others, however, have no special personality characteristics. To fulfill diagnostic criteria for schizophrenia, a person must have had at least two of the following symptoms for six months or longer (if untreated): delusions, hallucinations, disorganized speech, disorganized or bizarre behavior, and negative symptoms such as emotional flattening or lack of motivation. During this time, the person must experience a disturbance in social relationships, occupational duties, or self-care activities caused by these symptoms. Finally, there can be no medical causes or any other mental disorder present that could account for the person's symptoms.

In Thomasena's case, there are several possible medical and psychiatric causes that could explain her symptoms, and these would have to be carefully excluded before making the diagnosis of schizophrenia certain. First, she has a history of alcohol abuse; it is possible for chronic alcoholics to develop hallucinations and paranoia that are a direct result of alcohol's long-term toxic effects on the brain. Second, Thomasena's symptoms were reported to appear after a "mild stroke," suggesting another diagnosis—*organic psychosis* or *psychosis due to a general medical condition*. Distinguishing the latter diagnosis from late-onset schizophrenia can be difficult, and

Diagnostic Criteria

147

the treatment of the two conditions is virtually the same. Finally, Thomasena's husband died two years ago, and she may be experiencing complicated grief over his loss. A severe depression in older adults is frequently associated with psychotic symptoms that may in every way mimic schizophrenia.

Response to Vignette

Having completed your evaluation and come up with a preliminary diagnosis to guide your next steps, you would first try to persuade Thomasena to see a physician (preferably a psychiatrist). Before you attempt this, however, you or someone else on your pastoral staff should try to develop a relationship with Thomasena and establish at least a minimum degree of trust. Time to develop such a relationship, however, may be limited and depends largely on the severity of Thomasena's symptoms, current level of functioning, and rate that she is declining. Your first priority is to ensure Thomasena's safety. She needs a medical evaluation as soon as possible in order to rule out other possible causes for her psychotic symptoms—and some of these could be life-threatening (infection of the central nervous system, toxic effects of medication, an acute medical illness, and so forth). An acute, life-threatening cause for her symptoms is less likely for Thomasena, since her symptoms have been present for at least six months and are only gradually worsening. In this case, then, you may have at least some time to develop a relationship.

If she responds negatively to your suggestion that she see a physician, then you will need to involve the local department of social services. They will visit Thomasena in her home and decide if there is sufficient cause for concern to force her to see the doctor (if she still refuses). If there is sufficient cause, they will fill out commitment papers at the magistrate's office, and the sheriff will bring Thomasena to the doctor's office for a medical and psychiatric evaluation.

Treatment Within the Faith Community

The faith community can play a role in securing initial evaluation (as Sarah and Mary did in Thomasena's case) and in ensuring that a patient complies with the treatment plan once the diagnosis is established. As part of ensuring that the person receives an adequate evaluation, you may convince him or her to see a physician or contact social services, as discussed above. On the other hand, if the situation is urgent or social services cannot be reached (or won't respond promptly to the situation), you or a member of your pastoral staff or a member of the congregation can begin commitment proceedings by filling out appropriate forms at the magistrate's office. In either case, the sheriff will then take the person immediately to a psychiatrist for evaluation. It is probably best to involve family members in any commitment actions if they are available.

Once a diagnosis is made and treatment is initiated by the psychiatrist, a faith community can help ensure that Thomasena's treatment is carried out successfully. This includes ensuring that she gets to her follow-up doctor visits (providing reminders, transportation, and companionship during the trip), and encouraging her to take her medication as prescribed by the doctor. A fascinating study in 1975 used homemakers and ministers as volunteers to work with schizophrenics in the community after they were discharged from the hospital. These volunteers ensured that patients took their medication, monitored patients for worsening symptoms, helped them find jobs and housing, and gave them supportive counseling. This program resulted in significantly fewer readmissions to the hospital due to relapse of symptoms.[1]

Because schizophrenics sometimes have religious delusions or hallucinations with religious content, mental health professionals have sometimes confused culturally sanctioned religious beliefs with delusional thinking. In a study at the Veterans Administration Medical Center in Durham, North Carolina, we found that 13 percent of schizophrenic men experienced bizarre religious delusions; nearly twice as many schizophrenics, however, claimed that religion was very important in their lives but did not have religious delusions. This suggests that among schizophrenics, only a few experience religious delusions and many more have positive religious experiences outside of and unconnected with their psychiatric illness.

In the middle ages, elderly schizophrenics were often thought to be witches or to be possessed by demons and were burned at the stake or tortured. Modern-day attempts to "exorcise" schizophrenics by some fundamentalist Christian groups have had decidedly poor results.

Indications for Referral

All persons with psychotic symptoms of recent or new onset require a comprehensive medical and psychiatric evaluation to determine the cause of symptoms. Likewise, persons with a confirmed diagnosis of schizophrenia who have a significant worsening of their baseline symptoms require immediate referral for evaluation. Finally, any schizophrenic patient who stops his or her medication without approval from his or her physician should be referred; the likelihood of a relapse of symptoms within twelve months for patients who stop their medications is estimated to be around 70 to 80 percent.[2]

Treatment by Mental Health Specialist

All persons with schizophrenia should have their medications managed by a psychiatrist. The discovery of neuroleptic drugs in the early 1950s revolutionized the care of schizophrenic patients, who until then were often condemned to a lifetime of institutional care. With the advent of

1. S. Katkin, V. Zimmerman, J. Rosenthal, and M. Ginsburg, "Using Volunteer Therapists to Reduce Hospital Readmissions," *Hospital and Community Psychiatry* 26, no. 3 (1975): 151-53.
2. G. W. Arana and S. E. Hyman, *Handbook of Psychiatric Drug Therapy*, 2nd ed. (Boston: Little, Brown & Co., 1991), 15.

medicines such as chlorpromazine, schizophrenics could once again live in the community and even obtain meaningful employment. Today there are much safer drugs available, with many fewer side effects than the old drugs (haloperidol, risperidone). These medicines are very effective in relieving disturbing delusions and hallucinations associated with the disorder. Neuroleptic drugs, however, can have side effects including stiffness, tremor, restlessness, and in some persons, a chronic irreversible movement disorder called tardive dyskinesia. The biggest problem in treating schizophrenics is that they stop taking their medications. If patients refuse to take oral medication, the medicine can be given by intramuscular injection once a month. Failure to keep clinic appointments, however, can also be a problem.

In addition, all schizophrenic patients should have a case worker assigned to them by the local department of social services. Unfortunately, because of cutbacks in funding, social service agencies are overwhelmed with demands and frequently cannot give schizophrenics the time and commitment they need to lead successful lives in the community. This provides an excellent opportunity for the faith community to become involved.

Resources

Local Resources

Community mental health centers provide outpatient mental health care on a "sliding scale" fee basis to persons with chronic mental illnesses such as schizophrenia. In addition, the local department of social services can be helpful in coordinating services that these persons need. A collaborative effort between social service agencies and the local church would be ideal.

National Resources

To request a helpful "fact sheet" on late-onset schizophrenia, write the Mental Disorders of Aging Research Branch, National Institute of Mental Health (NIMH), 5600 Fishers Lane, Room 7-103, Rockville, MD 20857. The National Alliance for the Mentally Ill (NAMI) has groups in all states that provide emotional support to schizophrenic elders and their families, and can help people find local services; for more information, write NAMI, 200 North Glebe Road, Suite 1015, Arlington, VA 22203-3754, or call 1-800-950-6264. There is an excellent chapter by Peter Rabins on late-life schizophrenia in the *Handbook of Mental Health and Aging*, edited by J. E. Birren, R. B. Sloane, and G. D. Cohen (San Diego: Academic Press, 1992), pages 463-75.

Self-Help Resources

Any general psychiatry text will provide information about this disorder. We are not aware of any self-help books on this topic. The best place to call for such information (should it become available in the future) is the National Alliance for the Mentally Ill (NAMI), at 1-800-950-6264 (help line).

Because schizophrenic delusions and hallucinations may have religious content, these may be difficult to distinguish from normal religious experiences in different cultures. According to *DSM IV*, "Ideas that may appear to be delusional in one culture (e.g., sorcery and witchcraft) may be commonly held in another."[3] One way to distinguish pathological from normative religious beliefs or experiences is to determine whether the person is in control of these phenomenon and can switch them on or off at will (e.g., enter into a trance state). Even normative religious beliefs can be pathological if they are not within the individual's control. This is not always the case, however, since persons may have a religious vision or hear God's voice at times when they least expect it; nevertheless, such experiences are usually followed by prolonged periods of relatively normal functioning (unlike in schizophrenia, delusional disorder, or mania).

Cross-Cultural Issues

3. *DSM IV*, 281.

Depression with Psychosis

The Devil Came to Me

Fred, a 76-year-old widower and retired auto mechanic, makes an appointment with you to talk about a "personal problem." He comes into your office and sits down nervously in a chair. "How are you doing this afternoon, Pastor?" he asks.

You respond, "Good, Fred. What about yourself? I've missed you in church these past few Sundays. Is everything okay?"

"Well, I haven't felt much like going to church here lately. Listen, I've got something real important I need to talk with you about," Fred answers with an urgent tone in his voice. "I hope you don't think I'm crazy for telling you this, but I've got to tell someone." You encourage him to say what's on his mind. "Well, I've had this dream. In the dream, the devil came and spoke with me. He threatened me, saying that he was coming after me and nobody could stop him. Then I saw a bright figure, I think it was God. The bright figure started arguing with the devil."

Attempting to clarify, you ask, "When did you have this dream, Fred, and are you sure it was a dream?"

"Over the past couple months, Pastor; but the first time I had it was back about twenty years ago. You know, you're right, I don't really think it's a dream. I think the devil really is after me. I've also been hearing him say my name. Sometimes he says even more, like 'Fred, you're going to die.' He keeps repeating this over and over again."

You ask, "Does he ever tell you to do things, like hurt yourself or hurt other people?"

"No, but I think he's planning to hurt me. I'm really worried about this, pastor. Is there anything you can do?" asks Fred pleadingly.

You tell Fred that you need more information. Has he ever had problems with his nerves in the past? Yes, Fred admits to being treated for

Pastoral Care Assessment

depression on and off for the past twenty years, but he's been off all medication for about five years now. You ask him if he was ever in the hospital for his depression, and he confirms this. You ask what type of treatments he had, and he tells you that they gave him shock treatments and then put him on medicine. Has he ever had a drinking problem? No, not since his Army days. Any family history of nerve problems? Yes, his uncle committed suicide. You ask Fred if he has any physical health problems. Yes, he's got heart problems, diabetes, and high blood pressure, and he takes medications for each of these. Does he have any relatives nearby? Yes, a brother who lives in the same town. He hasn't seen his brother for about a month, though, since he hasn't felt like talking with anybody; before that, he visited him pretty regularly.

You ask Fred how his depression has been doing lately. He says it's been bad. He tells you that he hasn't been sleeping well at all, and that he's sometimes awakened by these voices. Fred tells you that he's lost about fifteen pounds in the past two months and really doesn't care much about eating or about doing much of anything except getting these voices to stop bothering him. He says his nerves are shot, he can't concentrate on anything, and he needs something to relax him. You ask him if he's been feeling guilty or ashamed about anything. Fred tells you that about twenty-five years ago, a woman invited him over to her place. He was married then, but his wife was out of town. He thought about going but decided against it. It was around that time that he first experienced the devil talking to him. He says that he feels guilty and ashamed about even having thoughts about that woman and feels God might be punishing him for that. You ask him if he's ever had thoughts of harming himself. He tells you that sometimes when the voices get loud at night and he can't sleep, he feels desperate, and one time last week he went into the shop and got his gun. He couldn't do it, though—he was too scared.

Fred looks anxious and tired; his clothes look and smell as if they haven't been washed for some time. He looks at the floor when he tells his story. His speech is slow but spontaneous, and at times he initiates conversation with a sense of urgency. He doesn't laugh or smile, and his emotions appear to fluctuate little, either up or down. His thoughts seem a bit confused and hard to follow. He does not appear to be hallucinating at present, and he explicitly states that he isn't. When you ask him if he thinks people are talking about him or planning some type of plot against him, he says that this thought has crossed his mind, and that this is why he hasn't been to church lately. He admits he's worried that some of the men in the church are out to get him because they think he's been messing with their wives. His memory for dates and times is reasonably good, and while he complains of problems with concentration, there are no objective indicators of this.

You ask Fred if he would allow you to talk with his brother, Bill. He agrees, so you call Bill on the telephone in another office. You find out from his brother that Fred has been acting strangely over the past couple of months. He confirms Fred's story about being hospitalized for depression and needing shock treatments about twenty years ago. When you ask what types of problems Fred was having, Bill tells you that it was something about the devil talking to him. How has Fred been doing over the past five years? His brother says that he's really been doing pretty well until recently and that he hadn't mentioned anything about the devil or dreams for some time now, despite being off all medication. Bill also confirms that Fred has never been a heavy drinker or abused drugs. He worked for years as an auto mechanic, building up quite a business over the years, but retired about four years ago. He was married until about ten years ago, when his wife died in a car accident. He has numerous friends in the community, but has not had much contact with anybody over the past six months. You ask if Fred ever had "highs" and "lows," and his brother denies this, saying that most of his mood swings went down rather than up.

Fred first talks about his problem as a dream, but then he reveals that he's not sure it's a dream—that it might be real. It also becomes clear that he is hearing voices that are threatening him and that he has a paranoid delusion about men in the church talking about him or planning to harm him. These are psychotic symptoms, and although they have content that is consistent with one religious worldview (e.g., the devil being out to harm him and God punishing him for past sins), they are bizarre and distorted ideas. You learn that Fred has a psychiatric history and that he once required hospitalization and treatment for depression, which was associated with psychotic symptoms like the ones he is describing now. His treatment history is also significant, as you learn that he has received electric shock treatments and medication in the past and has not been on medication for the past five years. It is important that you ruled out a drinking history, since these symptoms can also be due to alcohol intoxication or withdrawal. Information about health problems is also important, because a worsening of his heart problems, uncontrolled blood sugar due to his diabetes, or a reaction to one of his medications could all produce psychotic symptoms as part of a delirium. Arguing against this, however, is the duration of his symptoms (several months) and his prior history of similar problems, dating back twenty years.

Obtaining a social history is important in evaluating how much community support Fred has and in determining the best person from whom to obtain collateral information about this case (his brother). You have learned about the types of relationships Fred has been able to form and about the level of success that he has achieved at work. The fact that he was married, had numerous friends in the community, and operated a successful business argues against him having any significant personality

Relevant History

problem or having a chronic mental condition such as schizophrenia as the cause for his psychosis. You asked Bill about Fred's mood swings in order to help determine whether or not Fred is in the manic phase of bipolar disorder. Persons with bipolar disorder often have many friends and are very productive individuals because they are energetic and outgoing during manic or hypomanic phases of their illness. Also important is any family history of psychiatric or nerve problems, which can help identify psychiatric problems that Fred might be genetically predisposed to (e.g., depression, bipolar disorder, or schizophrenia). You discover that his uncle committed suicide, suggesting that there may be depression in his family. Finally, you ask about the symptoms Fred is having now and assess the severity of those symptoms. Clearly he is in great distress, to the point that recently he almost committed suicide, suggesting the need for immediate intervention (and the need to ensure his safety by assuring that someone is with him at all times, even when you are talking with his brother on the telephone).

Diagnostic Criteria

Fred has a *recurrent major depressive disorder with psychotic features* (delusional, paranoid thinking and auditory hallucinations). His psychotic symptoms are called "mood congruent" because they are consistent with his depressed mood—delusions of guilt or sin, feeling that he is being punished by God and that the devil is out to get him. He also fulfills the diagnostic criteria for a major depression (depressed mood or loss of interest, weight loss, difficulty sleeping, difficulty concentrating, social withdrawal, psychomotor agitation alternating with retardation, and suicidal thoughts for at least two weeks). Persons with psychotic depression often have delusions of being persecuted or of having an incurable illness involving the gastrointestinal system. Other psychiatric disorders that can mimic psychotic depression are the manic phase of bipolar disorder (which is often associated with bizarre religious delusions), late-onset schizophrenia (associated with paranoid delusions of persecution), dementia (delusions that are poorly formed, fragmented, and accompanied by significant memory impairment), or a late-life delusional disorder (a circumscribed, fixed, false belief from which a person cannot be dissuaded, regardless of evidence to the contrary). Finally, there is the possibility (although extremely remote) that Fred is telling the truth (which must always be considered) or that he is consciously making up the whole thing (factitious disorder).

Late-onset depression is frequently associated with psychotic symptoms, more so than is depression in earlier life. Up to 60 percent of women and 50 percent of men who have their first episode of major depression after the age of 60 will experience psychotic delusions. These persons have increased evidence for neurological conditions such as stroke, Alzheimer's disease, or other brain disorders. Fred has at least two physical conditions, diabetes and high blood pressure, that increase his chances of a stroke that might lead to depression with psychotic symptoms; however, he does not have a late-onset depression (since he had his first episode of depression before age 60), and he experienced psychotic symptoms nearly twenty years ago with previous episodes of depression (making recent neurological events as the cause for his symptoms unlikely).

Fred has a life-threatening psychiatric disorder that requires immediate professional treatment. He has numerous risk factors associated with successful suicide in late life: he is male, white, living alone, with physical health problems, psychotic symptoms, poor judgment, access to a means of suicide (a gun), and a recent suicide attempt. Thus, your first responsibility is to ensure his safety by keeping him under observation while not increasing his paranoia or anxiety to the point that he leaves your office. Because he is already having paranoid delusions involving men at the church, however, he may be easily "spooked" unless you proceed in a calm, matter-of-fact manner and build some degree of trust in your relationship. Your taking time to listen to him, show understanding and empathy for his situation, and gather significant details of his history are very important because if you establish some level of trust with Fred, you can facilitate both getting him to the doctor and helping the doctor make a more accurate diagnosis. Fred conveys his story in a somewhat confusing, disjointed manner (as typical for elderly psychotic patients), and a busy medical professional may not take the time to obtain a complete history by contacting relatives and so forth. Your summary of the important details of his case, then, could expedite both evaluation and treatment. If Fred either leaves your office or refuses to come in for treatment, then you must do whatever is necessary to ensure his safety and get him evaluated—including calling the sheriff or filling out commitment papers at the magistrate's office. If this becomes necessary, you need to enlist the cooperation of family members as much as possible.

Response to Vignette

Because of his paranoid delusions, Fred is alienated from the faith community. His primary need is for evaluation and treatment. Once this has been accomplished, reestablishment of relationships within the church becomes important. Because his condition is completely treatable, his psychotic symptoms will resolve and he will likely return back to his baseline level of functioning. He will then, however, need social relationships and religious resources to help prevent future episodes of depression. A supportive faith community can provide him with the social contacts he needs to prevent isolation and facilitate his recovery. The faith community can also encourage his compliance with medical therapies and regular doctor visits and monitor him for symptoms of recurrence.

Treatment Within the Faith Community

Indications for Referral

Any older adult with psychotic symptoms (or who appears to have psychotic symptoms) requires referral for professional evaluation and treatment, particularly when a reversible disorder like depression may be present. Psychotherapy is not indicated nor helpful for this type of depression, which needs immediate medical treatment. Fred has false, fixed beliefs that are not responsive to rational persuasion or argument (delusions).

Treatment by Mental Health Specialist

Psychotic depressions are known to respond rapidly to electroconvulsive therapy (ECT) or to a combination of antidepressants and antipsychotics (major tranquilizers). Hospitalization on a psychiatric ward is usually necessary both to ensure patient safety and to begin treatment with ECT or medication. Because Fred has been treated successfully in the past with ECT and medication, he will likely be treated in the same manner for this episode. Electroconvulsive therapy is effective and safe in older adults, whose psychotic depressions may not respond to medical therapies alone (including antidepressants and antipsychotics). Nearly 70 percent of the 1,500 ECT treatments per year done at Duke Hospital are performed on persons aged 60 or over.

Resources

See case 2, "Major Depression," for local, national, and self-help resources.

Cross-Cultural Issues

It may be difficult at times to distinguish psychotic delusions or hallucinations from real, bona fide religious experiences. This may be particularly true for persons from developing countries where spiritual phenomenon are given more credence than in Western countries. Also, Fundamentalist religious Christian groups or satanic cults may emphasize the work and role of the devil, including rituals involving communication with the devil or satanic beings. For persons with severe personality disorders or psychotic illness, it may be difficult to distinguish group-sanctioned beliefs and experiences from those of illness; nevertheless, persons within the group or particular culture can usually identify members with illness-based symptoms.

Delirium with Psychosis

I See Bugs Crawling on You

L eara is an 82-year-old widowed woman who has been a faithful member of your church for many years. She has recently been hospitalized to have her gallbladder removed, and you pay her a visit at the hospital while she is recuperating from her surgery. You knock on her door and then cautiously go into her room. You find Leara resting in the hospital bed but awake. The room is only dimly lit and the shades are drawn. "Hello, Leara, this is Pastor John."

As you first enter the room, Leara looks at you strangely and fearfully at first, but then a sense of recognition crosses her face as you turn on the overhead light. "Oh, Pastor, I'm so glad to see you. You don't know what I've been through."

You sit down at her bedside and take her gently by the hand, "Leara, what is wrong? How did the surgery go?"

Leara responds, "Pastor, they've got me in this strange place. It's terrible. I have this pain in my stomach, and I don't know what they've done to me. And there are things in here, crawling on my bed. Do you see them? I see bugs crawling on you, Pastor. Don't you see them?" she says, sitting up now in bed, becoming increasingly agitated.

You press the nurse's call button, and continue holding and stroking Leara's hand. "It will be okay, Leara. You are safe. Would you like me to pray with you for protection, safety, and help with the pain?" She agrees, and you begin praying with her. She seems to calm down a bit, but her level of alertness fluctuates between drowsiness and mild agitation. The nurse enters the room just as you finish praying. You say to the nurse, "Mrs. Willis says that she is seeing bugs on her bed and on people in the room, and that this is frightening her. Is there anything you can give her to make the bugs go away?"

Pastoral Care Assessment

Leara had surgery three days ago, and she has been disoriented on and off since awakening postoperatively; for the past twelve hours she has also been having visual hallucinations. Her doctors have been giving her meperidine (Demerol) for pain relief from the surgery and have continued her amitriptyline (Elavil, an antidepressant). They have added another medication, diphenhydramine (Benadryl), to help her sleep at night. Leara has been a faithful churchgoer for many years and has been active in the volunteer ministry in the local hospital. She is well liked and has a sharp mind for her age. She is living independently in her own house and had been getting along fine prior to her admission to the hospital. She has one daughter, who lives nearby and is also an active member of your church.

After notifying the nurse about the situation, you leave the room and call her daughter, informing her of the situation with her mother. You then return to the room and sit with Leara until her daughter arrives. Her daughter says that she was not aware of her mother having any problems, and she thanks you for your help. She tells you that her mother had been doing fine until this hospitalization. Six months ago, when she was admitted for a bladder infection, she became a little confused—but nothing like this. Leara has a history of mild congestive heart failure, and she had a mild stroke about two years ago; nevertheless, she had regained all her functions and, other than some mild memory problems, was doing fine. She does not have a history of alcoholism or of tranquilizer use. You call her daughter the next day. Leara is doing much better now. The hallucinations have nearly stopped, and she is not as anxious as before.

Relevant History

Leara is of advanced age, has a history of stroke, and experienced some mild confusion during a hospitalization six months previously. However, until her hospitalization, she was fully alert and functioning independently without problems. Her depression was under good control on medication. This information suggests that Leara was at risk for confusion and disorientation prior to this hospitalization but otherwise did not have a problem with chronic memory problems, dementia, or hallucinations (a very important point to establish). Also, her confusion and hallucinations appear to have started relatively suddenly after her gallbladder surgery. This suggests that her problems are related to her hospital stay, surgery, changes in her medications, or medical problems that have developed since she was admitted. Particular scrutiny should be paid to recent medication changes. She is receiving Demerol for postoperative pain relief, as well as two medicines with strong anticholinergic side effects (Elavil and Benadryl). Although unlikely, you always need to inquire about alcohol or tranquilizer use (Valium, Ativan, Xanax), because withdrawal from these substances can cause problems just like Leara's. Next, Leara has been lying in bed most of the time for the past three days and therefore is predisposed

Delirium with Psychosis

to develop either a urinary tract infection or a lung infection. Finally, note that her room was only dimly lit when you entered it, which may contribute to disorientation.

Leara is experiencing a *delirium with psychotic features*. Delirium is diagnosed when a person has a relatively rapid onset of symptoms (over a couple of days) that are temporally associated with a change in environment, a change in medical condition, a change in medication, or withdrawal of alcohol or other brain depressants. While persons with mild dementia are at increased risk for delirium, dementia and delirium are very different illnesses. Dementia is a slowly progressive, chronic problem with memory and orientation that develops over months or years; it is generally not treatable, except in certain rare cases, and is not associated with a decrease in alertness or fluctuating level of consciousness (see cases 14-16). Delirium, on the other hand, is almost always caused by a reversible or treatable medical cause. Persons with delirium experience a fluctuating level of consciousness, from being sleepy and semialert to being hypervigilant and agitated. Delirium is frequently accompanied by paranoia, delusions, hallucinations, or other psychotic symptoms. Delusions, if present, are usually fragmented and poorly formed (unlike with delusional disorder, schizophrenia, or acute mania, in which delusions can be quite complex and elaborate). Because they are rare in other psychiatric conditions, visual hallucinations in an older person almost always indicate delirium. The only exceptions to this are alcohol or drug abuse or withdrawal, and sensory deprivation from visual or hearing problems, which are also associated with visual hallucinations.

The cause for Leara's delirium and visual hallucinations is most likely a combination of her age, her predisposition due to other health problems (stroke, mild heart failure), her change in environment (hospitalization), and her medications (especially). Her age and health problems predispose her to disorientation because they cause poor blood circulation to her brain. The simple act of hospitalization itself represents a change in environment that can induce confusion in a vulnerable older person. Demerol is frequently given for postoperative pain, yet it is poorly tolerated by older adults and is frequently associated with adverse reactions including delirium. Also, both the antidepressant (Elavil) and the new sleeping pill prescribed by the doctor (Benadryl) have strong anticholinergic side effects that can cause an anticholinergic psychosis and symptoms such as Leara's because they impair the functioning of a chemical in the brain necessary for memory and orientation. There are a whole host of medical problems that can cause delirium, especially infection; Leara is already predisposed to infection in her bladder and lungs because of her bed rest after surgery. Finally, Leara's room was only dimly lit, causing her to have difficulty orienting herself; a well-lighted room is essential (along with a

Diagnostic Criteria

calendar and personal mementos) to help an older adult maintain orientation when in the hospital.

Response to Vignette

You responded beautifully to this situation. You clearly introduced yourself and turned on the light so that Leara could see you better. You sat down by her bed and, once she recognized you, established physical contact by holding her hand. You spoke calmly and softly, reassuring her with a prayer. You informed the nurse of the situation, called her daughter, and spent time with Leara until her daughter arrived. You provided the daughter with information that you know about these kinds of problems and informed her about the important elements in Leara's history that the doctors might want to know about in order to best diagnose and treat her condition. You then followed up the next day with her daughter. You may also wish to pay Leara a visit either in the hospital again or at home once her mental state has cleared completely.

Treatment Within the Faith Community

Although you happened to see Leara in the hospital, the same scenario could and often does take place when pastoral staff make a home visit to an elderly church member who has not attended services in a while because of physical health problems. Making a preliminary diagnosis and getting the person to see a doctor for a complete medical evaluation is essential because of the treatability of this condition and the poor outcome known to occur without treatment (high mortality rate). By simply monitoring and checking up on elderly church members who may be physically ill and have missed one or two church services, the faith community can more easily identify persons with these problems and obtain timely medical evaluation and treatment for them.

Indications for Referral

All persons with delirium, with or without psychotic symptoms, need immediate medical evaluation and treatment.

Treatment by Mental Health Specialist

Leara's medical doctors should carefully scrutinize her medications and probably stop the Demerol and Benadryl immediately. They would be wise to switch her to a different antidepressant without such strong anticholinergic side effects. They should also check her blood, urine, and lungs for infection and other medical problems. In addition, they should be sure that Leara's room is well lit at all times and that she has a calendar and personal items to help orient her. The nurses or the physical therapist should encourage and assist her to walk and sit up in her chair several times each day so that she doesn't spend so much time immobilized in bed. Having ruled out any treatable medical problems and stopped all but the most necessary of medicines, her doctors would consider giving her medication to stop her hallucinations. An antipsychotic medication such as haloperidol (Haldol) will help reduce Leara's hallucinations (whatever their cause) without excessively sedating her. This medication, however, has side effects and should be used at low doses and for the shortest possible period.

Uninformed physicians may mistakenly attribute the cause of an older person's delirium to dementia (chronic, irreversible memory problems) and not adequately search for the cause of the problem. In this case, members of the faith community should join with family members to request further evaluation or seek care from a geriatric specialist with appropriate expertise and interest in such problems.

Resources

See case 13, "Delirium," for local, national, and self-help resources. For more information, consult a good general medical text on delirium. One of the best available is *Harrison's Principles of Internal Medicine* (New York: McGraw-Hill), any edition, available at most public libraries or at the medical library in any hospital.

Cross-Cultural Issues

See case 13, "Delirium," case 18, "Schizophrenia," and case 19, "Depression with Psychosis."

Dementia with Delusions

I Don't Trust Him

Nellie is the 79-year-old wife of Al, a retired deacon in your church. You have known them both for many years. About five years ago, Nellie began having memory problems and three years ago was diagnosed with the beginning of middle-stage Alzheimer's disease. Al has been faithfully taking care of his wife during this time, despite her becoming more agitated and aggressive toward him and toward their two adult children, Carrol and John. Al approaches you after church and asks if you would have breakfast with him tomorrow; you consent and arrange a time and place to meet. You are aware that Al has been under a lot of stress lately caring for his wife, and anticipate that this is the subject he wants to talk to you about.

After breakfast the next day, Al begins to explain his situation. One day last month Nellie suddenly began to accuse Al of cheating on her and has been acting very cold toward him since. He reports that she has also been more irritable since then, and is even threatening at times. Al exclaims, "Pastor, she won't allow me to leave the house even to get groceries; and when I do, she gets upset and starts throwing things in the house. She was always the jealous type, but this is ridiculous. I've never been with another woman, and at the age of 81, I wouldn't know what to do with one if I had the opportunity."

You listen carefully, interjecting supportive comments whenever appropriate. You then ask, "What do your son and daughter say about all this, Al?"

Al responds, "Oh, they are as upset about it as I am and have tried to convince her that nothing is going on, but without success. Nothing that either I or they can say seems to have any effect. Maybe you could talk with her."

You agree to talk with Nellie, and Al brings her to your office the next day.

Pastoral Care Assessment

"Hi, Nellie!" you greet Nellie in a friendly voice as she walks into your office. You wish to speak with her alone, so you ask Al to wait outside. Nellie has on a stained blouse and a wrinkled skirt; she has on no makeup and her hair is only partially combed.

She responds to your greeting in a defensive tone, saying, "I don't know what Al has been telling you, but I'm doing just fine. Al is the problem, not me. I don't trust him."

You inquire, "What has Al done that makes you unable to trust him?"

She responds, "He's been over to our neighbor's house several times this week, and I think they are doing something over there. Wilma's always been a man stealer, and I caught Al flirting with her when we drove by the house some time back. I know they're up to no good, and don't you try to talk me out of it." Nellie's behavior is mildly agitated, impatient and suspicious. She doesn't smile, avoids eye contact, and talks quickly, sometimes losing her train of thought. With a frown she says, "I really don't want to talk anymore. Are we about done?"

You end the conversation and thank her for coming in to see you. You then ask to speak with Al for a minute alone. "I didn't get very far, Al. Is it okay if I talk with your son or daughter about Nellie? Maybe they will have some thoughts about this." Carrol and John live nearby and frequently visit their parents, helping with the caregiving tasks. Al gives you permission to call their children. Carrol confirms that Nellie has always been jealous of Al, without any justification as far as Carrol knows, but that things have really gotten out of hand in the past month. She is sure that Al is not having an affair and suggests that you call her brother John. A brief conversation with the brother confirms the story you received from Al and Carrol and provides additional information about Nellie and Al's marriage.

While the marriage has been relatively stable over the past thirty years, frequent fights and arguments characterized their marriage during the first twenty years, when the children were growing up. Al and Nellie came from markedly different backgrounds and consequently had different ideas about how to spend money and discipline the children. Al had been a drinker and a lady's man in his younger days, but he stopped all this after he married Nellie. She was jealous about his lovers, though, and frequently brought it up during their arguments. As for Nellie, she never dated anyone before Al and only knew him briefly before marrying him. Though controlling and domineering, she had been relatively stable emotionally and has no prior psychiatric or substance abuse history. However, she does have a family history of psychiatric problems. Her mother was manic-depressive, and her father was an alcoholic; she also had one older sister who died in a nursing home with "memory problems." Nellie is in relatively good health for her age, takes no medications, and hasn't been to see the doctor since he made the diagnosis of Alzheimer's disease three years ago. Her memory problems and ability to function, however, have slowly deteriorated during this time. She now has difficulty doing household chores and even needs help choosing clothes to wear; for the past several months, she has been losing her urine at night and soaking the bed. Consequently, Al has been sleeping in another room.

Although Nellie has no clear history of psychiatric problems, she was raised in an unstable home, and married Al at least partly to get out of that environment. She became quite dependent on and possessive of Al. While she has always been a jealous person, this did not become a problem until about a month ago, when she suddenly accused Al of being unfaithful. This was associated with increasing agitation and irritability and further decline in her ability to care for herself; in fact, on gathering further history from Al, you learn that the agitation and the functional decline actually preceded her accusations of unfaithfulness by about two months. From your conversations with Al and his two children, there is no evidence to suggest that Al has been or is having an affair with their neighbor or with anyone else. Nellie has Alzheimer's disease and a family history of memory problems.

Nellie has a *dementia with psychotic delusions*. She had been experiencing a slow decline in mental functioning for the past three to four years, but this has become more rapid over the past three months. Her delusions began suddenly within the context of this mental and functional decline. Nellie's symptoms now are consistent with a diagnosis of Alzheimer's disease, late middle-stage. Less clear is the role that recent, undiagnosed medical problems might be playing in her three-month decline, and this would certainly need to be investigated. Delusions associated with a medical-induced delirium, however, tend to be less well formed and more transitory than Nellie's delusion. Delusions of jealousy can also be seen in patients with late-onset delusional disorder, schizophrenia, mania, and psychotic depression, although there is little evidence that Nellie has any of these other conditions.

Delusions are actually quite common in older adults with dementia, occurring in at least 25 percent of such cases. For example, read the following description of Alzheimer's original patient:

> Around March 18, 1901 the patient suddenly asserted, without any reason, that her husband had gone for a walk with a neighbor. From then she remained very cool towards him and the lady. Soon after she started to have difficulty in remembering things. Two months later, she started making mistakes in preparing meals, paced nervously and without reason in the apartment, and was not careful with the household money. . . . She asserted that a wagon driver who often came to her home might do some-

thing to her and she assumed that all conversations of the people around her were about her.[1]

Approximately one-third of demented patients with delusions have a single delusional belief, whereas the remaining two-thirds have multiple delusions. The majority of these delusions are paranoid in nature, and usually involve persons breaking into their homes or stealing their possessions. Other delusions include belief that living or dead relatives are in the home, belief that one's spouse is unfaithful (about 5 percent), belief that the major caregiver is an impostor, and belief that the patient's home is not actually his or her own. Demented patients with delusions experience more behavioral disturbances than those without delusions, including agitation (72 percent vs. 15 percent), angry and hostile outbursts (31 percent vs. 4 percent), and urinary incontinence (31 percent vs. 11 percent).[2]

Response to Vignette

You listened carefully to Al's description of the situation and then met with Nellie to hear her story and assess her current mental state. You found that Nellie's mental state was indeed impaired and that her behavior was agitated and defensive—sufficient reasons to suspect her judgment and claims against her husband. You then spoke with both adult children to obtain collateral information that might either confirm or dispel Nellie's accusations. Even though Nellie has a psychiatric disorder that is commonly associated with delusions, it is always necessary to make sure that the accusations are false, since if they are true (which is always a possibility), there is no delusion.

Nellie needs medical evaluation to rule out any medical causes for her recent mental decline and, if none are found, to recommend symptomatic treatment for her delusions. You can encourage her to seek medical evaluation, and you or one of your pastoral staff may accompany her and her husband to the physician's office. There is little else that you can do for Nellie at this point, except be generally supportive and accepting of what she perceives as true. You can say something like this to her: "I know that you believe your husband has been unfaithful to you, and that must be difficult for you." She is likely, however, to be suspicious of your intentions as well, and will be a difficult person to support.

Providing emotional support for Al and other family members is an important task that you or your pastoral staff can undertake to help out the situation. He is obviously experiencing caregiver stress and needs fur-

1. G. Perusini, "Histology and Clinical Findings of Some Psychiatric Diseases of Older People," (translation) in *The Early Story of Alzheimer's Disease*, eds. K. Bick, L. Armaducci, and G. Pepeu (New York: Raven Press, 1987), 82-108.
2. M. S. Lachs, M. Becker, A. Sigeal, R. Miller, and M. Tinetti, "Delusions and Behavioral Disturbances in Cognitively Impaired Elderly Persons," *Journal of the American Geriatrics Society* 40 (1992): 768-73.

ther help with caregiving responsibilities and periodic respite from the caregiving role (see case 17, "Caregiver Stress").

The faith community needs to be mobilized to provide both emotional and practical support for this family. This includes emotional support for Nellie. Even though she may not on the surface express a need for such support, she is experiencing many terrifying changes in her life and needs love and prayer from members of her church. Nellie's family will need increasing outside assistance to care for her basic needs, including a break from caregiving duties and time to emotionally refresh themselves; church members may volunteer to spend the afternoon with Nellie or agree to help out with the cleaning, laundry, or other tasks that need doing either inside or outside the house. Confidentiality must be maintained at all times, however, and information released to other individuals in the congregation only after permission has been obtained from the family. See case 17, "Caregiver Stress," for more information.

Treatment Within the Faith Community

Any demented patients with a recent onset of delusional thinking need a complete medical evaluation to rule out treatable causes for the delusions. Once this has been accomplished, the next steps depend on the severity of the delusions or other psychotic symptoms. When these symptoms begin to interfere significantly with people's quality of life, with their ability to care for themselves, or with their social functioning, then evaluation by a psychiatrist (preferably one trained in geriatric psychiatry) is necessary.

Indications for Referral

Nellie needs to see a physician with experience and interest in working with persons with Alzheimer's disease. The physician will rule out new medical conditions, psychiatric conditions (depression, etc.), or substance abuse as the cause for her recent mental deterioration. If she were taking medications, these would have to be carefully scrutinized and their contributions to the problem assessed. If after thorough evaluation, Nellie's problem is determined to be secondary to her Alzheimer's disease, then an antipsychotic medication (major tranquilizer) such as haloperidol (Haldol) may be prescribed. If anxiety is a prominent symptom, then a low dose of a minor tranquilizer such as lorazepam (Ativan) or clonazepam (Klonopin) may be prescribed. Be aware, however, that delusions associated with Alzheimer's dementia may not respond readily to these medications; if significant improvement is not seen after several weeks of therapy, they should be discontinued.

Treatment by Mental Health Specialist

See cases 14-17 for local, national, and self-help resources.

Resources

See cases 14-17.

Cross-Cultural Issues

Alcohol Abuse and Dependence

The Retired Drinker

The family had a lifetime involvement with their local church. The couple, and later their two daughters, had been married there. The father, Mark, had been a founding member of the men's church group and was active in the group and other church activities until recently. Mark had spent almost forty years as a devoted employee working for a small company that had recently been bought in a hostile takeover by a giant out-of-state corporation. In a downsizing process, he was forced to take early retirement and had recently been talking about a permanent move across the country to Arizona. His spouse, Joyce, and their eldest daughter have requested a private pastoral counseling session.

The two women are very concerned over Mark's increased drinking. They tell you that in the past several months since Mark's forced retirement, he has become less and less active and has begun to drink alone at home. When confronted with the increased drinking, Mark becomes annoyed and insists that he has no alcohol problem—he simply needs a few drinks to get through the day. The family members report he is lonely, angry, depressed, and grieving over the loss of his life's work and over the separation from his longtime buddies at the workplace. Mark has complained to his spouse of feeling useless. He has recently been given his first citation for driving while intoxicated. He has "mysteriously" fallen twice in the past month. In the past week, he has begun the morning with an "eye opener" to steady his nerves and get rid of a hangover. To the family, Mark's plan to retire to Arizona appears to be a premature, unrealistic and impulsive attempt to escape his unhappiness and loss of identity.

Your pastoral assessment begins with examining Mark's drinking behavior, evaluating the consequences resulting from the drinking, and screening Mark for depression (see case 2, "Major Depression") and suicide

Pastoral Care Assessment

potential (see case 6, "Increased Risk for Suicide"). How much is Mark drinking and to what degree does he appreciate the negative impact of his drinking on himself and on his family? The stigma and shame attached to alcoholism is very strong in the older generation, often reinforcing denial. Your pastoral intervention needs to be persuasive in style, different from the heavy confrontational approach used with younger alcoholics. An intervention using a supportive style that builds self-worth has a greater chance of having a productive outcome. You might begin with an empathic question such as, "I am concerned—I haven't seen you in church lately." Give him a chance to tell you his story and express his loss and grief. Your goal is to help him see the need to seek help. It is important to have a list of treatment alternatives available for him in case he is open to treatment. When an addictive person is prepared to be treated, act as soon as possible to find assistance. Be prepared even to have the person taken to the treatment site. Treatment can be offered to Mark in a nonthreatening way if it is presented as a means to gain information about his alcohol use and its effects.

The underlying cause of an addictive process such as alcoholism is often a spiritual crisis. In this case, Mark has lost the primary means by which he has gained meaning in life, his work. He now faces critical questions about his identity and purpose for living. So far, instead of facing this crisis, he is using alcohol to escape a painful self-examination. This spiritual crisis can be a turning point for Mark that can help him transform the way he sees himself, finds meaning, and understands his life within God's providence. He will need your pastoral care and spiritual guidance to accomplish this.

Relevant History

Mark developed his attitudes toward drinking during the Temperance movement and Prohibition, before alcoholism was recognized as a disease. When he was young alcoholism was viewed as a moral weakness, little was known about the problem, and treatment was rare.

Diagnostic Criteria

Alcohol dependence is characterized by a group of symptoms indicating that an individual continues to use alcohol despite the significant problems resulting from it. In other words, he or she has lost control over drinking. Persons suffering alcohol dependence have a pattern of compulsive alcohol use usually resulting in tolerance and withdrawal. A craving to use alcohol is present. According to the *DSM IV* criteria at least three of the following symptoms are present at the same time over a twelve-month period:

1. The person develops *tolerance*, as defined by the need for increased amounts of alcohol to achieve the desired effect, or markedly diminished effects with continued use of the same amount of alcohol.

2. The person suffers *withdrawal symptoms*, such as physical discomfort, illness, or in 5 percent of the cases, severe complications (e.g., delirium, grand mal seizures), when alcohol is not available.
3. The person frequently consumes alcohol in larger amounts or over longer periods of time than intended.
4. The person has a persistent desire or makes unsuccessful attempts to control or cut down on alcohol use.
5. The person devotes a lot of time to activities related to obtaining alcohol, using alcohol, or recovering from its effects.
6. The person reduces or stops participating in important social, occupational, or recreational activities as a result of alcohol consumption.
7. The person continues to use alcohol in spite of persistent or recurrent psychological or physical problems caused or exacerbated by alcohol use.[1]

Alcohol abuse is a second diagnosis that can be thought of as a less severe form of alcohol dependence. The basic feature is a pattern of alcohol use characterized by negative, recurrent and significant consequences related to repeated use. If alcohol abuse alone is present, the person generally has control over drinking and may stop if he or she wishes. This diagnosis needs only one of the following criteria in the past twelve months:

1. Recurrent alcohol use resulting in a failure to fulfill major obligations at home or work (e.g., repeated neglect of household responsibilities).
2. Repeated use of alcohol in situations in which use is known to be physically hazardous.
3. Recurrent alcohol-related legal problems.
4. Continued use despite having persistent or recurrent social or interpersonal problems resulting from the effects of alcohol (e.g., arguments with friends or family members about the consequences of using alcohol).

Response to Vignette

Mark is suffering from several characteristic signs of late-onset alcohol dependence (which often begins after some type of major stress, as opposed to early-onset alcoholism, which is a lifelong problem). He has begun drinking alone, appears depressed and self-isolating, and is defensive when questioned by family members regarding his changing drinking pattern. He has also recently been cited for driving while intoxicated and has begun to drink in the morning to cope with hangovers. In addition, Mark has recently "mysteriously" fallen at least twice, which is both a common and precarious sign of alcohol intoxication among elderly alcoholics. This increased drinking is probably a maladaptive reaction to his forced retirement and dramatically altered self-identity, for which he was

1. *DSM IV*, 181.

unprepared. Men in the present and older generations are culturally trained to equate self-worth with work. Mark appears to have responded to the resulting feelings of loss, anger, grief, and guilt by self-medicating with alcohol. Mark will need help to see that moving across the country at this time is an attempt to escape the reality of his pain and would only aggravate his problems. Several factors argue for a positive prognosis. He has a family that is actively interested in helping him, the pattern of alcohol dependence is relatively new, and his faith and church network have been an asset in the recent past.

Treatment Within the Faith Community

A recent Gallup poll found that 40 percent of Americans indicated they have suffered harm as a result of someone else's drinking, and 17 percent reported they have suffered from their abuse of alcohol. It has been estimated that there are 3 million elderly alcoholics in America, and 85 percent of them never receive treatment of any kind.[2] Alcoholism is a huge social problem among seniors that often remains hidden. Older alcoholics tend to drink alone, live in shame, and self-isolate. The church, through members and religious caregivers, can play a critical role in making contact with the elderly who are at risk for addiction and help them seek appropriate care. The community of faith also needs to provide education, advocacy, and support group development for the elderly alcoholic, who is often devalued by a society fascinated only with the young. This devaluation is sometimes expressed by the belief that "an older person has nothing better to do than drink." The cultural prejudgment and the internalization of this belief by seniors who believe they have little worth is part of the reason seniors do not seek help, and is profoundly contrary to our faith values (see Isaiah 46:4). It is important to note that science has evidence that faith offers a powerful means to help elderly drinkers. Research has found that a strong devotion to faith is associated with a greater likelihood that elderly people will abstain from using alcohol.[3]

Indications for Referral

An assessment will need to be made as to whether or not inpatient detoxification is required. The following indicate the need for inpatient care: alcohol use is associated with imminent danger to self or another; the person exhibits other antisocial behavior; the person has a severe mental illness (e.g., major depression and suicidal thinking); previous attempts at outpatient treatment have failed; no support system is available. Involuntary hospitalization is the last resort, as it reduces the chance of future treatment compliance.

2. P. Krach, "Discovering the Secret: Nursing Assessment of Elderly Alcoholics in the Home," *Journal of Gerontological Nursing* 16, no. 11 (1990): 32-38.
3. N. Krause, "Stress, Religiosity and Abstinence from Alcohol," *Psychology and Aging* 6 (1991): 134-44.

Early Stages: Referral to a physician for assessment of the adverse effects of alcohol abuse, including any injuries sustained from falling, would be a priority. The therapist would encourage Mark to tell his story of alcohol abuse and empathize with his viewpoint in order to foster a therapeutic alliance. The mental health specialist would ask Mark to discuss his understanding of the negative consequences of alcohol abuse and assess Mark's account for denial and level of insight into his situation. Educating Mark about alcohol dependency would be employed to therapeutically address Mark's denial and resistance to treatment. It would be valuable to provide appropriate reassurance that help is available and that change happens with commitment.

If Mark recognizes he has an alcohol problem, the next step is to seek commitment to abstinence. Alcoholics Anonymous (AA) can provide the alcohol dependent person with a source of empathy, support, education, and continued support for his or her abstinence. Initially, Mark should agree to attend AA meetings several times a week. Over time, the Twelve Steps of AA are used to guide spiritual formation and to overcome "character defects." Members select "sponsors," who act as mentors for the recovering persons. The early stages of abstinence will require considerable support, and the therapist will make clear that occasional relapses are possible and need to be seen as "human slips," not "failures" that confirm the senior's sense of worthlessness. Family members can be coached to not "enable" the recovering person (e.g., to stop making excuses for him when he does not show up for church meetings), and affected family members should be referred to appropriate Twelve-Step groups (e.g., Al-Anon).

Later Stages: The therapist would continue to work individually with Mark as he recovers, in order to prevent relapse and work though temporary relapses if they occur. The sessions would continually review the reasons for the recovery process, provide support, reassurance, encouragement, and praise for ongoing work, and explore the roots of the addiction. It would be important to identify and address heretofore hidden family problems that may be unmasked as Mark becomes sober. Family sessions could be used to teach communication skills and explore underlying family dysfunctions (e.g., lack of intimacy or inability to express feelings) that may be related to the addictive behavior.

Local Resources

Local Alcoholics Anonymous (AA) groups can be found in most phone directories. Regional directories of AA meetings can be obtained though the General Services Office of Alcoholics Anonymous, Box 459, Grand Central Station, New York, NY 10163 (phone 212-870-3400). One can also obtain publications about AA, including a booklet entitled *A Clergyman Asks About A.A.*

Treatment by Mental Health Specialist

Resources

National Resources

The National Clearinghouse for Information on Alcohol and Drug Abuse (PO Box 2345, Rockville, MD 20852, phone 1-800-729-6686) provides free, useful materials about the problem of elderly alcohol abuse. The materials include "Alcohol and the Elderly" (pub. no. RP0469), "Nature and Extent of Alcohol Problems Among the Elderly" (NIAAA Research Monograph 14, pub. no. BK127), "Alcohol and the Elderly: An Update" (pub. no. PH251), "Alcohol Alert: Alcohol and Aging" (pub. no. PH251), and an annotated reading list. The National Council on Alcoholism (NCA) is a national nonprofit organization that offers information and referral services through two hundred state and local affiliates. They provide preventive educational programs for community organizations such as churches and senior centers. Persons seeking assistance can contact their area affiliate or call a national toll-free help line, 1-800-NCA-CALL, or write NCA, 12 West Twenty-First Street, New York, NY 10010.

There are several alcohol treatment programs that utilize specialized approaches with Native American seniors suffering from substance abuse problems. Alcohol dependence is a very serious problem among elderly Native Americans. For more information, contact Frances White or Leona Juneau, Tribal Elder Substance Abuse Program, Coeur d'Alene Tribal Sub-Agency, Plummer, ID 83851 (phone 208-274-3101); or Melveena Malatare, Pikuni (Blackfeet) Recovery Program, PO Box 489, Browning, MT 59417 (phone 406-338-3511); or Mildred Elm, Iskode Biiniisii Elder Alcohol and Other Drug Abuse Program, Family Resources Center, PO Box 189, Lac du Flambeau, WI 54538 (phone 715-588-9818).

Self-Help Resources

Family members and friends of alcoholics can find help through Al-Anon. This organization sponsors about 18,000 self-help groups in the United States for persons affected by someone else's drinking. Al-Anon groups follow the traditional Twelve-Step approach, and members participate anonymously. The organization has books, videos, cassettes for the hearing-impaired, braille literature, and large-print books that focus on understanding and coping with problems that result from alcoholism (PO Box 862, Midtown Station, New York, NY 10018, phone 1-800-356-9996 [USA] or 1-800-443-4525 [Canada]).

Cross-Cultural Issues

The lifetime prevalence of alcohol abuse and dependence has been found to be extremely high among elderly Korean American men at an astonishing 35 percent. In part, researchers attribute this high rate to Korean cultural attitudes that are "highly tolerant and permissive toward male drinking, and do not consider alcoholism a disease."[4] In a nation-wide study of hospitalized veterans, Hispanic and African American older men were less likely to complete treatment for alcoholism than other ethnic groups, while Native Americans were found to be the most likely to complete treatment. Specialized treatment modalities need to be explored when working with ethnic minorities.[5]

4. J. Yamamoto, S. Rhee, and D. Chang, "Psychiatric Disorders Among Elderly Koreans in the United States," *Community Mental Health Journal* 30, no. 1 (1994): 17-27.
5. B. M. Booth, F. C. Blow, C. A. L. Cook, and J. Fortney, "Age and Ethnicity Among Hospitalized Alcoholics: A Nationwide Study," *Alcoholism: Clinical and Experimental Research* 16, no. 6 (1992): 1029-34.

Over-the-Counter Drug Abuse and Dependence

I've Been Feeling Sick

Sam is a 71-year-old married gentleman who has attended your church with his wife, Betty, for many years. For the past month, Betty has been coming alone to services. Concerned, you ask her about Sam. "Betty, how is Sam doing? I noticed that you've been coming to church alone lately, and I was wondering if Sam's health is all right."

Betty responds, "Pastor, to be frank with you, I'm really worried about him. Over the past couple of weeks he's been so groggy that he can hardly keep his eyes open to read the paper or watch television, and two days ago he fell asleep while eating supper! I don't know what's wrong with him. His appetite has fallen off, he's gotten sick to his stomach a lot, and he's been complaining of pain under his right rib cage. He's also been talking crazy at times. I'm worried that his blood sugar is too high or something else is wrong. You know Sam, though; he won't admit to there being a problem, and thinks I worry too much."

You offer, "Would it be helpful if I paid Sam a visit at home? I've got a little free time this afternoon."

Betty eagerly accepts, "That would be wonderful, Pastor. And please, let me fix you some lunch."

When you arrive at their house, Sam is lying on the couch, asleep. Betty arouses him with some difficulty. "Hello, come on in," he says, after a period of struggling to wake up. He appears drugged, and you wonder if he even recognizes you. Sam slowly makes his way over to the dining room table. He is still in pajamas and doesn't appear to have bathed recently.

In a friendly and concerned voice, you ask "How are you doing, Sam? Your wife says that you've been a bit under the weather. Is that right?"

"Yes, I caught this cold about a month ago and can't seem to shake it. I've also been having trouble sleeping and been sick to my stomach. But nothing's been bad enough to see a doctor. This medicine I bought at the supermarket helps me a lot," he says, holding up a pint-size bottle of liquid cold medicine.

Betty interjects, "I think that cold medicine is what's causing your problems, Sam. You drink at least three bottles of that stuff every day."

Pastoral Care Assessment

Your first task is a careful evaluation of Sam. He looks groggy and disoriented and has a gray tone to his skin. Sam looks sick and in need of help. His level of alertness fluctuates. He speaks in a slow, sometimes garbled manner that is difficult to understand. While his memory is poor, Sam's demeanor is friendly, and he does not appear depressed. You need more history from his wife. Betty confirms that Sam has been sick with a cold for about a month, but it has been particularly bad over the past two weeks. He hasn't been to see the doctor for about two months and, as noted earlier, has been reluctant to see anyone about these problems. What other kinds of physical illnesses does Sam have? Betty tells you that he has high blood pressure, treated with two different medications; insulin-requiring diabetes; and arthritis, for which he takes over-the-counter pain pills. Does he have any history of psychiatric problems or substance abuse? Sam has no history of depression, other psychiatric problems, or problems with his memory, but did abuse alcohol until about two years ago. Both he and Betty swear that he hasn't used any alcohol since then. Sam has also had intermittent problems with painkillers and sleeping pills, but he is not taking any of these now. Besides his regular prescription medications, the only thing he takes is his cold medicine. You look at the bottle's contents and find out that it contains diphenhydramine (Benadryl), and acetaminophen (Tylenol), and 40 percent alcohol.

Relevant History

Sam has been sick for about a month but has worsened over the past two weeks, when he's become increasingly groggy, disoriented, and developed stomach problems with pain on his right side. Despite these symptoms and multiple other ongoing medical problems, he has not seen a doctor for about two months. His other medical problems are quite serious, as are their treatments. Sam's hypertension can predispose him to stroke, and the medications he takes can interfere with his mental functioning. His diabetes, managed with insulin, may cause either very high or very low blood sugar, which can also adversely affect his mental state. Sam is self-medicating with large doses of an over-the-counter cold medication that contains mostly alcohol, diphenhydramine (which has anticholinergic effects that can cause memory loss and disorientation), and acetaminophen. He also takes an over-the-counter pain pill (which also contains acetaminophen as the main ingredient) for relief of arthritis pain. Sam's past history is significant for alcohol abuse, but he has supposedly been "dry" for two years. Neither he nor his wife are aware of the high alcohol content in the liquid cold medication he now takes.

Sam is experiencing a delirium induced by *over-the-counter drug abuse*, and has probably unknowingly relapsed into chronic alcoholism. Delirium is indicated by the recent onset of fluctuating levels of alertness, disorientation, and excessive sedation, given no prior history of such problems. There is a specific substance that is likely responsible for these problems—the over-the-counter cold medicine. This cold medication contains a drug (diphenhydramine) that has anticholinergic side effects that can impair memory and concentration. Sam is taking large doses of this substance, enough to induce a delirious mental state. His prescription medications may also be interacting with the cold medication to cause these effects, as may either high or low blood sugar from diabetes or its treatment (insulin). Finally, his recent nausea, vomiting, and right-sided abdominal pain are a concern, given the large doses of acetaminophen he's been taking (in both the cold medication and the pain reliever). Such doses of acetaminophen or Tylenol can cause severe liver damage that may be irreversible (eight or more extra-strength Tylenol per day can cause such problems).

More than 40 percent of older adults use over-the-counter (OTC) drugs every day, and at least 66 percent take OTC drugs intermittently. Almost 80 percent of those who take OTC drugs also use alcohol, prescribed drugs, or both. Arthritis, insomnia, and constipation are the most common reasons for taking these drugs. Older persons most likely to use OTC drugs are those on limited incomes, with impaired mobility, and limited access to physicians. Over-the-counter drugs that are commonly abused by elders (and the health problems they cause) include the following: pain relievers (inflammation of the stomach, bleeding from the stomach, kidney damage, liver damage); laxatives (diarrhea, dangerous changes in the composition of blood, chronic colon dysfunction); cold preparations that contain antihistamines, phenylpropanolamine, or pseudoephedrine (disorientation, hallucinations, worsening high blood pressure, heart rhythm abnormalities, chronic sinus congestion); alcohol-based medications (relapse into alcoholism, liver damage); and caffeine-containing preparations (anxiety, difficulty sleeping, rapid heart rate). Abuse of OTC drugs is correlated with cognitive impairment, changes due to aging, and belief that OTC medications are not harmful.

You opened the door by asking Betty about Sam's health. Your willingness to visit and evaluate Sam in his home provided you with the important information you needed to make a recommendation. Your inquiring about what prescriptions and OTC preparations Sam takes and then read-

Diagnostic Criteria

Response to Vignette

ing the contents of the OTC preparations were crucial to your preliminary diagnosis. You would now strongly encourage Betty to take her husband to see a medical doctor, whether Sam agrees or not. You would also try to help Betty get Sam to a doctor or help mobilize other family members to assist.

Treatment Within the Faith Community

The faith community's primary tasks are monitoring, providing assistance to obtain medical evaluation, and assisting the person to comply with doctor-prescribed treatments (keeping visits, taking medications appropriately, and so forth). The faith community should monitor elderly members for unusual behaviors or changes in normal behaviors (unexplained absences from church, prayer or Bible groups, and so forth). For those members who are too ill to attend church meetings, regular telephone contacts can convey a sense of concern that will dispel loneliness, combat isolation, and help detect worrisome symptoms or behaviors. For monitoring to be successful, members of the faith community must have basic knowledge about health problems, their causes, and OTC drug preparations. Next, the faith community can help family members find the appropriate physician to conduct an evaluation (by maintaining an updated referral list), provide transportation (and companionship) to the doctor's office, and help explain treatment recommendations. Monitoring compliance and providing support by regular telephone contacts can be very helpful. Of course, this must be done in a nonintrusive manner, with the consent of the older adult or the older adult's family.

Indications for Referral

All persons experiencing significant side effects thought to be due to OTC drug abuse or dependence need immediate medical evaluation and treatment (especially those with symptoms of delirium: see cases 13 and 20). All medications, whether prescribed or OTC, should be brought with the patient to the doctor.

Treatment by Mental Health Specialist

Sam's physician should perform a careful mental status examination to test his orientation and memory, conduct a comprehensive neurological and physical examination, and carefully review his prescribed medications and any OTC medications he may be taking. Blood tests to check his blood sugar, blood composition (electrolytes, kidney function, liver function), and blood alcohol level are all needed. In addition, a urine test for other toxic substances should be conducted. In Sam's case, these blood tests show an elevated blood sugar of 300 (moderate) and abnormal liver function tests, as well as a significant level of alcohol in his blood. The alcohol in the cold medication, along with large doses of acetaminophen in the cold medicine and the arthritis pain reliever, have combined to cause severe liver damage that is responsible for Sam's stomach complaints.

Sam's physician should explain the risks of OTC drugs, educate him and his family about potentially harmful ingredients, attempt to break through his minimization or denial concerning their harmfulness, and suggest nondrug symptomatic relief for his complaints.

Local Resources

A call to the emergency room at your local hospital or to a local pharmacist can provide you with up-to-date information about medications or OTC drugs, their side effects, and drug interactions that can occur in older adults. Most hospitals are affiliated with a poison-control center that provides detailed information about medications and drugs, particularly in cases of drug overdose or abuse.

National Resources

Duke University Medical Center has a Drug Information Service that can be accessed by anyone in the country who has questions regarding OTC drugs, side effects, or interactions with other medications. The service can be reached at 919-684-5125 or 919-970-8110. The Carolinas Poison Control Center, at 1-800-848-6946, is especially helpful if persons have taken overdoses of medications or have taken substances that might be harmful to their health. Such services are also available in any large metropolitan area where a major medical center is located.

Self-Help Resources

There are numerous books on the market that provide information in layperson's language about OTC and prescription drugs. Reading about the drug can help alert the person about possible dangers in its use. If drug abuse is involved, whether prescription or OTC, and is out of control, the person can be helped by the simple principles that Alcoholics Anonymous teaches. In fact, actual involvement in AA (or a similar organization) may help.

Many home remedies sanctioned by various cultures may contain ingredients that when taken in large doses can have adverse effects on concentration or memory or cause damage to internal organs. Toxicology labs can analyze these substances if they are brought in for examination.

Resources

Cross-Cultural Issues

Prescription Drug Abuse and Dependence

My Pain Is Really Bad

Frances is a 72-year-old widowed woman who recently moved from across the state to be nearer to her son, the church's assistant pastor, Tom. She has joined your church and has been coming infrequently to Sunday services over the past couple of months. Frances was forced to leave her former home because of her worsening arthritis and her need for assistance with day-to-day activities of living. Her son Tom suggested this move when he found out how rapidly his mother's health and mental condition were deteriorating. Three months ago, the neighbors found her on the floor of her house, having fallen and been unable to get up; the house was a shambles, she was dirty and unkempt, and the food in the refrigerator was spoiled and rotting. Social services had demanded that she either be placed in a nursing home or move closer to family who could help care for her. Frances now rents a small apartment just down the street from her son and daughter-in-law, who visit her several times each week and help her with necessities of daily life. Unfortunately, her mental functioning has continued to deteriorate. Her medical doctors back home had prescribed about eight different medicines, and Tom was worried that these could be part of the problem. One day, Tom asks you to come see his mother with him.

On arriving at Frances's apartment at 10:00 A.M. the next morning, you find her sitting at her kitchen table with her head down in her arms. Shaking her gently to awaken her, Tom announces, "Mother, Pastor Don is here. He'd like to visit with you a while."

With a start, Frances wakes up and puts her glasses on. "Hello, Pastor Don," she says shakily. "It's good to see you today." She turns to her son saying, "My pain is really bad today, Tom. I had to take an extra dose of pain medicine today, and I guess I fell asleep."

As you look around the room, you notice dishes piled in the sink, papers and other garbage on the floor, and dirty clothes scattered about. There is a faint smell of urine in the air, covered up partially by room deodorant. Frances has the heat way up in the room. Feeling uncomfortably warm, you loosen your tie, pull up a chair at the table, and begin the conversation. "So how have you tolerated this big move, Frances? I bet it's been hard leaving your other family and friends to relocate down here."

Frances responds, "It sure is, Pastor. These past few weeks have been terrible. Tom and Clara have been very attentive to me, but they have their own lives to live, and I miss my old church crowd. My arthritis pain is worse, too, and so are my nerves." You inquire if she is taking any medicine to help with the symptoms. She responds, "My doctors give me pain pills to help with the arthritis and nerve pills to help calm me during the day and sleep at night. I don't know what I'd do without them."

"But Mom," Tom interjects, "I think you're taking too many of these pills. Remember, you asked me to fill the prescription two weeks before you were supposed to, and the pharmacist had to call the doctor to get authorization. I'm worried that you're taking too much of this stuff."

Frances responds, "Tom, dear, I've got really bad pain. The medicine the doctor prescribed isn't working as well as it used to, so I've needed to take it more often. It's all right; the doctor said I could take the pain medicine up to five times a day, and that's what I'm doing."

"But Mom, the doctor said that three months ago, after you got out of the hospital; should you still be taking so much?" He continues, "What about the nerve pills? You're taking those every few hours also. Every time I come over here you're so sleepy you can hardly talk; I think you're taking too many of these nerve pills, too."

Frances responds, "Tom, you know that I've tried to reduce the medication before, but I just can't seem to cut back. You just don't know how bad the pain is."

Pastoral Care Assessment

Frances is sleepy and having some difficulty staying awake; nevertheless, her memory and concentration are good for her age, and her thinking is generally rational. She is trying to cooperate and denies feeling depressed, but she doesn't look very happy. Instead, she focuses on her pain. Frances is shaky and unsteady on her feet and uses a walker to get about. Her hands are gnarled, with marked deformities, and when she gets up to move she does so slowly, wincing with pain. You discover that Frances has been taking pain pills for her arthritis for years now, and her doctor increased the dose after she was discharged from the hospital three months ago after a fall. She is taking Darvocet N-100 (propoxyphene) regularly for pain relief, and sometimes takes Percocet (oxycodone) when the pain gets really bad as it has recently (both contain narcotics for pain relief). Because the pain keeps her awake at night, she is also taking Valium (diazepam—5 milligrams) for sleep, and also needs it at least several times during the day to help keep her calm. She says that the Valium doesn't help her like it once did, and she still can't sleep at night. Frances has a number of medical problems in addition to her arthritis, including severe constipation and chronic lung disease (from years of cigarette smoking) for which she takes other medications. You learn from Tom that Frances sees several doctors, all specialists for her various conditions. She asks for prescriptions of her pain and nerve medications from each of them and has the prescriptions filled at different pharmacies. Tom has tried to put a stop to this, but says he cannot resist her begging and wonders whether she might really need it. Anyway, if he doesn't get the medication for her, she has the pharmacy deliver it to her apartment.

Frances has had arthritis and nerve problems since her mid-40s and has always depended heavily on medication. In her 20s and 30s she had a problem with heavy alcohol use because of marital difficulties. She stopped drinking entirely after turning 40, but then her nerve problems worsened and she began having health complaints. Frances has always been a nervous person but has never been to see a psychiatrist or been admitted to a psychiatric hospital; instead, she has relied on medical doctors to prescribe medications for her nerve symptoms. Frances's family history is significant for a younger sister with depression and a brother who died from the complications of alcoholism at an early age.

Relevant History

Frances has a long history of dependency on medications and, before that, dependency on alcohol. She also has a long history of nervousness and chronic anxiety, which have likely worsened due to her recent move and loss of community support. She has a family history of alcoholism and depression, which suggests a biological susceptibility to emotional problems that might increase the likelihood of drug dependence. She has several physical conditions that are likely to cause real pain (arthritis) and cause or contribute to nervousness (chronic lung disease, for which she takes medication that could worsen anxiety). She is now taking large doses of narcotic-containing pain medication and relatively large doses of Valium for her age, and is increasing the doses of these drugs because they have lost their effectiveness in controlling her symptoms. She is obtaining prescriptions from several different doctors and using several different pharmacies to purchase the medicine (without her doctors' knowledge). She has tried unsuccessfully to cut back on these medications, thus indicating that she has lost the ability to control her use of these substances. Frances is also experiencing a number of dangerous side effects from these medications: severe constipation from the narcotic-containing pain medication, impaired cough reflex that increases her risk of lung infection, declining mental function due to excessive sedation, and the increasing physical disability due to lack of activity and deconditioning.

Diagnostic Criteria

Frances fulfills the criteria for *prescription drug dependence* (specifically, opioid dependence and anxiolytic dependence). According to *DSM IV*, the criterion for prescription drug dependence is a maladaptive pattern of substance use leading to significant impairment or distress, as indicated by at least three of the following:

1. The person develops tolerance, as defined by the need for increased amounts of the substance to achieve the desired effect.
2. The person suffers withdrawal symptoms when the person cannot have access to the substance (or uses the substance to relieve or avoid withdrawal symptoms).
3. The person takes larger amounts of the substance over a longer period than intended.
4. The person makes repeated unsuccessful attempts to cut down or control use of the substance.
5. The person spends a great deal of time trying to acquire the substance (e.g., visiting multiple doctors and using multiple pharmacies).
6. The person reduces or stops participating in important social or recreational activities because of use of the substance.
7. The person continues use of the substance despite knowledge of ongoing physical or psychological problems that may be caused or made worse by the drug.

Frances shows clear evidence of five of these indicators (1, 3, 4, 5, 7), which is more than enough to qualify her for the disorder. This applies to both her use of narcotic-containing pain relievers and her use of the anxiolytic Valium.

Prescription drug *abuse* (as opposed to *dependence*, as described above) involves a maladaptive pattern of substance use that leads to significant impairment or distress, as indicated by any *one* of the following during a twelve-month period:

1. Drug use resulting in failure to fulfill major obligations either on the job, within the family, or concerning the self (ability to care for basic needs).
2. Recurrent use of the drug in situations that may be physically hazardous (or taking medication that might increase the risk of falling).
3. Recurrent legal problems due to use of the drug (e.g., stealing or—as in Frances's case—use of multiple pharmacies).
4. Continued use despite persistent social or interpersonal problems due to use of the substance (e.g., withdrawal from the church community).

If the person also fulfills criteria for dependence, then the latter diagnosis takes priority (as in Frances's case).

Elderly persons, while they make up only 12 percent of the population, use more than 25 percent of all prescription drugs. Persons over the age of 65 use an average of eight to ten prescription and nonprescription drugs regularly. In large community surveys of older adults, Valium has been found to be the fifth most commonly prescribed drug, being taken by 4 percent of elderly men and 7 percent of elderly women; other anxiolytics commonly used by older adults include flurazepam (Dalmane) by 4 percent of men and 5 percent of women, meprobamate (Equagesic or Equanil) by 1 percent of men and 2 percent of women, and chlordiazepoxide (Librium) by 2 percent of men and 1 percent of women. Overall, sleeping pills are used by 6 percent of older adults. Narcotic pain relievers are used by 2 percent of men and 2 percent of women. Over 90 percent of abusers of these medications have taken them for five years or longer. Older persons with health problems are even more likely to take these medications. More than one-third of patients (36 percent) seen at general medical clinics report receiving anxiolytic prescriptions for at least one year at some time in their lives, and 22 percent currently use these drugs.[1]

Response to Vignette

It appears that Frances may be dependent on both pain and nerve drugs. She needs professional help to come off these medications, and this may have to be done in a hospital. Your primary task is to make an assessment, educate Frances and her family, and help her obtain a comprehensive medical and psychiatric evaluation. This is a terrifying situation for Frances, and she will need much support and encouragement as she faces the difficult task of coming off these drugs and learning new, less potentially destructive ways of coping with pain and anxiety. Tapping into the person's spiritual resources is crucial at this time. In fact, the programs that have proved most effective for persons abusing or dependent on alcohol or drugs (whether prescribed, over-the-counter, or illegal) are Alcoholics Anonymous and Narcotics Anonymous, whose primary basis lies firmly on three spiritual principles: (1) admitting that one has lost control over an addiction and is unable to overcome the problem without help, (2) relying on a Higher Power to provide strength to resist falling back into addiction, and (3) making a commitment to others in a community and becoming accountable for one's actions to them. Thus, whatever the pastor or pastoral staff can do to help bolster Frances's religious faith and her involvement in the faith community will increase her chances of successful rehabilitation.

Treatment Within the Faith Community

The faith community can help identify individuals with prescription drug problems and obtain professional assistance for them. Church members can provide emotional support to the person during rehabilitation

1. H. Pinsker and K. Suljaga-Petchel, "Use of Benzodiazepines in Primary-Care Geriatric Patients," *Journal of the American Geriatrics Society* 32 (1984): 595-97.

and do whatever it takes to reintegrate him or her into the social life of the church. Just as persons in Alcoholics Anonymous must find sponsors who will be available to support them during times of weakness, persons recovering from drug abuse or dependence may rely on fellow church members who in turn commit themselves to providing help and encouragement. The helper may choose to call or meet with the person on a regular basis to show concern, support, and interest in the person's continued progress in rehabilitation.

Indications for Referral

Whenever a person meets criteria for drug abuse or dependence (whether prescription drugs, illegal drugs, or over-the-counter drugs), he or she needs immediate referral for professional assistance. You must be aware, however, that an older person may have a valid physical or psychiatric disorder that requires the use of narcotic pain medication, anxiolytic drugs such as diazepam, or other prescription medication. If a patient's use is being carefully monitored by a physician, then even if dependence on the medication is present, the benefits of use have been judged to outweigh the risks. In Frances' case, it is not clear that her conditions require that she continue to take large doses of narcotics and anxiolytics; it is clear, however, that no one physician is monitoring or coordinating her use of these substances.

Treatment by Mental Health Specialist

Frances needs to be evaluated by a doctor, preferably a family physician or a general internist, who will perform a comprehensive physical and psychological evaluation and coordinate her medical care to ensure that she does not have multiple doctors prescribing independently of one another. If it is established that she does not have an underlying medical or psychiatric disease that requires the doses of drugs she is now taking, then she will have to be carefully withdrawn from these substances. For this, she may need to be admitted as an inpatient in the hospital, given her age and other physical health problems. Nonpharmacologic measures to control pain and anxiety (biofeedback, psychotherapy, etc.) should be used as the other medications are tapered down.

Resources

See case 23, "Over-the-Counter Drug Abuse and Dependence," for local and national resources.

Self-Help Resources

The Physicians Desk Reference (PDR) contains information about virtually every drug being prescribed by physicians. An updated edition can be obtained at any local library. As noted earlier, books written for laypersons about commonly used prescription drugs (doses, interactions, and side effects) can be obtained at most local bookstores.

Persons from certain cultural backgrounds may be less willing to endure physical or emotional pain and be more likely to turn to medication for relief. In societies in which pain and suffering are accepted as part of life, by contrast, drug abuse and dependence are less common.

Cross-Cultural Issues

Somatization Disorder

I Need Surgery

Glenda is a 64-year-old widowed member of your congregation who has attended services intermittently over the past ten years since her husband's death. After not showing up for church for several Sundays in a row, she calls you and says she needs counsel. Glenda appears in your office the next day at her appointment time. After some small talk, she rapidly gets to the point. "Pastor, I need your advice. I just don't know what I'm going to do. I've got all these health problems, and nobody seems to care. I've gone to one doctor after another, and none have been able to help me. They tell me it's all in my head, but I know I'm hurting. What should I do?" she asks.

Responding gently, you inquire, "What types of health problems have you been having, Glenda?" For the next twenty minutes she produces a litany of symptoms, explaining each one in great detail: near constant pain in her back and shoulders, severe cramping abdominal pain, burning with urination, constipation and bloating, difficulty swallowing, dizziness, headaches, difficulty with balance, and a tight feeling in her uterus. She says that the worst problem involves uterine, rectal, and bladder areas; she feels that these organs have "dropped" and need to be removed. She exclaims, "Pastor, I need surgery to correct all this, but the doctors won't operate on me. I've seen at least a dozen different doctors, but after they get my medical records, they refuse to do a thing. I know that if they would just operate, they'd find the problem. Instead, they tell me I need a psychiatrist, and that just makes me angry."

You ask how long Glenda has been having these problems. She responds that she has had one or another of these problems since her 20s, but that they have all worsened over the past ten years, and especially over the past several months. Glenda admits that she has had several abdominal surgeries in the past for appendicitis and severe abdominal pain and to have her gallbladder removed, but none have completely relieved her. "I don't know how much longer I can take this, Pastor. I've lost my confidence in doctors and don't know where to turn to. Can you help me?" she asks in a desperate tone.

Pastoral Care Assessment

Glenda is a thin, pale woman who appears older than her stated age of 64. She is nicely dressed, although her hair is tousled and her makeup is heavy and smearing in places. Her eye contact with you is only intermittent, and she does not smile. She speaks rapidly, urgently, and is difficult to interrupt. The content of her speech centers around her physical symptoms and is unusually detailed. Her thinking appears logical, although she tends to wander off the subject and is sometimes difficult to follow. You cautiously explore whether she's had any strange or unusual ideas (delusions) or experiences (hallucinations), but she denies these. Her memory is good, and she is able to give dates and sequence of events without difficulty. Glenda does admit to having difficulty sleeping because of "my pain" and feeling tired much of the time. She denies feeling depressed but admits to feeling frustrated and angry with her doctors. When asked whether she has ever thought about suicide, she says that while she's thought about it, she doesn't think she could carry it out.

You need additional information about Glenda's history, so you ask to speak with her daughter, Linda. Linda lives with her husband and two sons a couple of blocks from Glenda's house, is also a member of your congregation, and frequently accompanies her mother to church. Linda appears relieved to speak with you about her mother. "Oh, Pastor, I don't know what to do with mother. She keeps doctor-shopping to get someone to operate on her, and I'm afraid someone is going to take her up someday. Besides a mild case of high blood pressure and some constipation, she's in good health, and none of the doctors has been able to find anything major wrong with her. I wish she would just get one doctor and stick with him; instead, she's been going to one specialist after another. She's had these physical complaints ever since I can remember, but they've gotten worse since Daddy died and especially since her dog was killed by a car several months ago. That old dog was a real companion to her, and she's taken his death very hard."

Linda tells you that Glenda has a college education and worked part-time as a practical nurse while raising her family. She has always been somewhat reclusive and does not have many friends outside of her family, although she has intermittently attended a women's Bible study at church. You ask if Glenda has ever had any emotional or psychiatric problems in the past, and discover that she became very depressed after her husband's death but seemed to recover pretty well on her own. She has never been to see a psychiatrist or other mental health professional in the past, and has never been a heavy drinker of alcohol. Linda does report, however, that Glenda has always taken a lot of medication and now takes a number of tranquilizers and pain pills that are prescribed by several different doctors. "I think they give her these pills to get her off their backs," Linda reports.

Glenda has many unexplained medical symptoms and many worries about medical illness that have come to dominate her life. She has sought evaluation from a wide variety of medical and surgical specialists, none of whom has been able to find any significant physical problems to account for her symptoms. She apparently does not have a trusting relationship with a single general physician who could coordinate her medical care. While Glenda has had physical complaints on and off since young adulthood, these symptoms have worsened since her husband passed on and especially since the recent death of her dog. She refuses to see a psychiatrist and attributes all her problems to real physical illness. She feels that her doctors have not taken her complaints seriously and is angry and frustrated with them. Although she denies having depression, she has a number of somatic symptoms of depression, has had thoughts about suicide, and is probably addicted to tranquilizers and pain medications (which she could also use quite effectively to commit suicide). Glenda lives a relatively reclusive lifestyle; nevertheless, she does have supportive and concerned family in the area and has made at least a few social connections in church. Finally, she appears to trust you enough to seek your counsel.

Relevant History

Glenda in all likelihood has *somatization disorder,* a chronic psychiatric condition characterized by a history of many physical complaints beginning in early adulthood and persisting for several years, during which treatment from multiple physicians has been sought. To meet *DSM IV*'s diagnostic criteria for somatization disorder, the person must have each one of the following at some time during the course of the illness:

Diagnostic Criteria

1. Pain symptoms from at least four different sites (head, abdomen, back, joints, extremities, chest, rectum, sexual organs, bladder).
2. At least two gastrointestinal symptoms (nausea, bloating, vomiting, diarrhea, food intolerance).
3. One or more sexual symptoms (sexual indifference, erectile or ejaculatory dysfunction, menstrual or uterine problems).
4. At least one neurological condition unrelated to pain (paralysis or localized weakness, difficulty swallowing, urinary retention, loss of pain sensation, visual or hearing problems, seizures, amnesia).

The final requirement is that after appropriate medical investigation, these symptoms cannot be fully explained by the presence of a general medical condition or the effects of a drug (drug abuse or drug withdrawal).

If a general medical condition is present, the person's symptoms or complaints must be out of proportion to what would be expected based on the medical evaluation. Finally, the medical symptoms cannot be intentionally produced (as in malingering).

Somatization disorder is one of a group of conditions called somatoform disorders. Other similar illnesses in this category include conversion disorder (a part of the body appears paralyzed or dysfunctional), hypochondriasis (there is an unusual fear of having an undiagnosed physical condition such as cancer), and body dysmorphic disorder (preoccupation with an imagined or exaggerated defect in physical appearance). Somatization disorder can also be confused with a major depressive disorder, which is often associated in older adults with complaints of pain or other physical symptoms. In depression, however, physical complaints usually have appeared only recently—during the depression episode—and have not been present for many years as in somatization disorder.

Chronic pain syndrome can also be confused with somatization disorder, particularly when the cause of pain has not yet been medically established. Delusional disorder can sometimes be confused with somatization disorder, particularly when delusions are somatic in nature; in fact, there may be a continuum that ranges from *concern* over physical symptoms to *obsession* with physical symptoms to psychotic level *preoccupation* with physical problems such that one believes that one's insides are rotting or has other bizarre physical complaints or explanations (delusions). Finally, some persons have a *conscious* need to assume the sick role (in somatization disorder, the motivation is unconscious). In these cases, the person feigns or pretends to be sick and may even harm herself or himself to make it look as if he or she needs medical attention. The latter condition is called malingering and in *DSM IV* is called a "factitious disorder."

Over a lifetime, a diagnosis of somatization disorder can be made in 0.2 to 2 percent of women and in less than 0.2 percent of men; between 10 and 20 percent of first-degree female relatives of persons with somatization disorder also fulfill diagnostic criteria for the disorder.[1] The condition is probably more frequent in older adults, particularly those who already have verifiable physical health problems. This makes it a very difficult disorder to diagnose, since many times the person is sick anyway, and sorting out truly physical symptoms from those that are psychologically based can be almost impossible. Persons with somatization disorder often have medical backgrounds (nurses, medical technicians, etc.) that make them knowledgeable about different physical disorders and their presentations. The course of somatization disorder is frequently lifelong, although symptoms may improve or worsen periodically (usually in response to psychosocial stress); typically, however, not a year goes by without the

1. *DSM IV*, 447-48.

person needing to seek medical attention for some unexplained physical complaint.

Obtaining as much outside information as possible is the key to making this diagnosis. Family members are usually the best source for such information, although it is also helpful to get information from the elder's personal physician (with consent, of course). At times, making the diagnosis and directing the person toward necessary professional help is all you can do. Often, however, you can make direct interventions that relieve suffering and feelings of isolation. Showing interest in and sincere concern about Glenda's complaints is important in winning her trust so that you can help her feel less abandoned. Exploring other psychosocial stressors that might be contributing to her worsening symptoms is important. In this case, Glenda may have not completely grieved over the loss of either her husband or her dog. Helping her to talk about these losses and what they mean to her can help with this process. It would not be helpful either to agree with her that all her symptoms are physical or to try to convince her that they are psychological; rather, you should simply validate her feelings of frustration, discouragement, and fear over not getting the medical help she wants and then help her to cope with these feelings. It is best to assume the role of a helping friend and counselor and to stay as far away from taking sides as possible.

Working with persons like Glenda can be time consuming and mentally exhausting, and this is why doctors and even family members may abandon such persons; nevertheless, just remember that these persons are often suffering deeply, feel intensely alone, and may reach a point where they feel like ending their lives. Finally, bear in mind that when persons with a presumed diagnosis of somatization disorder are observed over time, about one-third are eventually diagnosed with a real physical condition that could at least partially explain their symptoms.

Glenda needs loving concern, support, and acceptance from her faith community. Even the most devout and well-meaning Christian, however, may find it difficult to provide for these needs. Listening to the same complaints over and over again requires patience and understanding. Helping persons must be advised that their main objective is to simply convey to Glenda that she is not alone in this battle, that there are people who care deeply about her, and that they will not abandon her. Again, trying to convince her that her symptoms are psychological will only result in further alienation. However, placing an emphasis on God's healing power is often well-received and effective. When Jesus healed persons, he did not distinguish mental from physical causes for afflictions; he healed the whole person. Bearing this in mind, the helping person should pray for Glenda and pray with Glenda for such healing and wholeness. Indeed,

Response to Vignette

Treatment Within the Faith Community

this may produce more effective and long-lasting results than interventions by health professionals.

Indications for Referral

Glenda needs both medical and psychiatric care. If she does not have one, Glenda needs a compassionate and understanding general physician who will see her on a frequent, regular basis and coordinate *all* her medical care (including the prescription of medications). This will prevent her from seeing multiple physicians, none of whom know all the details of her case and each prescribing the same or different drugs. She may also need to be slowly weaned off addictive pain medications and tranquilizers and treated for concurrent problems such as depression. This may require expert psychiatric care (on either an outpatient or inpatient basis), which Glenda will likely resist. Nevertheless, if her personal physician requests this and the request is supported by her pastor, family, and church community, then she will likely comply.

Treatment by Mental Health Specialist

As noted above, Glenda needs a single general medical physician (family physician or general internist) to coordinate her medical care. This physician should set up a regular monthly or biweekly appointment with Glenda to perform a physical examination and any relevant blood tests, as well as monitor her use of medications. What is important in this visit is not so much what is done, but the physician's attitude of taking her complaints seriously and carefully monitoring her progress. Persons with somatization disorder and concurrent depressive or anxiety disorders are notoriously difficult to treat with medication because they experience many real or imagined side effects to even the smallest doses of antidepressants.

It is also important for Glenda to see a psychiatrist who has expertise in dealing with somatization disorder, who can confirm the diagnosis, explore possible psychodynamic explanations for unfounded or exaggerated medical symptoms, and rule out or treat other psychiatric disorders should they be present. If nothing else, the mental health professional should provide emotional support for her pain, suffering, and frustration over her illness.

Resources

Local Resources

There are few if any organizations that specifically help persons with somatization disorder, particularly since it does not fit nicely into any major category of psychiatric illness (e.g., depression, anxiety disorder, or schizophrenia). Family members may contact a county mental health center or department of psychiatry at a nearby university medical center, which may provide information about the condition and treatment options. Somatization disorder is probably closest to an anxiety disorder, and therefore organizations that specialize in this area may be helpful (see case 7, "Generalized Anxiety Disorder," for resources).

National Resources

The Department of Psychiatry at the University of Iowa, Hospital and Clinics, Iowa City (phone 319-356-1144), has a number of faculty that specialize in somatization disorders and who can be contacted for more information about these conditions (Dr. K. Tomasson, Dr. D. Kent, and Dr. W. Coryell). The Department of Family Medicine at the College of Medicine, University of South Alabama, Mobile (phone 334-460-7195), also has experts on this topic (Dr. F. deGruy and Dr. J. Crider).

Articles in medical journals discussing the symptoms and treatments for somatization disorder include the following: Simon and VonKorff, "Somatization and Psychiatric Disorder in the NIMH Epidemiologic Catchment Area Study," *American Journal of Psychiatry* 148 (1991): 1494-1500; Escobar et al., "Somatization in the Community," *Archives of General Psychiatry* 44 (1987): 713-18; and deGruy and Crider, "Somatization Disorder in a University Hospital," *Journal of Family Practice* 25 (1990): 579-84.

Self-Help Resources

If persons with somatization disorder become depressed or anxious over their condition, they may be motivated to read self-help books in order to cope. See the reading materials in this section for case 2, "Major Depression," and case 7, "Generalized Anxiety Disorder."

Cross-Cultural Issues

Somatic symptoms in somatization disorder may vary across different cultures. For example, persons in Africa or South Asia may be more likely to experience burning hands and feet or insects crawling under the skin than are persons in North America. While somatization disorder is rare in men in the United States, it may be more frequent in Greek and Puerto Rican men. In general, psychological conflict is more often expressed as physical symptoms by persons from developing countries, the uneducated, and those from cultures or societies in which having psychological symptoms is not acceptable.

Sexual Dysfunction

He Doesn't Love Me Anymore

Wayne and Ruth have been devout churchgoers for many years. Both in their 70s now, they have been married almost fifty years. You are surprised when Ruth calls you one day and asks if you do "marital therapy." Nevertheless, sensing the urgency of her request, you arrange to see the couple the next day. After Wayne and Ruth make themselves comfortable in your office, Ruth is the first to speak. "I'm embarrassed to even talk about this, but I'm afraid he doesn't love me anymore. Throughout most of our marriage, we have always had an active and fulfilling sex life. Here lately, though, Wayne doesn't want to touch me anymore. He even seems nervous when I snuggle up to him in bed at night. When I ask him what's wrong, he says he's just not in the mood. But we haven't been intimate in over three months, Pastor."

Taking a deep breath, you look over at Wayne, who appears very uncomfortable. "Wayne," you ask, "how do you see things?"

He begins hesitatingly, "Well, Pastor, I don't know what to say. I do love Ruth and always have. She should know that. But over the past three or four months I just haven't felt much like having sex. To be honest about it, Pastor, I've had trouble getting erections lately, and rather than hassle with it, I'd just as soon leave it alone."

More history is clearly needed at this point, so you should explore the problem further with Wayne, but probably alone for now. You ask Ruth to leave the room so that you can talk with Wayne for about fifteen to twenty minutes. The information you want to know is what was the frequency of their sexual relations ten years ago, five years ago, one year ago, and six months ago. This will give you some idea of how rapidly the problem has developed. You should ask Wayne if there is another woman in his life. This is a difficult but necessary question. Likewise, you need to ask Wayne if he still loves his wife and is totally committed to her. You

Pastoral Care Assessment

also need to ask if there is anything about his wife that turns him off. Assuming that Wayne loves his wife, finds her attractive, and is not involved with another, your next questions focus on the events and circumstances that surrounded the change in Wayne's potency.

At his age, the most likely cause for declining potency is health or medication. Illnesses such as diabetes or blood vessel disease can cause erectile difficulties from middle age onward, particularly as these conditions worsen in severity. Medications are another culprit, especially those used to treat heart disease or high blood pressure. Wayne tells you that he is in relatively good health, although about four months ago he was placed on a medication for his blood pressure by his family physician. It was not long after that when he attempted to make love to his wife he found that he had difficulty sustaining an erection. This upset him very much, because he had always prided himself in his sexual prowess, and it made him doubt himself and his masculinity. Thereafter, he tried a couple more times to have intercourse with his wife, but each time he was unsuccessful. Wayne recalls that the last time he tried he became extremely anxious, and he has not wanted to go through the experience again. For that reason, whenever his wife approaches him in a sexual way, he withdraws or gives excuses why he's not in the mood. You inquire about any recent stressors (deaths, financial troubles, etc.) and ask about depression, since these factors may affect Wayne's sexual interest and drive. He denies feeling depressed or down and cannot recall the occurrence of any recent life stressors.

You now meet with Ruth alone for fifteen to twenty minutes and get more details about her side of the story, without divulging any of the conversation you had earlier with Wayne. You learn that Ruth is less concerned about having intercourse than she is over the insecurity she feels because of Wayne's seeming rejection of her. She tells you that Wayne has never been a very expressive person and that she has always been somewhat insecure about his love for her, since he seldom says that he loves her. "Instead of giving me flowers or a card for my birthday, he fixes my car or builds something for the kitchen or house. Sometimes, I just can't figure him out," exclaims Ruth. "I wouldn't care if we never had sex again, if he would only let me get close to him again." You ask Ruth about the quality of their marriage over the years, how well they have got along, how frequently they have disagreed about things, and how they have resolved their differences. She reports that they have always had a good marriage and that that is why the current situation upsets her so much. You ask Ruth about her husband's mood, sleep, and appetite (symptoms of depression) and if there have been any recent life stressors. She confirms Wayne's negative report, although admits that this sexual problem has been "getting me down."

Finally, you would bring them back together and speak with them as a couple. At this time, it is important that you explore what effect their sexual problem has had on their spiritual life and relationship with God, both individually and as a couple. This usually reveals important information that you may utilize later in your counseling with them.

Ruth is clearly upset about the situation, and while Wayne is less demonstrative than his wife, he is also experiencing distress. Important questions to answer about their history include the following:

1. What was the quality of their earlier sexual relationship?
2. How satisfying is their marital relationship, and is either of them involved with another?
3. Specifically, what about the situation is upsetting to each person?
4. What does each person perceive as the cause of the problem?
5. What is the exact nature of the problem, and how rapidly did it develop?
6. What have they done to cope with the problem, and who else have they seen about it?
7. What other life stressors are affecting the marriage?
8. Is there untreated depression or other psychiatric illness in either partner?
9. Does Wayne have chronic health problems, does he take prescription or over-the-counter medications, or has he experienced any change in physical health or medication use?

These questions usually provide key information about the cause of sexual problems and clues about how they might be resolved.

It is likely that Wayne has a combination of *substance-induced sexual dysfunction* and *male erectile disorder due to psychological factors*. From the history, it sounds as if his initial erectile difficulties began after his physician placed him on a blood pressure medication (substance-induced sexual dysfunction). While this may have started the problem, it is likely that after several failed attempts at sexual intercourse, Wayne began having doubts about his physical capacity, virility, and masculinity that eroded his self-confidence. Each time he attempts sex with his wife, he becomes more concerned about his inability to obtain and sustain an erection than about focusing his attention on the pleasurable sensations associated with sex. This need to perform sexually often causes anxiety (performance anxiety), which then interferes with arousal and further contributes to erectile difficulties, making it increasingly more difficult to obtain an erection (male erectile disorder due to psychological factors). These two factors (medication effects and performance anxiety), on top of normal age-related declines in sexual interest and vigor, could easily explain Wayne's difficulties. Consequently, whenever Ruth makes sexual overtures toward him, Wayne is reminded of his erectile difficulties, feels anxious, and attempts to avoid situations that might lead to future experiences of failure. Ruth, not understanding the situation, interprets these behaviors as evidence that he is no longer aroused or excited by her because she is unattractive, and that he doesn't love her anymore because he doesn't want to get close to her. Consequently, the couple begins to drift further and further apart: Wayne wanting to avoid physical intimacy for fear of failure, and Ruth feeling afraid and angry over the perceived rejection by her husband. Thus, a simple medication side effect has set in motion a sequence of events that may lead to the breakup of a fifty-year marital relationship.

A large number of different medications affect sexual interest and performance. Most notorious in this regard are blood pressure medications, heart medications, and certain types of antidepressants, especially the selective serotonin reuptake inhibitors (SSRIs) such as Prozac (fluoxetine), Paxil (paroxetine), and Zoloft (sertraline). Switching to a medication in another drug class often results in complete return of sexual function. Besides medications, a number of physical illnesses can cause erectile difficulties in later life, including diabetes, peripheral vascular disease (progressive narrowing of blood vessels due to high cholesterol and other illnesses), and prostate surgery for enlarged prostate or for prostate cancer. These illnesses must be ruled out as a first step in the evaluation of any older man with erectile difficulties.

Information about normative sexual behavior in later life is necessary when counseling persons with perceived sexual difficulties. Many older couples remain sexually active until late in life. A study of men in their seventh decade revealed that 75 percent engaged in sexual intercourse at least once per month.[1] Nevertheless, Kinsey and other national surveys have demonstrated that the frequency of intercourse clearly decreases with age, with persons aged 16 to 25 engaging in sex 2.5 to 3.3 times per week, those aged 26 to 35 at 2.0 to 2.6 times per week, those aged 36 to 45 at 1.4 to 2.0 times per week, those aged 46 to 60 at 0.5 to 1.0 times per week, those aged 60 to 69 about twice per month, and slowly decreasing in frequency thereafter (mostly due to declining physical health).[2] Thus, sexual activity remains important for many older couples, particularly for those who enjoyed a fulfilling sexual relationship earlier in life. Older men who have been sexually inactive for some time, due to physical disability or loss of a spouse to death or divorce, may experience erectile difficulties when they attempt to resume sexual activity. For bereaved men,

1. W. H. Masters, "Sex and Aging: Expectations and Reality," *Hospital Practice* (15 August 1986): 175-98.
2. A. C. Kinsey, W. B. Pomeroy, C. E. Martin, *Sexual Behavior in the Human Male* (Philadelphia: W. B. Saunders, 1948).

this is called the "widower's syndrome"; here, an older man widowed and sexually inactive for many years marries a younger woman and consequently experiences difficulty resuming sexual activity.

Women also experience sexual dysfunctions in later life, especially problems with arousal and ability to experience orgasm. Declining estrogen production by aging ovaries often results in drying and shrinkage of vaginal mucous membranes, making sexual intercourse uncomfortable and physically painful. Estrogen supplementation can often help "tone up" mucous membranes and enhance the flow of secretions that will make intercourse more comfortable. In addition, vaginal lubricants (such as Johnson's Baby Oil) can be used to reduce discomfort.

Response to Vignette

You need to help Wayne and Ruth communicate with each other about their sexual difficulties, fears, and feelings of embarrassment and rejection that these problems have caused. They also need to be educated on the probable causes for Wayne's erectile difficulties, the normal feelings and psychological reactions that usually accompany these sexual dysfunctions, and ways of coping with the problem. First, informing Wayne about the possible association between his blood pressure medication and erectile difficulties should motivate him to see his physician and ask about other medications without this side effect. Wayne should have a complete physical examination to rule out other medical conditions that might be contributing to his erectile difficulties.

Second, you should explain to him the vicious cycle that can result when he becomes anxious over his erectile problem; in other words, as he become more anxious and preoccupied with getting an erection, he will be distracted from the pleasurable sensations involved in sex, which are necessary for sexual arousal. There are a number of behavioral treatments for this so called "performance anxiety."

Third, you should educate Wayne about the effects his behavior is having on his wife and their marital relationship. He may not understand that Ruth needs his attention and physical closeness more than she needs sexual intercourse; in particular, she needs reassurance that he still loves her and finds her attractive. Ruth needs help in understanding Wayne, why he behaves as he does, and what are typical male behaviors. Wayne also needs to be encouraged to open up emotionally to his wife and share with her his feelings and fears. This is what real intimacy is all about.

Finally, nongenital forms of sexual activity should be discussed with the couple as an alternative to intercourse that can provide pleasure and increase arousal for both. We found that persons from more conservative, fundamentalist religious traditions were less likely to experiment with different sexual practices that might help facilitate arousal and increase pleasure.[3]

3. H. G. Koenig and S. Herman, "Coping with Sexual Impotence by Elderly Men," *Journal of Religious Gerontology* 9, no. 1 (1995): 73-87.

We have been assuming, of course, that there is no underlying marital discord that might complicate the picture. Indeed, unresolved conflict and bitterness can interfere with sexual arousal and emotional intimacy, and if present, must be worked on at the same time that these other measures are implemented. Furthermore, it is a waste of time to work with couples to help them overcome sexual difficulties unless both are committed to the marital relationship. Finally, psychiatric conditions such as depression can interfere with sexual interest and arousal, and must be identified and treated appropriately.

Treatment Within the Faith Community

Because of the delicate, sensitive, private nature of sexual problems and their potential for embarrassment, it is of utmost importance to maintain confidentiality. This type of counseling should be reserved for the pastor or for pastoral staff who are trained to handle such problems. Nevertheless, having a supportive and caring faith community may help Wayne and Ruth better cope with the emotional distress resulting from their sexual and relationship problems.

Indications for Referral

Although you and your staff can help educate and direct Wayne and Ruth, as well as help facilitate communication between the couple, Wayne needs immediate referral to his family physician to rule out medical causes for his impotence. If medical problems and drugs are not the problem, and sexual difficulties persist despite education and appropriate counseling, then referral to a psychologist for individual or couples therapy is indicated.

Treatment by Mental Health Specialist

As noted above, a medical physician can rule out or treat medical conditions that may underlie the problem. Sometimes a urologist may be consulted who has specific interest and expertise in such problems. Wayne may be tested for adequate hormone levels in the blood (testosterone) or the presence of unusually high levels of other hormones (such as prolactin) that can inhibit sexual response. Treatments may be instituted that can help return hormone levels to normal and restore sexual functioning. Finally, a psychologist specialized in the treatment of sexual problems can suggest techniques to reduce performance anxiety and help persons focus on pleasurable sensations that may facilitate arousal.

Resources

Local Resources

Family physicians, general internists, or urologists (for men) or gynecologists (for women) are medical professionals with expertise in handling the medical aspects of sexual disorders. A local mental health center or psychology department in a nearby medical center may have experts in this area. Certified marriage and family therapists usually have considerable training in counseling couples with sexual problems and may be another local resource to pursue if available.

National Resources

No specific national organization exists that specifically deals with sexual problems in later life.

Self-Help Resources

Information about normal human sexuality and sexual disorders can be found in the *Comprehensive Textbook of Psychiatry*, fifth edition, volume 1, edited by Harold Kaplan and Benjamin Sadock (Baltimore: William & Wilkins, 1989). The Kinsey reports were among the first systematic studies to provide information about adult sexual practices in the United States; these include *Sexual Behavior in the Human Male* (Philadelphia: W. B. Saunders, 1948) and *Sexual Behavior in the Human Female* (Philadelphia: W. B. Saunders, 1954). A more recent article that reviews this topic is "A Review of Sexual Behavior in the United States," by S. N. Seidman and R. O. Riede, in the *American Journal of Psychiatry* 151 (1994): 330-41. Information about treatments for impotence and other sexual problems of men and women is contained in the book *Behavioral Treatment of Sexual Problems: Brief Therapy*, by J. S. Annon (San Francisco: Harper & Row, 1976). Helpful hints for spouses can be obtained from an article entitled "Coping with an Impotent Husband," in the *Illinois Medical Journal* 149 (1981): 29-33. Finally, a good overall text that provides a wide range of information on types of sexual problems, causes, and treatments is *Human Sexuality in Health and Illness*, by N. F. Woods (St. Louis: C. V. Mosby, 1979).

Cross-Cultural Issues

The continuation of an active sex life into the later years may have different value and importance for members of different cultures, and this will determine the seriousness and degree of disruption of the marital relationship that occurs when sexual problems do arise.

Insomnia

I Can't Sleep

Kathrine, a 70-year-old widowed member of your congregation, has been a faithful church worker for years. She heads up the children's ministry and frequently does secretarial work for the church. Over the past several months, you have noticed that Kathrine frequently nods off early in the service and sleeps right through your message and even the hymns. Fellow church members often have to nudge her during the service to interrupt her snoring. This is a new behavior for Kathrine and embarrasses her terribly, but she cannot seem to help it. Pastoral staff have pointed out to you that Kathrine has appeared more tired lately and has had difficulty carrying out the secretarial tasks assigned to her.

Concerned, you set up an appointment to talk with her. In a kind voice you ask, "Kathrine, you seem so tired lately. Are you doing okay?"

She responds, "Oh, Pastor, I feel so awful about my sleeping during church services. In fact, it's all I can do to force myself to get to church, feeling the way I do. It's just that since my stay in the hospital last May, I can't sleep at night. Although I had some problems sleeping before I entered the hospital, I was managing okay. In the hospital, my whole schedule got upset, and since being home, I haven't been able to get back on track. I've tried everything—including sleeping pills, and even a glass of wine before retiring—but they only help for a little while, and then I'm back to where I started. Do you think it has to do with my getting older?" She goes on to tell you that she goes to bed at around 9:00 P.M. and lies in bed for one or two hours before falling to sleep; after about two or three hours, however, she wakes up and can't get back to sleep. She then tosses and turns until daybreak, when she finally gets up, exhausted. She then feels tired all day, is irritable, and has difficulty concentrating on her tasks, both around the house and at church. You ask her if there is anything else going on in her life that she'd like to talk about. At first, she denies any other stresses (besides not sleeping), but then she admits to worrying a lot lately about her son, who has been sick with heart trouble.

"Pastor, what can I do?" she pleads. "I've been to see my family doctor now three times, and all he does is give me these sleeping pills and suggest that I increase the dose if I need to. I'm afraid of getting hooked on these pills, but I need my sleep." You validate how difficult this situation must be for her, and pledge to do what you can to help.

Pastoral Care Assessment

In order to help Kathrine, you need more information. Four areas need to be investigated further: (1) activities during the day, (2) sleep behaviors at night, (3) emotional problems, and (4) physical health problems.

First, you need to ask about what types of activities she is involved in during the evening hours. Does she watch exciting TV shows or listen to stimulating radio programs just before retiring? Does she call her son and talk with him each evening, causing her to think and worry about him after they hang up? What types of beverages does she drink during the evening hours? Is she drinking tea, colas, or coffee so that she can stay awake to watch her favorite TV program? What medications is she taking? Does she take a stimulating decongestant for her chronic allergy problems before retiring at night? Is she taking a stimulating antidepressant or any other medication that interferes with sleep? Does she use alcohol to help her fall asleep? If she can't sleep, does she take a sleeping pill at 3:00 A.M. and then feel the hangover effects the next day? Does she get enough physical activity during the day, so that she is tired enough to sleep at night? Does she take catnaps during the day when she is resting or watching TV? Is the bedroom used for any other activities during the day, such as eating or watching TV?

Second, you need to inquire about Kathrine's sleep behaviors at night. What is her sleep environment like? Does she live next to a train station, a nightclub, a busy freeway, or noisy neighbors that disturb her sleep? What is the temperature of the room? Best sleep occurs when the temperature of the room is cool (between sixty-five and seventy degrees). Is her room dark at night, or is there a lamppost next to her window? Does she feel safe at night, or is she realistically fearful of someone breaking into her house? Next, what does she do when she cannot fall asleep when retiring or after waking up in the middle of the night? Does she stay in bed, worrying about her sleep, or does she get up and go to another room and read a book or engage in some other peaceful activity until she is tired and ready for sleep?

Third, you need to inquire about symptoms of depression, anxiety, or any other emotional problems that might be contributing to her sleep disturbance. These are the most common causes of sleep disturbance in later life. Although you have already initiated this discussion, you will need to explore it further in future talks with Kathrine. You know that she worries about her son's health condition. How much does her son's health worry her, and why? Is it because he is her only major source of emotional support? What other things does she think about at night when she can't sleep? Her hospital bills? Her increasing disability from arthritis and fear of becoming dependent on others? Perhaps an argument that she had with her sister several months ago, with whom she has not spoke since? Is she afraid of dying in her sleep, as her husband did five years ago?

Fourth, are there inadequately treated medical problems that are causing insomnia? Is she experiencing shortness of breath from congestive heart failure after lying down that awakens her during the night? Does she have gastroesophageal reflux (heartburn) that interferes with her sleep when she lies down flat on her bed? Is she awakened by the need to go to the bathroom because of a water pill she is taking for her blood pressure or her heart disease? Does the chronic pain from her arthritis take a couple of hours to ease off after she takes her pain medication at night, and then returns in two or three hours after the pain medication wears off? Is Kathrine overweight and therefore at risk for experiencing *sleep apnea,* a condition in which people stop breathing during sleep and have little awakenings throughout the night that prevent them from getting the deep sleep they need. The answers to any of the above questions may reveal important clues to the cause of Kathrine's sleep problems.

Relevant History

On further questioning, you learn that Kathrine has had a history of sleep problems dating back five years after her husband passed away; prior to that time, she reports no problems. Family members tell you that she was appropriately sad and grieved during the year following her husband's death but has adjusted quite well since then. Her excellent performance working at the church, until just recently, provides further information suggesting successful adjustment to his death. When talking with Kathrine, she does not appear to be depressed, nor does she appear to be worrying excessively about her son's health. She has no history of depression, other psychiatric problems, or substance abuse, and has never needed counseling or nerve medication, other than for her sleep. Furthermore, she has no family history of sleep problems or psychiatric disorder.

You learn that she has taken sleeping medication for some time now, even before her May hospitalization. When you ask her about this, she reports that she took a relatively low dose of this medication and did not increase the dose over time. In the past several months, however, she has also been drinking two glasses of wine to help her relax at night. When you ask her about her sleep habits, you find that she frequently watches TV in her bedroom and eats meals there. Furthermore, if unable to sleep at night, she remains in the bed trying to fall off to sleep; and when she wakes up early in the morning, she stays in bed and worries that she won't be able to fall back to sleep. You also learn that she has arthritis, which has been progressing in severity over the past year; she is afraid to take pain medication because it worsens her constipation and she doesn't want to become "addicted to two medicines." She admits that her arthritis pain has been significantly worse since her hospitalization in May. Kathrine also has mild congestive heart failure and high blood pressure, for which she takes several medications, including a water pill and a high blood pressure pill.

Diagnostic Criteria

Although Kathrine will require further medical evaluation to determine the cause for her sleeplessness, she probably has a sleep disorder, or *insomnia*, which in her case likely has several different causes. First, she has some features of a primary sleep disorder, defined as a problem with falling asleep, staying asleep, or having nonrefreshing sleep that lasts at least one month, causes significant problems with social or occupational functioning, is not caused by another sleep disorder (such as sleep apnea or narcolepsy), is not caused by a mental disorder (such as depression), and is not due to the physiological effects of a medication or medical condition. She does not, however, meet all these criteria, because there are other factors that are affecting her sleep.

Kathrine has two medical conditions that may be affecting her sleep—worsening arthritis and mild congestive heart failure. Her arthritis pain is not adequately controlled during the night by her current medical regimen, and she probably gets short of breath while lying down because of her heart failure. She is also taking medications and other substances that may interfere with her sleep, including a drug that causes her to urinate frequently at night and a medication for blood pressure that may have insomnia as a side effect. Kathrine is also using alcohol as a sleep aid, on top of her regular sleeping medication. Though alcohol may reduce the time it takes to fall asleep, it interferes with the quality of sleep and leads to frequent awakenings during the night. Finally, her sleep habits are poor because she is doing things during the day and at night that will interfere with her ability to establish a regular sleep pattern (e.g., using the bedroom for activities other than sleep and staying in the bed at night even if she can't sleep).

Insomnia is a common problem among older adults. Surveys indicate that as many as 30 percent of persons aged 60 or over suffer from and complain of poor sleep on a regular basis.[1] This results in 20 to 25 percent of elderly persons regularly using sleeping pills.[2] Sleep problems are common after the death of a spouse, and almost 50 percent of bereaved elders experience sleep problems for at least one year following their loss.[3]

Response to Vignette

In response to Kathrine's plea for help, you should encourage her not to feel guilty about her sleep problem and share with her how common this

1. L. E. Miles and W. C. Dement, "Sleep and Aging," *Sleep* 3 (1980): 119-220.
2. "Drugs and Insomnia: The Use of Medications to Promote Sleep," *Journal of the American Medical Association* 251 (1984): 2410-14.
3. P. J. Clayton, J. A. Halikas, and W. L. Mauria, "The Depression of Widowhood," *British Journal of Psychiatry* 120 (1972): 71-78.

problem is. Nevertheless, you should make clear that her problem is not a natural result of getting older and that the majority of older adults sleep very well even into their 80s and 90s (and continue to require seven to eight hours of sleep). Remember that your primary role is one of providing information, reassurance, and support.

You might also offer Kathrine some suggestions to improve her sleep (see the list below). If implementation of these sleep strategies does not lead to significant improvement in sleep, then Kathrine needs further evaluation and treatment for possible medical causes of her insomnia. She should first see a good internist who will take the time to optimally manage her arthritis pain, congestive heart failure, and high blood pressure so that these conditions or their treatments will not contribute to her sleep problems. If sleep problems persist even after her sleep habits improve and her medical conditions and treatments are optimized, she should probably pay a visit to a neurologist who specializes in sleep problems. It is likely that the specialist will need to perform a complete sleep evaluation, including a sleep study that may involve an overnight stay in a sleep lab.

Religious resources may also be utilized to facilitate sleep. Kathrine might be encouraged to focus her mind on God and pray during periods when she cannot sleep. Alternatively, she might be encouraged to read scriptures at night or other inspirational books that might help her to cope better with her sleep, health, and other problems.

You should also offer Kathrine the following suggestions to improve her sleep:

- Follow a regular schedule: Go to bed and get up at the same time each day, and develop a bedtime routine each night that prepares your body to wind down (such as reading a book or taking a warm bath).
- Exercise regularly each day, but do so at least four hours before bedtime.
- Watch your eating and drinking habits. Remove all caffeinated beverages from your diet, including coffee, sodas, and tea; certainly do not drink any of these after 5:00 P.M. A warm glass of milk or a high protein snack (turkey or tuna) before bed may help.
- Do not drink any alcohol or smoke cigarettes before retiring to bed.
- Create a safe sleeping environment: Be sure doors are locked and smoke alarms are on.
- Create a sleeping environment conducive to sleep: Sleep in a well-ventilated, dark room (with a lamp that is easy to switch on and a telephone by the bedside). Use "white noise" to block out disturbing noises from outside the room.
- Use the bedroom only for sleep; if you are still awake fifteen minutes after retiring, get up and go into another room until you feel sleepy again. Do not use the bedroom for any activity other than sleep.

- Avoid worrying about your sleep: Pray or recite Bible verses to get your mind off sleeping.

Treatment Within the Faith Community

Support, loving concern, and tolerance from fellow church members will help Kathrine weather this difficult time in her life. As a pastor, you can do much to promote such attitudes and support within the congregation. Encouraging members to pray for her and with her might provide the encouragement and support she needs so badly. Confidentiality, of course, must be maintained and permission from Kathrine obtained before revealing personal information about her to others.

Indications for Referral

If Kathrine's sleep problems are not better after 4 weeks of sleep habit modification and optimization of pain control and other medical conditions, then she should be referred to a sleep specialist for proper evaluation and treatment. If there is any suggestion that depression, anxiety, or other emotional problems are causing her sleep problems, then referral for psychiatric evaluation and treatment is necessary.

Treatment by Mental Health Specialist

Elderly persons with persistent sleep problems that do not respond to the simple measures listed above should receive a complete medical and psychiatric evaluation to uncover treatable causes for their problem. If sleep problems persist after treatment of medical conditions is optimized, unnecessary medications and alcohol use discontinued, and psychological causes for insomnia ruled out, then judicious and cautious use of medication may facilitate sleep. Low doses of diphenhydramine found in over-the-counter sleeping aids such as Tylenol PM or other preparations may help sleep; however, caution must be displayed when using these drugs because they can impair memory and thinking ability if combined with other medications that also have anticholinergic effects. Sedating antidepressants such as trazodone may facilitate sleep without the addicting effects of sleeping pills. In general, the sleeping pills Restoril, Dalmane, and Valium should be avoided.

Resources

Local Resources

Geriatric medicine specialists, geriatric psychiatrists, general internists, and neurologists are physicians likely to be knowledgeable about geriatric sleep disorders.

National Resources

For general information and books about sleep, contact the Better Sleep Council (BSC), PO Box 13, Washington, DC 20044 (phone 703-683-8371). The Better Sleep Council publishes the *A to Zzzz Guide to*

Better Sleep, an excellent guide for improving sleep. To learn more about sleep disorders, contact the Association of Professional Sleep Societies, 604 Second Street, SW, Rochester, MN 55902. The National Institute on Aging also has numerous resources on geriatric sleep problems; write the NIA Information Center, PO Box 8057, Gaithersburg, MD 20898-8057.

Self-Help Resources

Useful self-help books include *101 Questions About Sleep and Dreams*, published by the Wakefulness-Sleep Education and Research Foundation (W-SERF) and available for about $5; they can be contacted at 4820 Rancho Viejo Drive, Del Mar, CA 92014. The AARP publishes a book entitled *The Sleep Book: Understanding and Preventing Sleep Problems in People Over 50* (around $10); contact AARP at 1909 K Street, NW, Washington, DC 20049.

Every culture has its norms and traditions concerning sleep. These cultural factors may have an immense effect on how much sleep older adults think they should get and on the meaning of sleep loss to them.

Cross-Cultural Issues

Elder Abuse

The Mother and Her Alcoholic Son

Mary is a 79-year-old widow who lives alone and experiences a constellation of physical problems. She can no longer drive her car, infrequently leaves her apartment, and has to walk with a cane. Several people in the church have recently commented that Mary is "going downhill." As her pastor, you are concerned with these reports of her deteriorating condition and accompany the parish nurse on a visit to Mary's home.

Mary's 49-year-old son, who is divorced, alcoholic, and explosive, has left the apartment just before your arrival. Mary looks upset as you begin your pastoral visit. She says, "I love my son dearly, but I am afraid of his temper." Mary reports that her son just left the apartment, out-of-control; he had screamed, thrown objects, and threatened her when she told him she could not give him more money for beer. She reports that last week it had been worse—he had slapped her and pushed her down. Large bruises are on her face, legs, and one forearm. Mary says that although her son is very helpful when he is not drinking, she is afraid to complain because he might stop coming to see her. She asks you and the parish nurse to pray for her and keep her problems secret.

Mary's situation is a clear case of elder abuse, and the destructive reality of her relationship with her son must be addressed. She has reported that her adult son has verbally threatened her, slapped her, and pushed her over; and she has been badly bruised as a result of his assault. The mother must have outside assistance to defuse the escalating violent behavior of the adult son and to create a safe home. The pastoral team will need to use their trust relationship with Mary, and preferably with her adult son as

Pastoral Care Assessment

well, to help both of them understand that it is essential to stop the abuse before Mary suffers permanent injuries or death. Most states require medical personnel such as the parish nurse to report elder abuse to the local department of adult protective services or department on aging. Eight states (Alaska, Connecticut, Georgia, Missouri, Nevada, New Hampshire, Ohio, and Oregon) explicitly obligate clergypersons by law to report elder abuse, while other areas (Guam, Minnesota, and Vermont) require reporting by any person who has knowledge or cause to suspect elder abuse. Some states impose legal penalties for not reporting elder maltreatment. In a situation such as this family's, a social worker is usually sent immediately by the local responsible agency to make an assessment and recommendations for appropriate interventions.

Relevant History

There was a pattern of domestic violence in the family between Mary and her husband when the now adult son was a young child, before the father had become involved in the church and had stopped drinking. The adult son was exposed to violence from his alcoholic father both in the form of observing assaults on his mother and receiving "beatings" as a child. Mary and her son have never talked about the domestic violence that occurred in the family in the early years. Mary always believed it was best "to keep family business private."

Diagnostic Criteria

Elder abuse is the maltreatment or neglect of an elderly person, usually by a relative or other caregiver. Elder abuse or neglect may take several forms:

- *Physical abuse* is the nonaccidental infliction of pain and injury or physical coercion (confinement against one's will). Most commonly this involves hitting, pushing, kicking, slapping, and striking with objects.
- *Psychological abuse* is the infliction of mental anguish with the use of verbal assaults, insults, fear, threats, intimidation, harassment, isolation, and humiliation.
- *Material abuse* is the illegal or improper exploitation or use of funds or other resources.
- *Neglect* means the refusal or failure to provide adequate food, clothing, medical care, or shelter. Neglect may be intentional (e.g., deliberate abandonment or denial of food); or it may be unintentional (e.g., nondeliberate nonprovision of food or health services because of ignorance or genuine inability to provide care). Some elders who are suffering from a mental illness may have self-neglectful behaviors that require interventions.

Several risk factors for elder maltreatment perpetrators have been identified. Most abusers are spouses or adult children of the victim. The abusive person is likely to be mentally ill or a substance abuser or both. Abusers characteristically are excessively dependent for financial assistance on the victimized senior as well as have a history of antisocial or violent behaviors.[1] Violence sometimes can be a learned, maladaptive response to high stress. Families that have a history of interpersonal violence have a greater risk of maltreating elders. Among the risk factors for suffering elder abuse are being female, advanced age, dependency, past abuse, intergenerational conflict, lack of a support system, cognitive impairment, and shared living arrangements with the abuser.

Response to Vignette

Mary is a victim of physical and emotional elder abuse and is in need of emergency medical care for her injuries. She should be examined by the parish nurse, and probably a physician, regarding her physical injuries. Does she have broken bones or has she sustained other injuries as a result of being pushed over by her adult son? She also needs prayer and pastoral care, as she requested, to seek guidance in a painful situation. Like many other elderly parents, she feels she is in a bind. If she reports her son's violence, will he stop seeing her altogether? If she does not permit outside help and the abuse is allowed to continue, and most probably escalate, how can she ever feel safe? She needs pastoral counsel to understand that the present pattern of emotional and physical abuse is not healthy for her or her adult son. It is important that the abuse not be denied but addressed. The mother and her adult son are in a cycle of abuse that will be increasingly dangerous to her and will only increase self-loathing, shame, and alcohol dependency in her adult son. The son must be therapeutically confronted with his unacceptable behavior and have his alcoholism addressed with an aggressive treatment plan.

Treatment Within the Faith Community

The church can play a critical role in the prevention of elder abuse and neglect through fostering public awareness about elder maltreatment and providing services to families at risk for being abusive. Unfortunately, although research indicates clergy are one of the most likely groups of caregivers to encounter cases of elder maltreatment,[2] a study utilizing a national sample indicates that clergy are among the least likely to refer abuse or neglect cases to helping agencies and are rated the least effective at treatment interventions when compared to thirteen other community helpers.[3] Training clergy to recognize and actively respond to elder abuse and neglect is imperative.

1. M. S. Lachs, and K. Pillemer, "Abuse and Neglect of Elderly Persons," *The New England Journal of Medicine* 332, no. 7 (1995): 437-43.
2. J. S. Crouse, D. C. Cobb, B. B. Harris, F. J. Kopecky, and J. Poertner, *Abuse and Neglect of the Elderly in Illinois: Incidence, Characteristics, Legislation and Policy Recommendations* (Springfield: Illinois Department of Aging, 1981).
3. B. E. Blakely and R. Dolon, "The Relative Contributions of Occupation Groups in the Discovery and Treatment of Elder Abuse and Neglect," *Journal of Gerontological Social Work* 17, nos. 1-2 (1991): 183-99.

In a study assessing stress among caregivers of seniors, the caregivers indicated that the greatest single assistance would be a support group in which they could discuss their problems and find emotional support. These caregivers also indicated that short-term respite and help with basic household chores would make it much easier for them to cope with their high stress levels.[4] These are exactly the sort of services that congregations can readily offer at-risk families.

Indications for Referral

Elder abuse is largely a hidden problem that is underrecognized and underreported. The National Center on Elder Abuse estimates that only about one in fourteen of the between 1.5 and 2 million cases of elder abuse are actually reported. A referral to an agency on aging for an evaluation for suspected abuse should be seriously considered when warning signs such as unexplained bruises, broken teeth, burns or cuts, dehydration, malnourishment, lack of cleanliness, excessive fear of staff or family members, signs of confinement (e.g., locked in room), unexplained sexually transmitted diseases, or overmedication and sedation are present.

Treatments by Mental Health Specialist

In the early stages of a treatment plan, a mental health specialist would work with Mary to increase her feelings of security and implement a safety plan if needed (e.g., safe-house placement, order from the court, hospital admission). The specialist would give emotional support and assist Mary in mobilizing her support network, including her faith community. It would be important to educate her about the likely pattern of increased severity and frequency of abuse over time by her adult son if action is not taken to change the dynamics between them. She needs to understand that denial of the abuse will not help him and that facing his problems is necessary if he is going to work on his alcohol dependency. In fact, this crisis may well serve as an opportunity to address long-hidden family issues.

In later stages of treatment, the specialist would help Mary develop more assertiveness skills and assist her in finding a women's or elderly persons' support group. If the son begins to address his problems, it would be helpful to work with the mother and son as a family in a reality-based, problem-solving counseling model. In the longer term, they may choose to explore underlying preexisting conflicts, such as their exposure to domestic violence early in the life of the family and how it may have contributed to the current abusive pattern.

Resources

Local Resources

The Older American Act of 1976 established nursing home ombudsman programs to respond to the abuse and neglect of residents of long-

---

4. S. K. Steinmetz, "Elder Abuse by Family Caregivers: Processes and Intervention Strategies," *Contemporary Family Therapy* 10, no. 4 (1988): 256-71.

term care facilities. This law requires that every resident of a nursing home have access to an ombudsman (advocate and resource person). Clergy who suspect abuse in a nursing home should report through their local state ombudsman. All area agencies on aging operate an information and referral telephone service that can refer people to a wide range of services that can help prevent elder abuse and neglect.

National Resources

Thirty-four states operate statewide, toll-free telephone systems for answering questions about and reporting elder abuse and neglect.[5] Pastoral caregivers should consult state government directories under the listing "Adult Protective Services" or "Department on Aging" or contact the National Center on Elder Abuse, c/o American Public Welfare Association, 810 First Street, NE, Suite 500, Washington, DC 20002 (phone 202-682-2470), for a referral to your state agency. Senior caregivers can call a nationwide toll-free Eldercare Locator number (1-800-677-1116) to identify services for elders in your community.

Self-Help Resources

The New England Journal of Medicine recently published a comprehensive review on the subject of elder abuse and neglect (Mark S. Lachs and Karl Pillemer, "Abuse and Neglect of Elderly Persons," *The New England Journal of Medicine* 332, no. 7 [1995]: 437-43). The National Center on Elder Abuse provides "Fact Sheets" on elder maltreatment, available free to the public, and has an extensive list of low-cost publications available; write c/o American Public Welfare Association, 810 First Street, NE, Suite 500, Washington, DC 20002 (phone 202-682-2470). Other organizations that provide information on elder maltreatment are the Clearinghouse on Abuse and Neglect (CANE), University of Delaware, Newark, DE 19716, and the National Committee for the Prevention of Elder Abuse, c/o Institute on Aging, The Medical Center of Central Massachusetts, 119 Belmont Street, Worcester, MA 01605.

Ethnic-minority elders are more likely to be investigated for elder abuse than are European-American elders.[6] In 1994, the National Center on Elder Abuse found that 21.4 percent of reported elder abuse cases were among African Americans, while 9.6 percent were among Hispanic

Cross-Cultural Issues

---

5. T. Tatara, *An Analysis of State Laws Addressing Elder Abuse, Neglect, and Exploitation* (Washington, DC: National Center on Elder Abuse, 1995).
6. M. S. Lachs, L. Berkman, T. Fulmer, and R. I. Horwitz, "A Prospective Community-Based Pilot Study of Risk Factors for the Investigation of Elder Mistreatment," *Journal of the American Geriatric Society* 42 (1994): 169-73.

Americans. Other research indicates that cultural factors may affect the perception and response to abusive situations. Korean-American elders, when compared to both African-American and European-American elders, were less likely to perceive a given situation as abusive or be willing to seek help.[7]

7. A. Moon and O. Williams, "Perceptions of Elder Abuse and Help-Seeking Patterns Among African-American, Caucasian-American and Korean-American Elderly Women," *The Gerontologist* 33, no. 3 (1993): 386-95.

Death and Dying

He Was Ready

Sam has been diagnosed with terminal brain cancer. He has had treatment to forestall tumor growth, but he has been told it is only a matter of months before his death. He is a decorated World War II veteran, a leader in the community, a devoted husband and father, and an involved believer. Sam holds a deep trust in God's providence here and in the hereafter. He tells you that at times he feels he entered eternity in this life the day he began to accept that "the man upstairs loves me just as I am." His concerns over dying focus on being a "burden to others" and having some input into the decision of where he would die. Overall, there is a warmth and confidence at the heart of Sam as he moves toward death. He believes with confidence that life is a gift and death is a return to the Giver. He is a remarkable man who is as open to his death as he has been to his life. You discuss in detail with Sam, his family, and his medical doctor his medical care choices. His family physician has had experience with palliative care (an approach to medical care that focuses on relieving pain and symptoms for the dying) and Sam makes the choice to receive hospice care at home and later in a residential hospice care setting if the demands become too great on his family and friends. He is thoughtful with details to the end of his days. He has given legal authorization (durable power of attorney for health care) to his wife of almost fifty years, Betty, to make decisions regarding his health care treatment should he become unable to do so for himself. His living will includes his specific instructions as to when to use or refuse medical treatment and when to place him in hospice care. He has made his wishes for medical care known to his medical doctor, his family, and you, his pastor.

The crisis of death places great demands on pastors but offers rich opportunities for ministry. It is critical that you work through your personal issues with death before you offer yourself in ministry to the dying. Becoming truly involved requires the risk of identifying with the person

Pastoral Care Assessment

in pain and may awaken deep-seated fears and unresolved conflicts that can lead to emotional turmoil in the helper. It is impossible to be present for others in times of grief and suffering when you are caught up in your own hidden emotions. There is an axiom among psychotherapists—"You cannot guide others any further than you have been yourself." If you have troublesome unresolved issues with grief and death, seek the counsel of a colleague in ministry or a professional counselor.

Be a good listener. Most dying people wish to talk about the reality of their impending death. Many dying people become isolated because friends and even loved ones may have a difficult time facing the finality of death. Your sacramental presence can open the way for the dying to say what they feel if you listen and give them time and emotional hospitality.

Relevant History

Sam is a devoted and knowledgeable Christian who has very definite ideas about his funeral service. You discuss his wish that his funeral be focused on worship and thanksgiving. He takes pleasure in knowing that favorite songs and scriptures will be a part of the planned service.

Diagnostic Criteria

"The Naturalness of Dying," by Jack D. McCue (*Journal of the American Medical Association* 273, no. 13 [1995]: 1039-43), is a valuable examination of current, often conflicted, thinking about death and dying in medicine. The author suggests that modern medicine needs to stop viewing the death of some elderly as a failure, especially when death is an expected and desired event. Doctor McCue suggests that some deaths are natural and courageous ends to life and should not become starkly unnatural with the overuse of medical technology.

Response to Vignette

This is the case of a person who is very intentional about his process of dying. He is knowledgeable about his choices of palliative care and hospice. He gives legal authority to his spouse to carry out his wishes if he becomes incapacitated or comatose; only 9 percent of Americans have such a "living will." He is an older person who faced death as a young man in war and has lived his life with gusto and deep satisfaction. He has an abiding trust in God. He is the sort of person who is an inspiration to those who minister to him. His funeral service can and should be a celebrative thanksgiving of several hundred people who have been touched by his generous life and saintly witness.

Pastors know by experience that Sam's reaction to death is not always the case. Human beings have a variety of responses to death and dying. In some cases death is anticipated and comes as a relief after extensive suffering. Sometimes people find death unacceptable and remain in denial and refuse to talk about their pending death. Others become angry and "rage against the dying of the light" (in Dylan Thomas's phrase) while still others feel depressed and despondent. Working with the dying can require many pastoral skills—patience, understanding, and acceptance among them. Generally, dying persons sort through these feelings and come to some degree of acceptance. What is critical in pastoral work is communicating the ultimate care and concern of God as the person makes the journey toward death.

The seventeenth-century Anglican divine Jeremy Taylor wrote in *The Rule and Exercise of Holy Dying* (1651), "It is a great art to die well, and to be learnt by men in health." The church is called to speak to the reality of death in a death-denying society that dresses up the dead for burial as if they were still alive. Death is a fact of life, and talking about it can lessen our fear and help us live in the present. Christians understand death as a bridge from this life to eternity in God.

Treatment Within the Faith Community

There are many means by which congregations can provide spiritual, emotional, and practical support for the dying and their families. For example, the terminally ill at First United Methodist Church in Tempe, Arizona, are encouraged to write a spiritual journey during their last months and days; and later, with the writer's permission, portions are used in the funeral service. The church keeps records of members' deaths on a computerized system that automatically reminds pastors to visit or write the bereaved family members on monthly and yearly anniversaries. The Genoa United Methodist Church in Houston, Texas, assigns a care leader to each person in the church who is dying. When the death occurs, the caring team of several persons visits the bereft family. The day of the funeral, the caring team takes a meal to the family's home. The caring team continues to contact the family to give support after the death. The First United Methodist Church of Schenectady, New York (518-374-4403), has a "Dark Night" worship service during late Advent, reminding the church of the difficulty of the season for the widowed.[1]

Research suggests that persons with a strong faith may have less anxiety, depression, and general distress about death than persons without strong faith. It is also interesting that persons who believe that the most important aspect of religion is that it offers life after death have higher levels of depression and distress about dying. It would appear that the study supports the case that a living faith commitment comes prior to lowered discomfort about death.[2]

Indications for Referral

If members of the family are not coping well with the pending death of a loved one, an assessment for complicated bereavement (see case 1) is called for.

1. R. P. O'Hara, "Congregations Offer Hope," *Circuit Rider* (Sept. 1995), 5.
2. K. A. Alvarado, D. I. Templer, C. Bresler, and S. Thomas-Dobson, "The Relationship of Religious Variables to Death Depression and Death Anxiety," *Journal of Clinical Psychology* 51, no. 2 (1995): 202-4.

Treatment by Mental Health Specialist

If a family is having a particularly difficult time facing the anticipated loss, a family therapist could be useful in facilitating communication. In a family group setting, the therapist would encourage family members to express their feelings about the experience of loss before the actual death occurs.

Dying persons may experience depression, severe anxiety, psychosis, or a number of other psychiatric symptoms that require treatment by a mental health specialist. The indications for referral are the same as when these symptoms occur in an elder who is not dying. The dying process should be a relatively peaceful one; when it is not and psychiatric symptoms are interfering with the dying person's ability to relate to loved ones, then referral to a specialist becomes necessary. A psychiatrist with an interest in treating older persons, some experience in treating the mental disturbances of dying persons, and a thorough knowledge of psychopharmacology should be sought. Symptoms of pain, depression, and anxiety frequently overlap, and certain medications prescribed for the relief of depression (the tricyclic antidepressants) can also help relieve both anxiety and pain. Although dying persons frequently experience mild delirium during the final stages, prominent and frightening delusions and hallucinations require direct treatment with antipsychotics.

Resources

Local Resources

The cost of a traditional funeral and in-ground burial is between $5,000 and $6,000. Memorial societies are nonprofit organizations, staffed almost completely by volunteers, which advocate economical funerals and freedom to conduct funerals to conform to one's faith values. Memorial societies arrange agreements with funeral providers for members to reduce costs. Membership cost is low. They are found in all areas of North America and provide useful educational materials on planning affordable funeral options. You may obtain information about your local memorial society by calling 1-800-458-5563 or by writing Funeral and Memorial Societies of America, 6900 Lost Lake Road, Egg Harbor, WI 54209.

National Resources

Hospice is a medically coordinated, interdisciplinary team approach that focuses on compassionate methods of caring for the terminally ill. Hospice care focuses on pain and symptom control (called *palliative care*), with the goal that one can live one's last days with dignity and comfort, at home or in a homelike environment. According to the National Hospice Organization's Hospice Facts Sheet (August 1995), about 70 percent of persons served by hospice care are 65 years of age or older, and most hospice patients have terminal cancer. The great majority of the persons working in hospice care (mostly volunteers) report their faith is "very important in their lives." Seventy-five percent of the more than two thousand hospices in the United States are Medicare-certified or pending certification. Most managed care plans and private insurance plans include hospice benefits. You can locate a hospice in your area by calling the Hospice Helpline at 1-800-658-8898 or by writing 1901 North Moore Street, Suite 901, Arlington, VA 22209.

Self-Help Resources

A *Gentle Death*, by Marilynne Seguin and Cheryl K. Smith (Toronto: Key Porter Books, 1994), is an informative and well written book about how one can make and take choices about death and dying within the contemporary medical system. *The Pastoral Role in Caring for the Dying and Bereaved*, edited by Brian P. O'Connor et al. (New York: Praeger, 1986), offers several thoughtful chapters on pastoral care responses to the dying. *Death, Grief and Caring Relationships*, by Richard A. Kalish (Monterey, Calif.: Brooks/Cole Publishing, 1981), is a thorough and helpful text on many aspects of death and dying. *The Denial of Death*, by Ernest Becker (New York: Free Press, 1973), is a provocative and brilliant appraisal of the psychological dynamics of death.

Faith communities differ in the manner of dealing with death and dying. Christians could learn much from the Jewish practice of remembering the dead in each Sabbath service for a year.

Cross-Cultural Issues

PART THREE

Resources

A Plan to Meet the Needs of Older Adults

As we indicated earlier, pastors and their staff will be increasingly called on to meet the mental health needs of older congregants. These older congregants and their families will simply have nowhere else to turn, as public funds for mental health services become more and more scarce. In thinking about and discussing this issue with clergy around the country, we have come up with a plan that we think will enable churches both to meet the needs of their older members and to put into practice the Judeo-Christian principles that are the bedrock of their faith.

Be aware of and understand the twenty-five major psychological and spiritual needs of older adults. Although space does not allow us to go into the details of each need here, we will list them (not in order of importance):

- a need for meaning and purpose
- a need for a sense of usefulness
- a need for vision
- a need for hope
- a need for support in coping with loss and change
- a need to adapt to increasing dependency
- a need to transcend difficult circumstances
- a need for personal dignity
- a need to express feelings
- a need to be thankful
- a need for continuity with the past
- a need to accept and prepare for death and dying
- a need to be certain that God exists
- a need to believe that God is on their side
- a need to experience God's presence
- a need to experience God's unconditional love
- a need to pray alone, with others, and for others
- a need to read and be inspired by Scripture
- a need to worship God, individually and corporately

Be Aware of and Understand the Needs

- a need to love and serve God
- a need for fellowship with others
- a need to love and serve others
- a need to confess and be forgiven
- a need to forgive others
- a need to cope with the death of loved ones

It is essential that pastors be aware of these needs, understand how they are met, and realize their psychological and spiritual consequences in order to organize and teach others how to address these needs.

Realize That One Person Cannot Do It Alone

Given the sheer numbers of older persons in congregations and their level of need, a pastor does not have the time to individually address each congregant's situation (in many areas of the country, more 50 percent of the members in the average congregation are aged 65 and older). Moses encountered the same dilemma after he had led the Israelites out of Egypt and was trying to deal with all the people's problems on his own: "Moses took his seat to serve as judge for the people, and they stood around him from morning till evening" (Exodus 18:13 NIV). Jethro, his father-in-law, saw this and asked Moses, " 'What is this you are doing for the people? Why do you alone sit as judge, while all these people stand around you from morning till evening? . . . What you are doing is not good. You and these people who come to you will only wear yourselves out. The work is too heavy for you; you cannot handle it alone' " (Exodus 18:14, 17-18 NIV). Jethro then made the following suggestion:

> "You must *be the people's representative before God* and bring their disputes to him. *Teach them* the decrees and laws, and *show them* the way to live and the duties they are to perform. But *select capable men [and women]* from all the people—men who fear God, trustworthy men who hate dishonest gain—and appoint them as officials over thousands, hundreds, fifties and tens. Have them serve as judges for the people at all times, but have them bring every difficult case to you; the simple cases they can decide themselves. That will make your load lighter, because they will share it with you. If you do this and God so commands, you will be able to stand the strain, and all these people will go home satisfied." (Exodus 18:19-23 NIV, emphasis added)

Develop a System of Assigned Responsibilities

Based on the above advice from the Scriptures, we suggest that the pastor first recognize what his or her primary responsibilities are. Then, he or she should select capable and dependable people from his or her staff and congregation, and assign the less urgent duties and tasks to them.

1. For a more fully developed discussion of these needs, see H. G. Koenig, T. Lamar, and B. Lamar, *A Gospel for the Mature Years: Finding Fulfillment by Knowing and Using Your Gifts* (Binghamton, N.Y.: Haworth Press, 1997).

Responsibilities of the Pastor

Following the principle of Exodus 18:19-23, we see that the pastor's primary responsibility is to act as the people's "representative" before God. In other words, the pastor seeks a close and living relationship with God and works to live an exemplary life before the congregation. This is sought through prayer, holy living, and study. The pastor brings the needs of his or her congregation before God, seeks to discern the purposes of God, and tries to interpret God's response with the people. Just as important as being the people's representative before God is seeking to "teach" and "show them the way to live." In other words, the pastor in his or her sermons and daily relations gives guidance, motivates, and inspires the members of his or her congregation to participate in the ministry of the church to the disabled, infirm, less fortunate older adults in the congregation.

We believe that the most important areas in which the people of faith need teaching and motivation are summarized in the great commandments: (1) "Love the LORD your God with all your heart and with all your soul and with all your strength," and (2) "Love your neighbor as yourself" (Deuteronomy 6:5, Leviticus 19:18 NIV; with parallels in Matthew 22:37-40; Mark 12:30-31; Luke 10:27). Both the Hebrew Scriptures and the Greek New Testament make these commandments the very foundation of the Judeo-Christian faith. An emphasis on these two commandments will provide the necessary framework upon which to build and implement the rest of the plan of ministry that we are suggesting. People of faith need to develop a solid, personal, fulfilling relationship with God, as well as understand the importance of loving and serving one another, and we are unlikely to do so unless we are genuinely inspired.

The next responsibility of the pastor involves selecting capable persons in the congregation to take on leadership tasks. Specifically, appointing persons to lead small groups of eight to ten persons that meet regularly in homes. The pastor will need to educate and equip these persons to take on the responsibilities of home group leaders (see below). Regular meetings between pastor, pastoral staff, and home group leaders every two to four weeks can both serve an educational purpose and facilitate the sharing of difficult problem situations. When difficult cases arise, these can be addressed (preferably without mentioning names) at the group meetings, and the pastor or pastoral staff can give the home group leaders specific guidance on how to address the problem; for these more difficult situations, the pastor will need to take a more active leadership role.

While the pastor's primary concern must be that of meeting the spiritual and psychological needs of congregants, he or she must be aware of and alert for potential medical and legal issues that could arise, and have a plan on how to respond. If an older person with serious depression who is receiving ministry in a home group suddenly commits suicide, then family members may become angry and decide to sue the church for not referring the person soon enough to a mental health specialist. In potentially suicidal cases, it is essential to make a timely referral to a health professional. It is the pastor's responsibility to closely monitor the activity of home group leaders in order to identify these situations before they get out of hand, ensuring that there is communication with mental health professionals if the need is indicated. As time permits, the pastor should also be involved in networking with community social service and mental health agencies, as well as in advanced counseling with difficult cases and in hospital visitation.

Responsibilities of the Pastoral Staff

Pastoral staff play important roles in this plan of ministry. First, church staff must be knowledgeable about mental health and social service resources that exist in the community. Where can an older congregant or a family member receive support and information about Alzheimer's disease? What home health agencies in the area are reliable and cost-effective? Where can information be obtained about social security, Medicare, assistive devices, home services for the disabled, and so forth? Which nursing homes provide the best care? Which health professionals have the expertise necessary to deal with problems that older congregants are likely to have? Pastoral staff should establish a *referral network* of health professionals who are competent, available, sensitive to older persons' religious values, and easy to communicate to and work with. Lines of communication should also be set up with community mental health and social service agencies, as well as an area agency on aging. These relationships will facilitate the flow of information and collaboration in difficult cases. Pastoral staff should also be primarily responsible for advanced counseling with older adults and their families when complex problems arise and should coordinate hospital and nursing home visitations.

Responsibilities of Home Group Leaders

The tasks of home group leaders include

- providing a time and place for the group to meet (usually once per week)
- acting as a group discussion facilitator
- identifying and clarifying individual needs
- assessing and, initially, managing problems as they arise
- communicating closely with pastor and pastoral staff

Initial management of problems typically involves personal counseling, locating practical resources (with help from pastoral staff), and mobilizing and directing other group members to help out. At all times, individual confidentiality must be maintained, and the specific nature of problems should be revealed only after explicit permission has been obtained from the older person or the older person's family or both. If the problem is not resolved or becomes more complicated, then the home group leader should (with permission) involve the pastor or the pastoral staff. If referral for professional assistance becomes necessary, this should be a joint decision with the pastoral team.

The content of small group discussions may vary widely, either focusing on the past week's sermon or more directly on the spiritual and psychological needs of older adults.

Responsibilities of Church Members

The most important part of this ministry plan is the active involvement of all older congregants (and preferably younger members as well) in home groups. The pastor must repeatedly encourage and affirm active participation in these groups. What works best is that the pastor choose the home group leaders, and the church members choose the specific home group they wish to attend (often the one closest to their home). The responsibilities of church members in these home groups are to

- regularly attend and prepare for meetings
- listen to and support other members during group meetings
- involve themselves in small group prayer
- contact other group members during the week by telephone or in person to provide support, encouragement, prayer, and monitoring
- provide practical assistance with needs (preparing meals, providing respite, doing home chores, providing transportation, and so forth)

Church members who are severely disabled, physically ill, in nursing homes, or hospitalized should be given special assignments by their group leader or pastor. These assignments typically involve praying for specific needs of other members of the congregation. In summary, each church member is helped to identify what their special talent or gift is, and then is encouraged to use this talent to serve God through serving others.[2]

2. See Koenig, Lamar, and Lamar, A Gospel for the Mature Years.

Empowerment in the Mental Health Network: Building Your Team

> *Properly conceived, referral is a means of using a team effort to help a troubled person.*
>
> *—Howard Clinebell,*
> Basic Types of Pastoral Care and Counseling

Basic Types of Pastoral Care

A parish-based clergyperson in the United States is more likely than a mental health specialist to have a diagnosed severely mentally distressed senior seek his or her assistance.[1] Most of those who consult clergy never make any contact with a mental health professional.[2] Numerous studies indicate that fewer than 10 percent of persons who seek pastoral help are referred to mental health specialists.[3] Experts estimate that the rate of referrals should be close to three times the present rate given the severity of the problems taken to pastors.[4] Clergy indicate that they feel seminary training has not adequately prepared them to respond to the serious emotional and family problems encountered in the parish, yet many report they are unlikely to seek additional training in counseling.[5]

It is basic to responsible ministry that pastors be prepared to recognize the mental health needs of older adults and make effective referrals, especially in crisis situations such as suicide and major depression, psychosis, severe dementia, drug and alcohol dependency, elder abuse, and psychological trauma. Clergy are woefully unprepared to respond to mental health emergencies.[6] The central task of a pastor within the mental health network is to identify the needs of the person who seeks assistance

---

1. An earlier version of this section appeared as "Building a Network," in *Circuit Rider* (May 1996), 10-11 (written by Andrew J. Weaver and Harold G. Koenig).
2. A. A. Hohmann and D. B. Larson, "Psychiatric Factors Predicting Use of Clergy," in *Psychotherapy and Religious Values*, ed. E. L. Worthington Jr. (Grand Rapids, Mich.: Baker Book House, 1993), 71-84.
3. A. J. Weaver, "Has There Been a Failure to Prepare and Support Parish-Based Clergy in Their Role as Front-Line Community Mental Health Workers? A Review," *The Journal of Pastoral Care* 49, no. 2 (1995): 129-49.
4. R. R. Lee, "Referral As an Act of Pastoral Care," *The Journal of Pastoral Care* 30, no. 10 (1976): 186-97.
5. D. K. Orthner, *Pastoral Counseling: Caring and Caregivers in the United Methodist Church* (Nashville: General Board of Higher Education and Ministry of The United Methodist Church, 1986).
6. Weaver, 129-49.

and connect the person to a larger circle of specialized helpers. This section of the book makes several suggestions as to how pastors can become more empowered within the mental health network.

1. Develop a working relationship with at least one, preferably several, mental health professionals who have a comprehensive knowledge of the mental health services for seniors in your community and are willing to work with you as a colleague. Seek out mental health specialists who are open to people of faith and have some appreciation of the scientific fact that religious commitment can be a positive coping resource for seniors in times of crisis. Do not be timid; be assertive. Interview the mental health specialist on the telephone before you refer a senior in need who will be trusting your counsel. Ask the specialists direct questions to assess their skill level, expertise, and fee schedule. Ask them detailed questions about their experience, training, and education. What sorts of cases have they worked with in the past? What specialties do they have? How do they develop a treatment plan for various crisis situations and other mental health problems? How easily can they be located in a crisis? Are they willing to do some low fee work? Keep a record of available providers to whom you can refer your older congregants in an emergency.

2. Develop a list of professional and community resources before you are faced with a mental health emergency. Where is the nearest hospital emergency room, in case an elderly parishioner becomes suicidal or psychotic? Where is the local mental health center located? How can you contact social services, and what can they do for you in an emergency? Where are the local senior centers? To whom do you report elder abuse in your area? If you live in one of the several states that mandate elder abuse reporting by clergy, what are the procedures for reporting? Where can you take a homeless mentally ill older person for mental health care? Most areas have published listings of the human resources for the elderly in their region. Using these, develop appropriate plans of action with your mental health colleagues.

3. Continued education is a must. Pastors report that no matter how long they serve in the parish, counseling skills, unlike other ministry skills, do not increase without continuing education.[7] Referral skills are closely related to evaluation skills, since the clinical evaluation usually guides the course of action. Research tells us that training clergy in diagnostic skills enhances their ability as pastoral counselors as well as their effectiveness in making referrals.[8] Clergy with the highest rates of referrals have attended a workshop or seminar in the area of mental health in the past year.

4. Pastor refer thyself. Pastors in emotional turmoil are going to be

7. Orthner.
8. N. A. Clemens, R. B. Corradi, and M. Wasman, "The Parish Clergy As a Mental Health Resource," *Journal of Religion and Health* 17, no. 4 (1978): 227-32.

limited in their ability to help those who ask for their assistance. A significant number of pastors report having a poor psychological profile. They feel isolated, suffer emotional distress and poor self-esteem, lack hopefulness, and find it difficult to reach out for help.[9] This indicates that numbers of clergy and their spouses need counseling, whether they recognize it or not. By contrast, pastors who feel greater competence as counselors are more willing to seek outside assistance for their personal and family problems and are much less prone to alienation and burnout. Apparently, those who trust in their ability to help others are more likely to seek help for themselves as well as enjoy a greater satisfaction in ministry.[10]

9. Orthner.
10. Ibid.

Summary and Conclusions

Congregations across the United States are swelling their ranks with more and more older adults (about 50 percent among mainline denominations). These persons have special mental and physical health needs that must be addressed by pastors and their staff. This trend will only continue over the next thirty years, as our population ages and federal dollars available to care for these needs diminish. For this reason, pastors need to know about the most common mental disorders that occur in later life, including how to assess and diagnose them, what types of treatments can be initiated in the faith community, when referral is necessary, and whom to refer to. This book identifies twenty-nine of the most common mental health conditions that occur in later life, provides illustrative cases, lists local and national resources available to help with management, and suggests when and to whom to refer for professional help.

Because of the important role that religion plays in the lives of many older adults and religion's now demonstrated relationship with better mental health, it is important that pastors, theology students, and chaplains be knowledgeable about assessment, diagnosis, and treatment options for elders with emotional or mental illness. Part of treatment involves directing the elder toward professional help, if needed, and mobilizing persons in the local community to help meet needs for support and companionship of both the person in need and the caregiver. Maintaining strict confidentiality is essential. Knowing when to refer is also crucial, given the medical-legal atmosphere of liability if a poor result should occur. Also, knowledge about the wide variety of treatment options will help allay anxiety and fear over not knowing what to do.

One of the best ways the pastor can intervene is to establish a system of delegated responsibility within the faith community, inspire and motivate members of the congregation to deepen their faith and relationship with God, and then help them identify and use their talents and abilities to help those in greater need than themselves. These ministries can bring fulfillment, purpose, and usefulness to the caregiver.

John Wesley, the founder of the Methodist church, lived to be 88. Many of his most productive years in service came after age 60. Wesley wrote in his diary in 1788 on the occasion of his eighty-fifth birthday:

241

I am not so agile as I was in time past. . . . I have daily some pain. . . . I find likewise some decay in my memory in regard to names and things lately passed. . . .

> My remnant of days
> I spend to His praise
> Who died the whole world to redeem:
> Be they many or few,
> My days are His due,
> And they all are devoted to Him.[1]

---

1. John Wesley, *The Journal of the Rev. John Wesley, A.M.*, ed. Nehemiah Curnock, vol. 7 (London: Epworth Press, 1938), 408-9.

Glossary of Terms

addiction: The condition that arises when a medication or drug causes physical *tolerance* (the need for increasing doses to achieve the desired effect) and *withdrawal symptoms* (unpleasant, intolerable symptoms) when use of the drug is stopped. Someone who is addicted to a drug is also *dependent* on that drug.

adult day care: A day care center offering health-related and rehabilitation services to physically and mentally impaired elderly people.

Alzheimer's disease: A form of *dementia* that causes a severe, progressive, irreversible deterioration of intellectual functioning.

Alzheimer's unit: A special section in a skilled nursing facility that is physically designed to care for Alzheimer's patients (with open areas to allow patients to wander and move about freely). The nursing staff at such a unit is specially trained to handle the unique problems of persons with Alzheimer's disease.

anticholinergic: Causing dry mouth, difficulty passing one's urine, blurred vision, and effects on heart rhythm. Frequently in older persons, this can cause confusion and disorientation and sometimes frank *psychosis*. Some medications have this as a major side effect.

antidepressant: A nonaddictive medication that is used to treat depression. There are many different kinds of antidepressants; all work about equally well (60 to 80 percent of the time). Side effects, however, vary between antidepressants.

antihistamine: Often an over-the-counter medication taken to relieve hay fever symptoms or allergies, an antihistamine can also be taken at bedtime to help with sleep, because it has sedation as a side effect. Such medications can have adverse effects in the elderly because of their *anticholinergic* side effects.

aphasia: Loss of the capacity to use or understand language.

bereavement: Usually indicates the loss of a spouse through death, although it can refer to the death of any very close friend or family member.

Benzodiazepine: A minor tranquilizer like Valium that can be addictive in some persons, particularly those who have a past history of drug or alcohol abuse. Persons with anxiety disorders, such as panic disorder, have a biological need for this type of medication.

bipolar: Refers to a psychiatric disorder in which a person experiences extreme highs (mania) and extreme lows (depression) that may alternate with each other.

cognitive: Having to do with the ability to think or reason. Sometimes used to describe memory processes. The operation of the mind, as distinct from emotional experience.

commit: Oftentimes, mentally ill persons become at risk for harming themselves or harming others; if such a person refuses to see a mental health professional, then family members, friends, a pastor, or a physician may decide to commit the person. This involves going to the magistrate's office and filling out commitment papers. A sheriff will then pick up the mentally ill person and take him or her to a doctor's office for evaluation.

compulsion: The need to perform a certain behavior over and over again in order to relieve anxiety. Examples of repetitive behaviors include washing hands, taking showers, checking locks on doors, and counting tiles on the ceiling. A person with a compulsion sometimes loses control over his or her ability to stop these behaviors. An indicator of obsessive-compulsive disorder.

delusion: A fixed, false belief that a person cannot be dissuaded from. Delusions may be plausible (e.g., a belief that someone is following or stealing from the person) or bizarre (e.g., a belief that there is an antenna that is sending out signals planted in the person's brain).

delirium: A temporary state of impaired mental alertness, often associated with hallucinations, delusions, or agitation; memory and concentration are disturbed, and persons are frequently disoriented with respect to time and place. Delirium is different from *dementia*, which causes more permanent memory and concentration problems and does not impair level of alertness.

dementia: A clinical term describing a group of brain disorders that cause a relatively permanent impairment of thinking, memory, and judgment; it does not impair level of alertness.

dependence: Often used synonymously with *addiction*; both *tolerance* (need for increasing amounts of a substance to achieve the desired effect) and *withdrawal symptoms* on stopping the substance (worsening of symptoms for which the medication or drug was taken, or appearance of new unpleasant symptoms) must occur for dependence to be present.

disorder: In this text, a disorder is a psychiatric condition that causes impairment in a person's social, occupational, or mental functioning or otherwise significantly interferes with a person's quality of life (or the quality of life of others around a person).

durable power of attorney for health care: Legal authorization given to a person of your choosing (usually a spouse, close relation, or trusted clergy member) to make decisions for you about health care treatment if you become unable to do so for yourself. It may include such matters as when to use or refuse medical treatment or provisions about *nursing home* placement.

family care homes: Provide custodial care for two to six unrelated adults, including room and board, personal care and hygiene assistance, supervision and activities; no medical care is provided. Many of these are not licensed by the state.

geriatrics: The branch of medicine that specializes in the conditions of the elderly.

gerontologist: A *psychologist*, sociologist, nurse, *social worker*, physician, or pastor who specializes in the medical, mental, or behavioral aspects of aging.

geropsychiatrist: A psychiatrist who specializes in the mental health problems of older adults. There is now special board certification in this field (certificate of added qualifications).

grief: A normal emotional reaction to the loss of anyone or anything that is very important to the person; this usually refers to the temporary sadness that follows the loss of a spouse or other loved one.

guardianship: When an *incompetent* person is unable to make decisions for himself or herself (and has not yet signed over a durable *power of attorney* to someone), a family member, close friend, or court-appointed stranger appeals for guardianship. Court proceedings are held to appoint a guardian to make financial or health care decisions (or both) for the *incompetent* person.

hyperthyroidism: A medical condition in which the body's thyroid gland (just underneath the Adam's apple in the neck) produces too much thyroid hormone. Excess thyroid hormone can cause nervousness, shakiness, increased blood pressure, and rapid heartbeat. In some cases, especially in older adults, a condition called "apathetic hyperthyroidism" can occur, in which high thyroid levels result in depression.

hypochondriasis: A preoccupation with and fear of having a disease that the doctors haven't diagnosed yet. Frequently, older persons fear that they may have cancer despite repeated reassurance to the contrary by their physicians. This is different from *somatization*, in which a person has many physical complaints but no objective basis for those complaints.

incompetent: Unable, because of a mental or neurological condition, to make rational decisions and weigh the risks and benefits of alternative choices. This is usually a legal definition (made by a judge in a court of law), but the testimony or deposition from the examining physician often carries heavy weight.

insomnia: Difficulty sleeping; either being unable to fall asleep at night, waking up frequently during the night, or waking up too early (two hours before usual) in the morning and being unable to get back to sleep.

living will: Written instructions making known what one wants done if, for example, one is gravely ill and the only way one can be kept alive is by artificial means.

meals-on-wheels: A program that delivers nutritious meals to housebound seniors for little or no cost.

Medicaid: A state-run health insurance program for persons without health insurance or those who cannot afford to pay for their medical care. Federal funds partly support the program.

Medicare: A federal health insurance program that helps defray medical expenses for Americans aged 65 and older.

memorial service: A service for the dead held without the body present, which does not require extensive mortician services.

narcotic analgesic: A drug derived from opium or synthetically made that provides relief from pain and sedation. Narcotic analgesics include Darvocet, Percocet, Dilaudid, Morphine, Codeine, Demerol, and others.

nursing home: Nursing homes provide twenty-four-hour care and medical supervision. They are divided into intermediate care facilities (for patients who require periodic, low level nursing care and some physician input) and skilled care facilities (for patients who require continuous nursing supervision and care that is under the direction of a physician); often, both intermediate and skilled care are provided in a single facility.

obsession: The mental state, occurring in obsessive-compulsive disorder, of having recurrent thoughts about something or someone. The recurrent thoughts are difficult to stop and difficult to control.

ombudsman: A person designated to advocate and protect the rights of persons living in long-term care facilities. An ombudsman is given authority to investigate elder or dependent adult abuse and initiate corrective action.

panic: A state of extreme fright that comes on without warning. It lasts about five minutes and then spontaneously subsides. Often associated with difficulty breathing and rapid heart rate.

paranoia: A mental state in which persons are fearful that other persons are trying to hurt them or harm them in some way. While this may be true to some extent, the paranoid person perceives this to be far more severe than the circumstances indicate.

parish nurse: A nurse working in a congregation promoting physical, emotional, and spiritual wellness. Parish nurses train and coordinate volunteers, develop and facilitate support groups, liaison within the health care system, refer to community resources, and provide health education. A 1994 survey estimated a national total of two thousand parish nurses functioning in congregations.

personality disorder: A lifelong, maladaptive pattern of reacting to stress and relating to other people that causes distress and turmoil in the life of the person or those surrounding the person.

phobia: A persistent, unrealistic fear of an object or situation. For example, claustrophobia (fear of closed places) or agoraphobia (fear of leaving home or other safe environments).

power of attorney: A competent person signs over to another person the right to make either financial or health care decisions for him or her, should he or she become incompetent. A durable power of attorney allows an easy transition to guardianship, should the person remain incompetent.

psychiatrist: A medical doctor (physician) who is specially trained to handle psychological problems. He or she can administer medication, hospitalize patients, and administer electroconvulsive treatments. A psychiatrist may treat with psychotherapy, medication, or both.

psychologist: A doctor with a research degree (Ph.D.) who is trained to use a variety of treatment modalities including individual and group psychotherapy, cognitive therapy, behavioral modification, psychodynamic psychotherapy, and family systems therapy.

psychosis: A mental condition, either temporary or long-standing, that involves hallucinations or delusions or paranoia; this is often what people refer to when they say a person is "crazy."

psychotherapy: A process in which an individual seeks to resolve personal problems or achieve growth through verbal communication with a mental health professional.

rest home: Also called "domiciliary care," a rest home is a residential facility that provides twenty-four-hour supervision and personal care services to adults who can no longer live at home but who do not need the constant medical supervision available in *nursing homes*. Rest homes are licensed by the state.

schizophrenia: A chronic mental disorder associated with auditory and visual hallucinations and bizarre delusions. When people worry about "going crazy," this is the condition they are usually worried about. However, most persons with this condition have little insight into their condition and do not worry about it.

serotonin: A brain chemical that plays a role in controlling mood and emotions. Certain *antidepressants*, known as "serotonin reuptake inhibitors" help to replenish this chemical in the brain when it is deficient, as in states of depression or anxiety disorders.

sleeping pill: A medication used to help people fall asleep more quickly and sleep longer. Most of these medications (especially *benzodiazepines*) are addictive; in other words, the longer you take them, the more of them you have to take to get the desired effect (*tolerance*).

social worker: A trained professional who assists seniors and their families in understanding the processes of aging, as well as coordinates access to available services.

somatization: A preoccupation with one's bodily functions. Persons who somatize may convert psychological problems into physical ones. They frequently have many, many physical complaints. It is often difficult to distinguish such persons from those who have a real physical illness, especially in the elderly.

substance abuse: Excess, abnormal, or illegal use of drugs or alcohol.

tolerance: The need for increasingly greater doses of a drug to achieve a desired effect. Some people refer to this as *addiction*.

tranquilizer: A medication used to produce sedation or a calming effect. Major tranquilizers include Haldol, Prolixin, Thorazine, and Mellaril. These medications are used to treat psychosis. Minor tranquilizers include Valium, Xanax, Ativan, Klonopin, and Librium (*benzodiazepines*) and are used to treat anxiety.

visiting nurse: A trained nurse who visits persons in their homes to monitor their physical condition and implement medical care.

withdrawal symptoms: Unpleasant, intolerable symptoms that occur when the use of a drug or medication is stopped. An indicator of *addiction*.

List of Agencies

Numbers in parentheses after addresses indicate the case studies in which more information on the agency can be found.

AARP (American Association of Retired Persons), 601 E Street, NW, Washington, DC 20049. Telephone: 202-434-2277 and 1-800-424-3410 (1, 14).

AARP: Health Advocacy Services, 1909 K Street, NW, Washington, DC 20049 (16).

AARP: Housing Activities, 1129 Twentieth Street, NW, Suite 400, Washington, DC 20036-3489 (16).

Al-Anon, PO Box 862, Midtown Station, New York, NY 10018. For free literature and meeting information call 1-800-356-9996 (USA) or 1-800-443-4525 (Canada) (22).

Alcoholics Anonymous, General Services Office of Alcoholics Anonymous, Box 459, Grand Central Station, New York, NY 10163. Telephone: 212-870-3400 (22).

Alzheimer's Disease and Related Disorders Association (ADRDA), 919 North Michigan Avenue, Chicago, IL 60611. Telephone: 1-800-621-0379; in Illinois: 1-800-572-6037; for drug fact sheets, call 1-800-272-3900 (14).

Alzheimer's Disease Education and Referral Center (ADEAR), PO Box 8250, Silver Spring, MD 20907-8250 (14).

American Association of Suicidology, 2459 South Ash, Denver, CO 80222. Telephone: 303-765-8485 (6).

American Bar Association's Lawyer Referral and Information Service, 750 North Lake Shore Drive, Chicago, IL 60611 (14).

American Psychiatric Association, 1400 K Street, NW, Washington, DC 20005. Telephone: 202-682-6000 (8, 9).

American Psychological Association, 750 First Street, NE, Washington, DC 20002. Telephone: 202-336-5500 (8).

The American Suicide Foundation, 1045 Park Avenue, New York, NY 10028. Telephone: 212-410-1111. Provides information on preventing suicide.

Anxiety Disorders Association of America, Department A, 6000 Executive Boulevard, Rockville, MD 20852. Telephone: 301-231-9350 (7, 8, 9).

Association for the Advancement of Behavioral Therapy, 305 Seventh Avenue, New York, NY 10001. Telephone: 212-647-1890 (8).

Association of Professional Sleep Societies, 604 Second Street, SW, Rochester, MN 55902 (27).

Better Sleep Council (BSC), PO Box 13, Washington, DC 20044. Telephone: 703-683-8371 (27).

Carolinas Poison Control Center. Telephone: 1-800-848-6946 (23).

Clearinghouse on Abuse and Neglect (CANE), University of Delaware, Newark, DE 19716 (28).

Council on Anxiety Disorders, Winston-Salem, North Carolina. Telephone: 910-722-7760 (voicemail) (7).

D/ART Public Inquiries, NIMH, 5600 Fishers Lane, Room 15C-05, Rockville, MD 20857 (2).

Dean Foundation Obsessive Compulsive Information Center, 8000 Excelsior Drive, Suite 302, Madison, WI 53717-1914. Telephone: 608-836-8070 (10).

Duke University Medical Center Drug Information Service. Telephone: 919-684-5125 (23).

Eldercare Locator. Telephone: 1-800-677-1116 (28).

"Gift From Within" (PTSD organization), #1 Lily Pond Drive, Camden, ME 04843. Telephone: 1-800-888-5236. Also, e-mail joyceb3955@aol.com; also http://www.sourcemain.com//gift**** (9).

GriefNet, griefnet@rivendell.org. Telephone: 313-761-1960. Also: major-domo@falcon.ic.net *and* goshorn@fortnet.org (1).

Hospice Helpline, 1-800-658-8898. 1901 North Moore Street, Suite 901, Arlington, VA 22209. Locates hospice programs throughout the United States and provides general information (1, 29).

Iskode Biiniisii Elder Alcohol and Other Drug Abuse Program, Mildred Elm, Family Resources Center, Box 189, Lac du Flambeau, WI 54538. Telephone: 715-588-9818 (22).

Legal Counsel for the Elderly, 601 E Street, NW, fourth floor, Washington, DC 20049 (14).

Mental Disorders of Aging Research Branch, National Institutes of Mental Health (NIMH), 5600 Fishers Lane, Room 7-103, Rockville, MD 20857 (2, 18).

National Alliance for the Mentally Ill (NAMI), 200 North Glebe Road, Suite 1015, Arlington, VA 22203-3754. Telephone: 1-800-950-6264 (2, 8, 18).

National Anxiety Foundation, 3135 Custer Drive, Lexington, KY 40517. Telephone: 606-272-7166 (8).

National Association of Area Agencies on Aging, 1112 Sixteenth Street, NW, Suite 100, Washington, DC 20036 (14).

National Center on Elder Abuse, c/o American Public Welfare Association, 810 First Street, NE, Suite 500, Washington, DC 20002. Telephone: 202-682-2470 for referral to your state agency (28).

National Citizens Coalition for Nursing Home Reform (NCCNHR), 1424 Sixteenth Street, NW, Suite L-2, Washington, DC 20036 (16).

National Clearinghouse for Information on Alcohol and Drug Abuse, PO Box 2345, Rockville, MD 20852. Telephone: 1-800-729-6686 (22).

National Committee for the Prevention of Elder Abuse, c/o Institute on Aging, The Medical Center of Central Massachusetts, 119 Belmont Street, Worcester, MA 01605 (28).

National Council of Senior Citizens, Nursing Home Information Service, 925 Fifteenth Street, NW, Washington, DC 20005 (16).

National Council on Alcoholism (NCA), 12 West Twenty-First Street, New York, NY 10010. Telephone: 1-800-NCA-CALL (1-800-622-2255) (22).

National Depressive and Manic-Depressive Association (NDMDA), PO Box 1939, Chicago, IL 60690 and 730 North Franklin Street, Suite 501, Chicago, IL 60610. Telephone: 1-800-826-3632 (2, 5).

National Institute of Mental Health, Panic [and anxiety] disorder information line. Telephone: 1-800-647-2642 (7). Barry Liebowitz, Mental Disorders of Aging Research Branch, 5600 Fishers Lane, Room 7-103, Rockville, MD 20857 (14).

National Institute on Aging Information Center, PO Box 8057, Gaithersburg, MD 20898-8057 (12, 16, #7).

National Mental Health Consumers' Self-Help Clearinghouse, 1211 Chestnut Street, tenth floor, Philadelphia, PA 19107. Telephone: 1-800-553-4539 (8).

Obsessive-Compulsive (OC) Foundation, Inc., PO Box 70, Milford, CT 06460. Telephone: 203-878-5669 (7, 10).

Obsessive-Compulsive Information Center, Department of Psychiatry, University of Wisconsin, 600 Highland Avenue, Madison, WI 53792. Telephone: 608-836-8070 (7).

Panic Disorder Education Program, National Institutes of Mental Health, Publications List, Room 7C-02, 5600 Fishers Lane, Rockville, MD 20857. Telephone: 1-800-64-PANIC (1-800-647-2642) (8).

Phobics Anonymous, PO Box 1180, Palm Springs, CA 92263. Telephone: 619-322-2673 (8).

Pikuni (Blackfeet) Recovery Program, Melveena Malatare, PO Box 589, Browning, MT 59417. Telephone: 406-338-3511 (22).

Samaritans, 500 Commonwealth Avenue, Kenmore Square, Boston, MA 02215. Telephone: 617-247-0220 (twenty-four-hour helpline); also 617-536-2460 (6).

Shepherd's Center of America, 6700 Troost, Suite 616, Kansas City, MO 64131. Telephone: 816-523-1080 (15).

Society for Traumatic Stress Studies, 60 Revere Drive, Suite 500, Northbrook, IL 60062. Telephone: 708-480-9080 (9).

Tribal Elder Substance Abuse Program, Frances White or Leona Juneau, Coeur d'Alene Tribal Sub-Agency, Plummer, ID 83851. Telephone: 208-274-3101 (22).

Widowed Person's Services, American Association of Retired Persons (AARP), 601 E Street, NW, Washington, DC 20049. Telephone: 202-434-2277 (1).

Index